YOU ARE THE KINGDOM

AN EXPLORATION OF
DISCIPLESHIP
THROUGH THE GOSPEL
IMAGERY OF THE KINGDOM
AS DIVINE PRESENCE
IN THE WORLD

PETER VARENGO

COVENTRY
PRESS

Published in Australia by
Coventry Press
33 Scoresby Road
Bayswater Vic. 3153
Australia

ISBN 9780648725176

Copyright © Peter Varengo 2020

All rights reserved. Other than for the purposes and subject to the conditions prescribed under the *Copyright Act*, no part of this publication may be reproduced, stored in a retrieval system, or transmitted in any form or by any means, electronic, mechanical, photocopying, recording or otherwise, without the prior permission of the publisher.

Scripture quotations are from the *New Revised Standard Version Bible*, copyright 1989, Division of Christian Education of the National Council of the Churches of Christ in the United States of America. Used by permission. All rights reserved.

Cataloguing-in-Publication entry is available from the National Library of Australia http://catalogue.nla.gov.au/.

Cover design by Ian James - www.jgd.com.au
Text design by Film Shot Graphics FSG – www.fsg.com.au

Printed in Australia

The Kingdom of God is within You
(Luke 17:21)

Jesus had hang-ups,
and the greatest of them all was his persistence with the
kingdom – not a domineering oppressive power,
but a life-giving and active God-presence in our world,
for which he gave his own life.

Like faith,
such presence is never an ethereal concept,
but a reality embracing every dimension of being human,
and every aspect of our lives in the here and now of each
day.
It was precisely that daily experience
of work, relationships, and chance encounters
that became both the source and the place for Jesus'
message and of his passionate mission.

I propose that discipleship
is the personal and collective response to the Jesus-
kingdom, understood at God's life-giving presence in our
world,
lived in the reality of each day
and expressed through the imagery of the parables.

Contents

Preface
The Parables of the Kingdom 6

Introduction
Hearing versus Listening to the Word of God 11

The Kingdom
Obsession and Mission
Matthew 13:1-52; Luke 8:4-18; 13:18-21 16

The Shepherd
A Window into God
Luke 5:4-7; John 10:14-15 40

Spirit
The Energy of the Kingdom
Acts 2:1-12 63

Calling
Called by Name into the Kingdom
Matthew 9:36 to 10:8 79

Relationship
Vines and Branches – Oneness of Life in the Kingdom
John 15:3-16 97

Self
The Treasure Within – The Person of the Kingdom
Matthew 13:1-52 113

Beatitudes
The Values of the Kingdom
Luke 6:20-26 131

The cross
The Banner of the Kingdom
Luke 24:13-26 152

Resurrection
The Impossible is Real
Mark 16:1-8 169

Forgiven
A Kingdom of Healing and Forgiveness
Luke 15:1-32 188

Eucharist
Breaking Bread in the Kingdom
Matthew 26:26-30; John 6:53-57 208

"Opus operandi"
The "Doing" in the Kingdom
Luke 10:25-37 228

Community
Foot Washing in the Kingdom
John 13:1-20 244

Mission
The Stranger in the Kingdom
John 21:1-19 262

Destiny
The Kingdom – Presence in Absence
Mark 16:15-20; Matthew 28:1-10 287

Kingdom-person
Mary – The First Disciple of the Kingdom
Luke 1:1-56 307

Preface

Peter Varengo has many friends at Our Lady of the Southern Cross – a parish comprising St John the Baptist in Clifton Hill, Victoria, and St Joseph's in Collingwood – where he served as parish priest from 2007-12. He continues his ministry in the parish, celebrating Mass with the Italian community and accompanying the many families he has befriended over the years in both their joys and sorrows. I first started to grasp how widely known and loved Peter is after repeatedly hearing his name turn up in the neighbourhoods of the parish. Many people in the area connect him to the church and the church to him. They tell stories about him with affection. When a local car mechanic discovered that I attend the parish, he began to tell me about his family's long connection to St John's and how Peter celebrated his and his brother's weddings, buried his father with them, and baptised their children. He credited Peter as the reason his family stayed in the church despite their feelings of betrayal and disappointment with its leaders. "He's the real thing", he said of Peter. "He cares about the people." The stories that neighbours tell of Fr Peter are family stories. They are stories of faith.

In *You are the Kingdom*, Peter articulates a vision of discipleship that interweaves our faith in Christ with the patterns of our ordinary living. Our experience of following Jesus quickens with our commitment to recognising the activity of God's life-giving presence in the contours of what we most intimately know: our families and friends, our work and leisure, our successes and failures, our daily encounters. As a pastor, Peter reminds us that Jesus announced a kingdom that continues to break into our here and now. He thus urges us to look for the realities intended in Christian language and symbol by considering the complexities of our own lives rather than by clinging to abstract concepts or hiding in formalised precepts. Any kind of theologising that neglects the fullness of who we are, that permits us to ignore parts of ourselves or our communities (and thus undermines Christian hope), mistakes the invitation of the kingdom for yet another spirituality of convenience. Peter suggests that spaces nearest to us, ambiguous and ambivalent as they often are, contain the deepest promises of the gospel.

Many readers will especially enjoy the personal stories that Peter tells throughout this book. He narrates some of his most powerful insights into Scripture in terms of his own life experience. When discussing the Scriptural metaphor of the shepherd, for example, he tells a story of visiting a Bedouin camp near Bethlehem. The guide for his group pointed out a shepherd standing on a nearby hillside and explained that for thousands of years the truth of a Palestinian shepherd has not changed: a shepherd is born a shepherd, lives and dies a shepherd, and has purpose only in caring for the sheep. Peter explains how this insight illuminates the depiction of Jesus as the good shepherd in the Gospel of John – how Jesus is who he is because of us, and how he calls us to imitate him in giving of ourselves according to the needs of others. The exegesis here exemplifies the kind of living *into* Scripture that Fr Peter proposes throughout his chapters.

A spirituality that refuses to flinch from the complexities of our lives must also deal with our limitations and weaknesses. Here again Peter treats his subject with the same honesty and vulnerability he sees as crucial to authentic discipleship. He tells the story of visiting his mother in northern Italy, later in life after his father had died, and remarking that his mother should cut down the few grape vines she caringly, if tediously, tended. They seemed worth rather less than the maintenance they required. Reproached by his mother, Peter realises how things possess meaning and connections to people and places that far outstrip their instrumental, use-value, and this forever changes how he hears Jesus speak about our shared life with images of vines, branches and the vinedresser. By weaving them together, the words of Jesus with his mother's response, Peter creatively brings us to an essential insight that he repeats, namely: that God loves us as we are, in all our brokenness and incompleteness, and that if we should truly love God and neighbour we must also and honestly love ourselves.

I was delighted that Peter asked me to write the preface for *You are the Kingdom*. I hope it will be widely read and shared in the Australian Church. For those of us in the parish of Our Lady of the Southern Cross, the message beautifully complements the witness of its author.

Christiaan Jacobs-Vandegeer
St John the Baptist, Clifton Hill
January 2020

The Parables of the Kingdom

The nature of the kingdom
    The mustard seed – Matthew 13:31-32; Mark 4:30-32; Luke 13:18-19
    The leaven – Matthew 13:33
    The rich fool – Luke 12:13-21
    The yeast – Luke 13:20-21

The values of the kingdom – (Beatitudes)
    The rich fool – Luke 12:13-21
    The crafty steward – Luke 16:1-8
    The rich man and Lazarus – Luke 16:19-31
    The Pharisee and the tax collector – Luke 18:9-14

Healing and forgiveness in the kingdom
    The lost sheep – Luke 15:4-7
    The lost drachma – Luke 15:9-10
    The prodigal son – Luke 15:11-32
    The Pharisee and the tax collector – Luke 18:9-14
    The unforgiving servant – Luke 18:23-35

Suffering, death and resurrection
    Dragnet into the sea – Mathew 13:47-50
    Wheat and darnel – Mark 4:26-29
    The barren fig tree – Luke 13:6-9

The kingdom: community and mission
> Labourers in the vineyard – Matthew 20:1-16
> The Good Samaritan – Luke 10:29-37
> Washing the disciples' feet – John 13:1-20

Relationships: God – self – others
> The sower – Matthew 13:3-23, 36-43
> Treasure in the field – Matthew 13:44
> Pearl of great value – Matthew 13:45-46
> The lost sheep – Matthew18:12-14
> Labourers in the vineyard – Matthew 20:1-16
> The wedding banquet – Matthew 22:1-14
> The sower – Mark 4:1-20; Luke 8:4-15
> The banquet – Luke 14:15-24
> Vine and branches – John 15-10

Introduction

Hearing versus Listening to the Word of God

A blur of unrecognised sounds, words oozing out from an anonymous technological gadget by my bedside. Thus ends another day, only to be re-awakened into blurred consciousness a few hours later by a similar whirring sound, slowly shaping itself into some half-distinguishable word-message. It is time, a new day, unfolding to the rhythm of a tsunami of words pounding us incessantly from the four corners of the compass, and engulfing in its choking grip every instant of our daily routine. "Words, words, words. They have a plentiful lack of wit", would muse Hamlet to his friend Polonius – words of encouragement and compassion, words of war and of peace, words of affection and of condemnation, words of excitement and of deep pain, words of life, and words of death. The mind is buzzing, unable to escape the entrapment of words spoken, sung, read, or just thought or mumbled to ourselves.

However, by a strange paradox, often this very superabundance of communication creates distance between speaker and hearer, heightening anonymity, leading to estrangement from the message delivered, and to loss of meaning and of relevance of the words themselves. But there is an escape. Our consciousness automatically shuts down and we become de-sensitised, unaware of the messages bombarding us on all sides, until that instant of uneasy emptiness full of silence strikes us uncomfortably, while we jog down the street, or stand by the kitchen sink. Yes, paradoxically, we are jolted into reality when struck by the "sounds of silence" of Simon and Garfunkel's happy memory.

In this world of communication overload and of unheard words, if communication is to become life-giving and growth-producing, we need to make a deliberate decision for listening, shifting the focus from hearing words to listening and perceiving the message behind them. This is the technique underlying the Word of God and exemplified by Jesus' parables. By tapping into the life experience of his contemporaries, Jesus draws the attention of his hearers to hearing the words, and then to listening to the message. However, such a shift of focus depends on the hearer converting and becoming a listener, allowing the superabundance of words to envelop us and turning into a conscious challenge both at personal and communal level. Alternatively, the word is dead, losing its very nature and transforming power, reduced to nothing beyond a meaningless amorphous sound offering a "plentiful lack of anything".

In the Christian economy, however, the Word is never dead or empty but ever-present and life-giving, taking on a uniquely powerful and personal meaning. God could not find a more apt way of communicating life and love to us than becoming personified in "the Word", and God does not have bad words or amorphous sounds. God's Word is not the effect of some electronic impulse, but a living and life-giving reality embracing the whole of human experience. The Word incarnates the very presence of God in human affairs, an active life-giving presence embodied in the very nature of the human story (John 1).

However, just as the over-profusion of words can choke our existence, when we fail to listen to the Word of God, as believers we can become equally anesthetised to it. As the parable of the Sower warns us, even this "living Word" can become empty and meaningless. Choked by the plethora of concerns and lacking any personal appropriation, the Word of God becomes disempowered of all its potential to bear fruit. We need to become listeners, or our faith will be simply a superficial ritual, precisely an amorphous sound, and we will never be truly believers. Whether through liturgy or biblical reflection and personal prayer, the Word of God is not about information but about transformation, never about some historical reportage of long ago, but for us and about us today.

By confronting us with our reality and delving to the very core of our being, the word of Scripture is meant to express and nourish that lived and living human-divine relationship with our God and with each other called spirituality. Only by listening today and appropriating the word we hear, we will be able to discover our own self and experience God immersed in that personal self. Spirituality does not consist in a one-way monologue reminding God of our personal agenda, but in the listening within the silent depth of the heart, as Benedict invited us to do centuries ago, and then incarnating that message in our life-experience.

The living Word of God truly embraces us on every side and in every insignificant skerrick of existence, and we can never escape its challenging message or deny its appeal in whatever situation we may find ourselves. It is of the very nature of God to communicate his Word of life and love, and God cannot resist communicating with us and offering us the gift of fullness of life. However, we can resist and refuse God's appeal by separating word and life and ignoring the absolute interconnectedness between hearing and listening. Too often, we leave our Sunday gathering satisfied with having completed a performance, ticked all the boxes, or fulfilled a precept, only to abandon the Word inside the door of the church. We have heard the sounds, but we have failed to capture and then live the message addressed to us. Listening is the diamond drill of our Sunday gathering and we have to retell the message encapsulated in those words not as passive hearers, but as active actors committed to making those narratives our personal on-going stories.

It is all a matter of awareness and of attitude on our part. As if in a mirror, we are those thousands fed by Jesus out of nothing (John 6:1-15). We encounter blind Bartimaeus ignored by most, and yet trusting by the side of the road on our life journey (Mark 10:46-52). We are Myriam, distraught and desperate, called into reality just when she is seeking for a dead body in an empty tomb (John 20:11-18). We crouch in the dust, gripped with terror and we breathe judgment and justification (John 8:1-11) at the same time, facing an execution. Like the disciples of Emmaus, we may not expect or recognise the Lord, but he falls in step with us along the road to reassure us and enter the intimacy of our home (Luke 24:13-34). This is our experience; this is our story; and our God is right there in the midst of it all.

That is why Scripture shuns any theoretical and abstract dissertation, but delves deeply into the language of images and personal experiences. Parables are the diamond drill of biblical communication because they speak out of daily experience in order to awaken an experience of God in our daily life; a God-experience that Jesus called the kingdom. God's grace is abundant, universal, and always fruitful, but this fruitfulness depends on our readiness to accept and foster its potency for life within the soil of our daily experience. May we be people who, having encountered the Word, are aware of God's presence and goodness sowed abundantly in the field of life, yes even in the thorny and less savoury moments of our stories!

The Kingdom

Obsession and Mission
Matthew 13:1-52; Luke 8:4-18; 13:18-21

That same day Jesus went out of the house and sat beside the lake. Such great crowds gathered around him that he got into a boat and sat there, while the whole crowd stood on the beach. And he told them many things in parables, saying: 'Listen! A sower went out to sow And as he sowed, some seeds fell on the path, and the birds came and ate them up. Other seeds fell on rocky ground, where they did not have much soil, and they sprang up quickly, since they had no depth of soil. But when the sun rose, they were scorched; and since they had no root, they withered away. Other seeds fell among thorns, and the thorns grew up and choked them. Other seeds fell on good soil and brought forth grain, some a hundredfold, some sixty, some thirty. Let anyone with ears listen!

Then the disciples came and asked him, 'Why do you speak to them in parables?' He answered, 'To you it has been given to know the secrets of the kingdom of heaven, but to them it has not been given. For to those who have, more will be given, and they will have an abundance; but from those who have nothing, even what they have will be taken away. The reason I speak to them in parables is that "seeing they do not perceive, and hearing they do not listen, nor do they understand . . .

. . . He put before them another parable: 'The kingdom of heaven may be compared to someone who sowed good seed in his field; but while everybody was asleep, an enemy came and sowed weeds among the wheat, and then went away. So when the plants came up and bore grain, then the weeds appeared as well. And the slaves of the householder came and said to him, "Master, did you not sow good seed in your field? Where, then, did these weeds come from?" He answered, "An enemy has done this." The slaves said to him, "Then do you want us to go and gather them?" But he replied, "No; for in gathering the weeds you would uproot the wheat along with them. Let both of them grow together until the harvest; and at harvest time I will tell the reapers, "Collect the weeds first and bind them in bundles to be burned, but gather the wheat into my barn.

He put before them another parable: 'The kingdom of heaven is like a mustard seed that someone took and sowed in his field; it is the smallest of all the seeds, but when it has grown it is the greatest of shrubs and becomes a tree, so that the birds of the air come and make nests in its branches. (Matthew 13:1-13, 24-32)

The kingdom: God at play here and now

It may sound irreverent, but I am convinced that Jesus had hang-ups. We only need to look at the gospel narratives to see that one leitmotif keeps on recurring with obsessive persistence, the kingdom. Although in our modern parlance, the term "kingdom" may hold a certain political/social dissonance for some people, in the Gospel narrative, the notion of kingdom is clearly Jesus' hang-up, dotting the whole story and underlying every theme. Jesus was obsessed with the kingdom, and, through his life and ministry, he makes no secret that his mission is to establish the Reign of God. He introduces most of his parable with "the *kingdom is like*", and then proceeds to illustrate various dimensions of this kingdom, making no secret of the fact that his life and ministry is to establish the kingdom of God. In turn, at the end of the story, the same kingdom becomes the mission of the disciples for all time. Significantly, on the last Sunday of the liturgical year, the Church invites us to celebrate the Feast of Christ the King, a celebration that represents the grand finale of a symphony, harmonising the various biblical and liturgical themes that have accompanied us across the previous ten months of our liturgical life and over the daily unfolding of our Christian story.

I am not too conversant with children's stories these days, but I am old enough to remember grandma launching into imaginative, even if repetitive, yarns that inevitably began, "*Once upon a time...!*" and always ended with the mandatory "*... and they lived happily ever after!*" In between these two bookends, grandma's imagination had no limits, and somehow, we would be swept away in a world of powerful but benevolent kings, of gracious queens, of beautiful princesses and of brave knights. Indeed, such was their benevolence, graciousness, bravery, and beauty that nothing could resist their power in those epic battles between good and evil. The good king inevitably conquered his enemies and all kinds of evil, so that in the end everybody truly *"lived happily ever after!"*

Unfortunately, as we grow older, imagination gives way to rationality and headiness, and often the price of confronting difficult and stark life experiences is the loss of our capacity to dream and to hope of ever achieving happiness, now or ever after. However, Christian belief is of little consequence if devoid of hope, and the belief in God's kingdom proclaimed by Jesus and celebrated through liturgy is precisely a call to hope in the power and life-giving presence of a Benevolent King totally enmeshed into the human story, yes even into the most tragic experiences of loss and death.

In the Old Testament, kingdom was both the apex of past memories and the catalyst of future expectations. The glory of the Davidic era was the sign of God's faithfulness to his promise and of Israel self-awareness of nationhood, of its identity as God's own chosen people, and of its final destiny of universal liberation by God's promised Messiah. Unfortunately, over time, such self-awareness and expectations took on strongly political and social overtones and lost their theological and spiritual significance as a sign of God's universal presence embracing the whole of history. Consequently, Jesus' contemporaries and disciples alike never fully understood the imagery of kingship that he proclaimed. Yet, Jesus became obsessed with the image of kingdom underlying all his teaching, and never desisted from this obsession. To the very last, facing his accusers, he boldly proclaimed:

> *I am a king. For this I was born, and for this I came into the world, to testify to the truth.*
> (John 18:37)

In that bold self-proclamation, while engaging the original understanding of kingdom, Jesus moved right away from a socio-political interpretation and gave a totally new and transforming significance to the ancient image. Dominating the climax of Jesus' story stands a crucified One, ridiculed as king (Luke 22:63), telling a condemned criminal that today he will be with him in his kingdom (Luke 23:43), and pleading with the Father to forgive his executioners (Luke 23:34).

In this way, Jesus reversed all previous expectations and present presuppositions of human kingship of power and control. The Gospel king is a strange king indeed, who does violence to all human expectations of royalty and kingship. With outstretched arms nailed to a cross as if to embrace the whole world, and with the last breath of his earthly existence, on Golgotha, he exhibits none of the power, splendour and riches that usually accompany our expectations of mythical all-conquering heroes. On the contrary, this crucified king identifies with the most violent and dehumanising aspect of earthly experience.

Nothing could be more dissonant and contradictory than a kingdom proclaimed through crucifixion, and a dying king pleading for someone else's life while thrusting his own in the hands of God. Yet this is Jesus' revelation of kingdom: a unique kingdom realised today and exercised not in control and power but through leadership of service, compassion, hope, and complete availability to others in love. Devoid of physical or sensory identity, yet reaching beyond time and space, Gospel kingdom is not about domination but about liberation, about a God-King setting people free from inner and outer oppression. It is about lame and paralytics walking again, about blind and dumb people exploding into song of wonder at what they experience for the first time in the world around them, and discover the richness and beauty that they are.

Jesus' kingdom is not about cold and domineering structures and systems, but a reality that is alive, active and life-giving, where people like you and me, while going about the roller coaster of our daily living and dying, are both actors and beneficiaries at the same time. Jesus' kingdom *is not from this world* (John 18:36), as he reassures a fear-ridden Pilate, but its full realisation takes place totally *in this world*. Jesus' kingdom is a presence, the active compassionate presence of God impregnating every insignificant skerrick of human experience, a way of being, a state of mind, and a lived relationship between God and each person, individually and collectively.

The words of Jesus to the repentant thief on the cross express it so eloquently and clearly: "*Today you will be with me in paradise*" (Luke 23:43), sharing together the very life of God. Bonded together with our king and with each other in a deeply personal and life-giving relationship, our king will empower us to conquer all negativity in our life and to live in peace and joy, happily ever after, even through and after the most excruciating death by execution, victims of one's mistakes or of human injustice. On the cross, arms wide open to embrace the world even in its pain and death, Jesus identifies completely with our human history to the point of absolute injustice and mind-shattering pain. At the same time, those arms wide open stand in total but trust-filled abandonment to the Father who, through the resurrection, will conquer even death, while bringing life, love, and hope to the world. Like in old grandma's stories, the powerful and benevolent king will conquer all evil, even death on behalf of his people, and if we have the courage to trust this most unlikely king, we too will be able *to live happily ever after.*

The kingdom of God excludes none of the realities of humanity, and the full gamut of human experience is the stage where God wants to be and where God is at play. People matter to God not because of what they are, but simply because they are people, and the only way we can encounter God and experience the full reality of the kingdom is in the here and now, with real people struggling with life and embracing love. Our life is the stage where the kingdom is played, and if we are not prepared to seek and find our God on the stage of daily reality, then we will never meet God. No matter how much we protest faith in a personal God, or pray to an idol of our own making, we will never discover or experience the kingdom outside of our place and time, or beyond those whom we meet casually or by design.

Because this kingdom defies bounds of space and time, one small word, *today*, becomes particularly significant. For the repentant thief, that *today* became the moment of encounter with God and of salvation, and for us *today* must become our moment of salvation and of encounter with God through each other. *Today* we must carry written in our hearts the sentence of hope "Jesus of Nazareth King of the Jews". *Today*, encountering us, others must be led to murmur in prayer "*Jesus, remember me when you come into your kingdom*". *Today* we are invited to live in hope and joyful peace, in the sure knowledge that our God-King will continue to live, and rejoice, and grow, and struggle with us to ensure that in the end we will all live happily ever after.

The language of the kingdom

Jesus' parables play precisely this tune of the kingdom as the active presence of God embracing every aspect of daily life, and it is only through the experiences of daily life that we experience the kingdom and encounter our God.

> Parables are stories describing situations in everyday life which, as Jesus used them, conveyed a spiritual meaning. In general, the teaching of each parable relates to a single point, and apart from the details may, or may not, have a particular meaning. Jesus used this method of teaching because: (a) it gave vivid, memorable expression to the teaching; (b) led those who heard to reflect on his word and bear responsibility for their decision to accept or oppose his claim; (c) it probably reduced specific grounds for contention by hostile listeners.[1]

Paradoxically, such rational head-language based on philosophical/theological categories would be incomprehensible to anybody in biblical times, and certainly to Jesus' audience. Even in our culture, while we may understand the rational concepts, this kind of communication is inadequate as we try to express deep personal dimensions of the heart and of our psyche, such as love,

---

1 *The New Oxford Annotated Bible*, (1991), Oxford University Press Inc.

faith, relationship, togetherness, and indeed, God himself. These are expressions of the heart and they can only be expressed through the heart-language of images and storytelling, appealing much more effectively to the personal experience and to the deepest sentiments of the reader and/or listener. Likewise, faith is not so much a matter of words but primarily a matter of deep personal relationship where verbal expressions are often inadequate. The deeper the relationship, the harder it is to find the adequate vocabulary to express it. It is then that we resort to the language of images, like a handshake to express welcome, a bouquet of flowers as a sign of gratitude and good wishes, or a kiss to express the love between two people. Thus, by engaging our imagination, we overcome the limitations of head-language and enter the realm of heart-relationship.

That is why Scripture cherishes images and narrative language, as it tries to give expression to the personal relationship between God and people, a relationship so deep and so intense that only the open-ended message of imagination can express. Throughout Scripture, our relationship with God is expressed and made real by a variety of images ranging from peaceful bucolic scenes to the tragic plight of someone beaten by robbers. We encounter shepherds and sheep, farmers and vinedressers, food and drink, wedding feasts and self-righteous leaders, loving parents and wayward children, vines and wheat, lambs and wolves, shepherds and kings, bread and wine, simple meals and rich banquets – a whole gamut of life situations drawn from the immediate daily experience of both storyteller and listener, and speaking directly to the people who lived that experience in the flesh.

However, precisely because images are most eloquent when drawn from daily experience, they can be so culturally specific that even their rich imagery may appear foreign and at times unintelligible outside its socio-cultural context. The Old Testament is a millennial story of a rural and pastoral people whose very livelihood depended almost exclusively on nurturing and caring for a small but invaluable flock. Hence, the rich imagery of vines and vinedressers and of sheep and shepherds that spoke *to* and *of* the life of those people. Such was the relationship between shepherds and sheep that the flock became the symbol of their lifestyle, and the expression of the social, political, and religious culture of Israel. Most of all, that rural setting identified their understanding of God and of their individual and collective relationship with Yahweh. Indeed, so intense was the power of the image that Yahweh self-identified and proclaimed himself the Shepherd of Israel, totally given over to the care and welfare of his chosen flock. Sung in the psalms and proclaimed by the prophets, through the oracle of Ezekiel, Yahweh would declare,

> *I myself will be the shepherd of my sheep, and*
> *I will make them lie down, says the Lord God*
> (Ezekiel. 34:15).

From the distance of millennia from biblical times, we too live in a world of signs and symbols. We instinctively respond to a series of three-coloured set of lights signposting our road and highways, and intuitively react to ubiquitous multi-ranged electronic beeps filling our house, or we welcome someone at the door with a handshake. These, like hundreds of similar sensory perceptions, impregnate our daily life and shape our behaviour to such an extent that our response to them is automatic, to the point that, most likely, we notice their presence only when they are absent. Our life is full of gestures, words and symbols whose meanings go way beyond the immediate experience. However, symbols and images express far more than their literal meaning and carry important messages that are often too personal or too deep to express in words or rational arguments. We clap our hands in affirmation and approval and we say "sorry" in support and sympathy. As we drive along, we automatically stop when a bright red light appears in front of us, or we pull over to the side at the sound of a screaming siren because we associate that piercing sound with urgency, danger, life, and death. We extend a hand in welcome and we hug a child in affection. We use expressions such as, *"It's hard to describe; you had to be there!... It's like...!"* or *"You are the sunshine of my life!... I give all my heart to you!"* It is not the beep from the microwave that readies my coffee, nor the bright red light ahead that stops me on my busy travels. What really shapes our behaviour is the unconscious yet all-important message these signals project, a message that is often nothing short of life or death. Obviously, we do not take these expressions literally; but these sensory perceptions project us into another level of awareness, awakening deep human emotions and calling us to wonder, rejoicing, and love. In the words of Joseph Campbell, "a myth is the music we dance to even when we cannot name the tune".[2]

That is the power of the symbol: to appeal to our senses in order to deliver a message that is often so deep and personal that we seem unable to express fully through rational language or logical categories. At the same time, unless we are able to perceive,

---

2 Joseph Campbell, *The Power of Myth*, New York: Doubleday, 1988.

understand, and react to the message beyond and behind the signal, then the latter remains a useless and meaningless piece of coloured plastic or a strange gesture of two people extending an arm to each other. Unless the sign of the red light, the handshake or the noxious beep is there, then we will never be able to communicate, and in some cases to survive. The real power of images and symbols lies in the message they convey and, in our capacity, to understand the message and behave accordingly.

It is the message that we need to be able to perceive and act upon beyond the sign/symbol/image. The immediate sensory expressions become life-giving when they drive at that inner level of our psyche where self-identity resides, and faith responds. Writing about the image of the Good Shepherd, Barbara Davis identifies stories as a "dynamic creative force of great love and energy, of practical compassion and faithful commitment".

> Images can show us the unknown faces of our own souls and generate the energy for change... Myths and images can help us to perceive inner spiritual reality by speaking to truth that is greater than facts... (and) represents all those most deeply held experiences, beliefs and values that are at the heart of our stories and have the power to continue to fire and fuel our lives.[3]

---

3 Barbara Davis, *We are Caught into this Mystery*, Sisters of the Good Shepherd, 2002), 9.

The message of the kingdom

The parables of Jesus are a masterpiece not only of storytelling and of teaching techniques, but they are a masterpiece on the use of images and symbols.

Jesus of Nazareth was fully caught up in his world and time, and revealed the kingdom through the categories and within the experiences of his world and time, in many ways different and yet so much like ours in its expressions and values. That is why the language of the kingdom is drawn almost exclusively from the categories that people knew, and the daily experience they could relate to. And so, ours is a kingdom of fishermen and pearl seekers, of shepherds and farmers, of rich and paupers, of powerful leaders and rejects of society, of mothers and of prostitutes, of self-giving fathers and of self-indulgent children, of barren trees and explosive fruitfulness of vines, of magnanimous landlords and of ungrateful workers, of bread and wine at a lavish banquet and of selfish exploitation of the king's generosity at the wedding table, of children full of laughter and of grieving widows burying their only son. The kingdom is as small and yet as powerful and life-giving as the tiniest seed, as large as the ocean teeming with life and energy, and as simple and delicate as a wild flower of the fields.

Jesus did not come to dispense agricultural instructions about shepherds and vinedressers, or to expound new theories of social behaviour or revolutionary theories of governance, or tenets of personal relationship between people. Underlying all the parables stands one absolute conviction giving meaning to his whole life and driving his ministry. Jesus' obsession with the kingdom stemmed from his absolute and unshakable conviction that our God is the living and life-giving presence in our life story and in our daily lives. This was the rationale and the diamond drill of his mission, and he staked his life in order to reveal this living presence of God in our midst, a God drawing us into himself in a deep relationship of love, and at the same time energising us into a community of love with each other.

Ours is a God obsessed with each of us individually as the shepherd for whom the flock was the very reason of his life, or the merchant of pearls who is prepared to risk his whole life's fortune just to gain possession of that one stone which could well prove a fake. This is a God who is not put off by human weakness, rejection, or even by the betrayal of a wayward and ungrateful child, but against all the accepted mores of time and place, or the demands of strict retributive justice, he waits for his child to return home, regardless of what this son/daughter may have done (Luke 15:11-32). Our God shuns self-righteousness but longs to enter into a deep personal relationship with each of us, where the human response is not some vacuous routine or pseudo-religious practice, but honest self-appraisal, trust and abandonment on our part (Luke 18:9-14). Our God is generous to a fault, lavishing his love and life on us with extravagant handfuls in our life-story and waiting for the fruitfulness even amid the thorny wastefulness and ungratefulness of our life (Mark 4:1-20).

The challenge of the kingdom

Such radically new and controversial revelation offered to us by Jesus through the image of the kingdom is both affirming and challenging.

Jesus is a great realist and does not hide the fact that when we take seriously the kingdom he came to establish, we both encounter and create confrontation and division, first within ourselves and then in the world where we live. Jesus' whole life and message is always an eloquent sign of God's living and active presence in our life, demanding a response from the believer, who is thereby constantly called to confront themself, to reassess personal values, and to see and do things in a new and unexpected way. To accept this kingdom demands that we be prepared to jettison the superfluous, to remain open to the unplanned, to readjust our bearings and course of action, to seek advice and/or companionship, and to remain alert.

Among the plethora of parables illustrating these challenges we have the rich fool (Luke 12:13-21), the watchful slaves (Luke 12:35-48), the narrow door (Luke 13:22-30), the wicked tenants (Matthew 12:1-12; Mark 13:32-37). The acceptance of God in one's life and experience does not admit compromise, 'yes-but', or excuses and alibi. The kingdom is expressed and realised in a community of love energised by God's love for each and all of us, and love is an absolute, denying all conditions or selectivity (Luke 10:25-37). We either love someone or we do not, and that one fundamental injunction immediately creates dissonance and turmoil in our hearts, especially when we are victims. Yet, we are asked to love the enemy or the perpetrator of injustice and violence.

The imagery of the kingdom as understood and revealed by Jesus sometimes reminds me of a dissonance suddenly distorting the melodic flow of an uplifting musical masterpiece. Occasionally, during a musical performance, a melodic passage seems to slide into an unexpected strain of disconnected notes, a jolt in key, tonality and timing that just do not seem to belong to the melody dominating the preceding bars. Somehow, the tone changes and the melody appear to break up into a sound that strains the ear and does violence to the whole performance. This is dissonance, a distortion of musical sounds as much as of life experiences, often unexpected where things just do not seem to be right any more, making us cringe, and at the same time raising a new awareness in us, forcing us to take notice, even if we do not like what we hear or see.

For all its unpleasantness, however, musical dissonance is an important technique deliberately introduced by the composer with a clear double intent: it awakens a new awareness in the listener and, more importantly, dissonance invariably will explode into a completely new musical theme, sometime of stunning beauty and unexpected power. The immediate temptation could be to dismiss the experience, keep on repeating mantra-like the original melody, or silence the grinding unpleasantness by turning off the sound. However, if we have the wisdom and the courage to resist the temptation to avoid silencing the disharmony and allow that distortion to take us into another level of sound experience, we will soon find ourselves bathing in an exhilarating new symphonic masterpiece. That is the power of dissonance: to bring about wonder, newness, and beauty, and this is the power of the parables as used by Jesus.

The Word of God is alive and active, speaking to us and about us, and precisely because of this personal intentionality, often it makes us cringe, sounding perhaps threatening and disconcerting to a spirituality of sugar-and-honey Jesus, comfortable and personally satisfying against a cosy background of individualism and me-and-God alone type of faith. The kingdom is not about individualism, because our faith can only be lived and expressed in communion with others, and that is rarely cosy, comfortable or satisfying. It should never be such. Yes, we need to be jolted out of a comfortable but false understanding of the kingdom, and Jesus does precisely that with great realism. Through the dissonance of this teaching, he jolts us out of passivity and privatisation, into a new awareness of that kingdom which he once described as violent, adding that *'the violent take it by force'*(Matthew 11:12).

> *I came to bring fire to the earth, and how I wish it were already kindled! Do you think that I have come to bring peace to the earth? No, I tell you, but rather division! (Luke 12:49)*

Language can be so inadequate at times and more so when language and associated imagery carry strong cultural connotations. The fundamental thrust of Jesus' whole life and mission was to reveal a revolutionary concept and experience of God as Father. But while this may give rise to a powerful sense of life-giving, security, care and loving commitment, I sometimes find myself wondering what kind of God calls me to hate father and mother, children and every other family member as well (Luke 14:25-27), or what kind of awareness it awakens into consciousness for a deserted mother and her fatherless children. Devoid of its cultural-existential context, language often sounds quite meaningless if not downright offensive, as Jesus often claims in the Gospel, where we encounter the word "hate" in relation to family members. Jesus' demands are just as challenging as they sound, and he appears to place seemingly unreasonable conditions on his followers.

Such challenging remarks constantly put us on the alert and demand a personal decision right in the existential situations of life.

We have to choose between love and hate, violence or peace, justice or oppression. We cannot ignore these contrasting dualities. They demand decisions. Faith has nothing to do with feeling good within the cacoon of our self-styled religious securities. Faith demands that, once we have said yes to God in faith, we continually struggle, question, and pummel within ourselves to live out that *yes* in a world that upholds counter-values, questioning and challenging any form of God-presence.

The "yes" of faith in the kingdom must be a disturbing confrontation to a world focused entirely on achievement at all costs, a world that proposes alternatives threatening life and love, while canonising individualism at the expense of community, justice, and human dignity. In all these situations, not only we have to struggle to come to terms with the contradictions and diverse compulsions arousing within ourselves, but also, if we are to achieve that communion of love that Jesus came to establish, we must take a stand against these negative energies for the sake of the world at large,

Jesus took a stand for what he preached and lived by, and that cost him his life, precisely at the hands of those who tried to silence him, because they found his teaching and his presence too harsh a dissonance to accept in their lives. In contrast, he listened to the dissonance around him, walked with trust through the disharmony thrown at him, and the conclusion was the most powerful symphony of all times: life forever in spite of death. For Christian believers, that is also both our destiny and our mission, so long as we are prepared to accept the dissonance and disharmony within ourselves, and be challenging and disturbing for the world around us. Then we will truly know fullness of joy in the communion of love of the universal kingdom of God-with-us.

Commitment to the kingdom

At the very beginning of his public ministry in the synagogue at Nazareth, Jesus introduced himself to the world as the one sent

> *to proclaim release to the captives, and recovery of sight to the blind, to let the oppressed go free, to proclaim the year of the Lord's favour.*
> (Luke 4:18-19)

Such self-proclamation re-echoes clearly Jesus' words at the opposite end of Matthew's story where he enjoined on his disciples the mission to *"go therefore, and make disciples of all nations"* (Matthew 28:19). Jesus' yearning to set the world alight with this new awareness of presence becomes the unavoidable call of the believing disciples to commit themselves to continue his mission in the establishment of the kingdom of peace, healing, and hope in our world.

The God revealed to us by Jesus is not the passive idol in the sky, or the stern accountant checking the balance sheet when we die. Jesus declared himself the one sent to bring Good News, to set people free, to bring health, sight, and peace, and left us joy as his parting gift before he died. These are not otherworldly utopias, but daily actualities that will only become reality through the decisive commitment of the believer. Jesus is yearning to set the world alight with the transforming fire of love and compassion, but the time soon comes when this God-entrusted mission will demand the active involvement of the disciples in the here and now. Is our life a fire setting the world alight with hope and love, or a flickering candle that only seems to enhance the deep darkness around, incapable of generating warmth and joy within us and all around us?

> The kingdom of God was at the heart of the life and teaching of Jesus. It was not a political vision, nor simply a place you go to after death. It is a reality to be experienced now, at its heart is a way of seeing. The kingdom of God implies a non-dual way of seeing reality. Kingdom consciousness cannot be earned; it is already given. It is something to become conscious of, to awaken into. It is characterised by abundance, generosity, mercy and compassion. It is not about generating more action plans or moral crusades. It allows us to see people and creation as God sees them... Instead of operating exclusively from egocentric minds we learn to put on what Paul calls *the mind of Christ*. If we are honest many of us do not want to do this; we prefer to live inside our own small minds.[4]

Because the kingdom is here, then we are caught up in the drama not just as spectators or consumers of kingdom gifts. We must become actors who, while praying that God's kingdom may come, take on the responsibility of realising the kingdom in the here and now. Through his personality, as much by what he did and

---

[4] Michael J. Cunningham, *Salesians – Contemplatives in Action*, Thornley House, Bolton: Don Bosco Publications, 2012), 48.

said, Jesus' life and mission became a disturbing presence for those he encountered, and so must be the life of the disciple and believer. The kingdom Jesus proclaimed and handed over to us is not a pie-in-the-sky-when-we-die, but a responsibility placed in our hands. It is up to us to reveal the God of our life or the kingdom-energy will dissipate and die.

> *I was hungry and you gave me food; I was thirsty and you gave me drink; I was a stranger and you made me welcome; naked and you clothed me, sick and you visited me, in prison and you came to see me* (Matthew 25:35-37).

This is the Magna Carta of the kingdom and the identity-mission of the believer. Having been healed, we must become healers. Having been nourished, we must become nourishers. Having experienced the gift of peace given to us at the Resurrection, we must become peacemakers. Having been cured of our blind paralysis, we must walk in compassion with the lame, rejected, blind, and hopeless of our streets and affluent residences. Having been vitalised by the active presence of God, we must become the leaven of life and growth for others. Significantly, the liturgical feast of Christ the King was instituted by Pope Pius XI in 1925, precisely as a counter cultural statement of community and social awareness in a world where individualism was becoming so dominant as to ignore and crush all human dignity, and eventually exploding in the global tragedy of World War II. The kingdom is here, declared Jesus, and as we pray, "*thy kingdom come on earth as it is in heaven*", we commit ourselves to make it happen.

To accept God in one's life does not allow for neutrality, and therefore faith becomes a commitment to the kingdom in the here and now, to live with contradictions and doubts, and to make decisions that often run counter to one's personal preferences and plans. To accept God into one's life means choosing uncertainty simply on the certainty afforded by one's belief in this all-embracing *presence* called *kingdom*, even in the face of contradiction or the lure of more comfortable choices. Our lives can never be disengaged from our faith lived fully in the reality of each day, but lived in such a way that people will take notice. Our lives must create dissonance within ourselves and all around us, a dissonance between honesty and self-righteousness, between transparency and pretence, between altruism and self-centredness, between individualism and community. The communion of love of the kingdom will only eventuate when our lives transpire honesty and coherence of belief, challenging both apathy and self-seeking neutrality, and proposing a vision that may well run counter to the dominant culture of time and place, but life-giving and transforming of "the within" through "the without".

Years ago, during a casual conversation, a friend of mine who prided himself of being the ultimate atheist, challenged me with a disturbing comment, creating in me precisely the kind of dissonance that I was trying to engender in him. Pointing the finger of reproach at Christianity, he paraphrased a famous line of Mahatma Ghandi, "I can accept Christianity, but I have a real problem with Christians". Then, to justify his decision, he added, "If you Christians are like us non-believers, then the world has no need of you". Biased and uninformed though the comment may sound, this person had understood that if one is a Christian, then this person's life should make a difference to their world and to the world at large.

Here was someone who had taken a stand for his unbelief, reproaching those who claim belief of refusing to make decisions that challenged him or anybody else. Life does not have to be perfect, but the questioning within and outside of oneself has to be constant, niggling, and life-long. Our commitment will always be short of the mark, challenging our inadequacies, and creating discomfort and uneasiness in a world that espouses divergent views within the unity of the family, or personal agenda as much as on the global scale of economics, politics, culture, traditions and religious beliefs. If we claim faith, then our life must be a counter witness and a screeching dissonance in such a world, and we must have the courage to take a stand, even if that may on occasion be painful and dissonant to our self-centredness and our personal agenda.

Confronting the challenge of the Gospel, Francis of Assisi famously expressed the intense dissonance engendered by the awareness of God's living and active presence in our life and world, and prayed that he become an instrument of transforming dissonance for the world around him. He did not seek consolation or the comfort of peace as his own personal experience, but that through his life of absolute trust and transparency, he might become a sign and instrument of the kingdom of peace, joy, hope, and forgiveness for the whole world.

> *Make me a channel of your peace.*
> *Where there is hatred let me bring your love;*
> *where there is injury your pardon, Lord;*
> *and where there's doubt true faith in you.*

> *Oh, Master grant that I may never seek*
> *so much to be consoled as to console;*
> *to be understood as to understand;*
> *to be loved as to love with all my soul.*
> *Make me a channel of your peace.*
> *Where there's despair in life let me bring hope;*
> *where there is darkness, only light; and where there's sadness, ever joy.*
> *Make me a channel of your peace.*
> *It is in pardoning that we are pardoned;*
> *in giving to all men that we receive;*
> *and in dying that we're born to eternal life.*

This is the prayer of the disciple, and this is our identity and mission in the kingdom.

The Shepherd

A Window into God
Luke 5:4-7; John 10:14-15

Which one of you, having a hundred sheep and losing one of them, does not leave the ninety-nine in the wilderness and go after the one that is lost until he finds it? When he has found it, he lays it on his shoulders and rejoices. And when he comes home, he calls together his friends and neighbours, saying to them, "Rejoice with me, for I have found my sheep that was lost." Just so, I tell you, there will be more joy in heaven over one sinner who repents than over ninety-nine righteous people who need no repentance. (Luke 15:4-7)

I am the good shepherd. I know my own and my own know me, just as the Father knows me and I know the Father. And I lay down my life for the sheep. (John 10:14-15)

The question of God

"The Name of God is Mercy", and each one of us, for eternity and from eternity, is the object of an unconditional and eternal love affair of God with humanity. This is the spiritual and theological ID

card of Pope Francis, proclaimed with the flavour of an obsession from the very beginning of his pontificate, and then proposed to us as the rationale for the Jubilee Year of Mercy (2016). We can be grateful and have reasons to rejoice at the positive and encouraging vision and pastoral insights such a pronouncement opens up on life as a whole. More importantly, as a fundamental thesis of faith, those affirming words drive at the core of life and faith and they raise a plethora of crucial questions that challenge both our God-image and our self-image, demanding confrontation and personal appropriation. Who is this God, so obsessed with humanity? Who are we to become God's unconditional love-obsession? What kind of God is *our/my* God? What does this divine recklessness do to my private cherished idea of God and to my self-image? As a number of parables suggest, who am I really, if this God considers me so precious and worth more than the whole world?

If the Year of Mercy (2016) was to become "a program of life (and) impetus to conversion as demanding as it is rich with joy and peace",[5] as Francis proposed, then we must face these questions with honesty and a deep sense of faith, and allow the challenge to change us both within and without.

Jesus' whole life and mission, as well as his teaching and healing, had but one clear intent: to reveal the true face of God, challenging the tried and true but most of all the comfortable concept of his contemporaries, for whom God was El Shaddai, the "Distant One" to be honoured, feared, and worshipped. Jesus took on a critical and revolutionary stand against this static and passive belief, by bringing God into the reality of daily life and revealing a revolutionary human-divine relationship that could only be

---

5   Pope Francis, *Misericordiae Vultus*, 15.

compared to the relationship between a child and its parents. From a purely political standpoint, the Jews, faithful to their ancient traditions, were justified in condemning Jesus to death as a dangerous revolutionary. Unfortunately, by the time of Jesus, such inert tenets had reduced Yahweh to an inert distant God, truly the distant one to be feared and kept at arms' length with repetitious rituals. In contrast, Jesus' address of God as *Abba* was so radical for the faithful Israelites of his time as to be threatening and world shattering of all the religious, social, economic, and political construct of Israel. Yet, faithful and trusting in this *God-Abba*, Jesus did not flinch before the harshest opposition, and paid with his life for his obsession of being bonded with God so intimately and so intensely that it could only be expressed through the image of child-parent association. Jesus called God "*my Father and your Father*" (John 20:17).

Because of its intense relational connotations, *Abba-Father* is Jesus' favourite expression and the most powerful image of God in the Gospel. "Abba" is a rare Aramaic term used affectionately by children towards their "daddy" and, because of its intense relational and affective weight, it remained one of the very few untranslated and authentic words originally uttered by Jesus and transmitted literally by the authors of the Gospel narratives. Even when the gospel narratives adopt other God-images suggesting vital dimensions of the divine presence in human history, nevertheless they always carry intense relational connotations and convey messages of God's bond with humanity clustered around the concept of God's compassion and mercy within the reality of daily life. Consequently, to understand the gospel message about God and about ourselves, it vital that we perceive the message behind the symbolic imagery of the narrative.

The language of images – the language of faith

Our life is full of gestures, words and symbols whose meaning goes way beyond the immediate experience. Moreover, far more than their literal meaning, it is this message that we need to be able to perceive and act upon beyond their symbolic representation, a message that is often too personal or too deep to express in words or rational arguments. Personal experiences sometime are difficult to express, and relationships can be experienced but never fully described. The more intense the emotion and the deeper the relationship, the more difficult it becomes to find the words to express adequately the experience. Consequently, a person becomes "a ray of sunshine", a heavy downpour of rain has something to do with "cats and dogs", and the heart transcends its anatomical structure to become a giving of oneself to another person in love. When we have difficulty in expressing the deeply personal reality of an event, we resort to images. Engaging our imagination overcomes the limitations of head-language and we enter the realm of heart-communication and, by going beyond the limitations of speculative language, we are projected us into the realm of relationship.

The fundamental message that the Word of God tries to convey is to express the personal relationship between God and real people; and this kind of depth relationship is so intense that only the open-ended message of imagination can express it. That is why images and symbols are the diamond drill of biblical narrative and communication, confronting both mind-set and behaviour about ourselves and about God, far beyond our immediate experience.

Jesus' parables are masterworks of the use of images. Thus, within the rural culture of biblical times, we read of wheat and weeds, of shepherds and sheep, of farmers and vinedressers, of sowing and vine-tending, of food and drink, of wedding feasts and lost coins, of children leaving home and women giving birth, of violence in the streets and poor widows giving their last penny in almsgiving. This is the richness of life situations drawn from the immediate daily experience of both storyteller and listener.

Jesus is not about proposing a new ethical code or agricultural instructions, but by tapping into the immediate experience of his listeners, he projects us into a totally other level of reality for which we do not have an adequate vocabulary or expression. The kingdom is about the level of a divine-human relationship and of God's interference in the daily reality of the human story. Culturally conditioned though parables and symbols may be, Jesus' use of images like fatherhood and motherhood reach deeply and powerfully into the very core of our being, and demand that we become actors of the narrative by delving into a personal appropriation of the message.

Two elements predicate on the parables of the gospels. First, the parables are conspicuously inconclusive, remaining unfinished and open-ended and leaving the listener or reader to fill in the ending and the lived message at the personal level. Secondly, most of these archetypal stories, while breaking through all limits of rationality and of human justice, often exaggerate a situation beyond the bounds of equanimity or even possibility. Jesus not only reflects his own cultural conditioning; but the hyperbolic style of his parables invariably forces the listener to confront a situation that appears illogical and radical in the extreme, and to make a decision for or against the human-divine relationship proposed by the story.

In Mathew 18:10-14, a real shepherd would not leave ninety-nine sheep in a desert place to go looking for a single stray one, and in Luke 15:8-10, the poor widow could not possibly invite friends to celebrate her find, as that would far outweigh the cost compared to the value of a few small coins. As for the father who gives his son his demanded share of the property (Luke 15:11-32), it would be inconceivable and almost blasphemous in that cultural setting.

In this perspective, it is essential then that we unravel the husks of time and place, so we can hear the pith of the message telling us of that human-divine relationship which the Word of God is trying to convey to us.

Unwrapping the husk

One such image that I believe to be fundamental for understanding our relationship with God and God's relationship with each and every one of us is the image of the *Good Shepherd*. In a pastoral setting such as biblical Palestine, images of sheep and shepherds take on a unique but understandable dominance in conveying the fundamental message of faith-relationship that underscores both the Old and the New Testament.

Beside dominating much of the biblical language in both the Old and the New Testaments, he image of the Good Shepherd overflows very early into the Christian iconography, and one of the first representations of Christ in the ancient catacombs of Rome is precisely a graphic depiction of Jesus inspired by the parable of the Good Shepherd (John 10:1-6).

However, I must confess to having been a very slow learner in reading the message conveyed by such imagery. Consequently, the rich biblical symbol of sheep and shepherds remained quite unappealing and unintelligible to me, even through years of exposure to Scripture reading, teaching and pastoral work. Besides, I must confess that for a long time the thought of being likened to a sheep did not really appeal to me. By contrast, precisely because of my cultural upbringing, the image-parable of the vine and the branches that Jesus adopted and left to us as his Last Will and Testament (John 15:1-4) spoke to me with far greater power of the relationship that God craves to establish with each of us individually and all of us collectively. To this day, an undulating landscape covered with luscious vines as far as the eye could stretch is both enticing and life-giving.

As a youngster, I grew up in a part of the world where shepherds were looked upon as strange and aloof people, and rather odd winter visitors. They were those people who would appear at the onset of autumn on the river flats on the edge of town. By now, heavy snow would have obliterated the higher reaches of their mountain pastures and driven the shepherds to lower levels in search of small plots of greener grasslands that they would lease from the local farmers for their flocks. They would set up a couple of tents in some grazing paddocks and watch their flocks forage placidly. Some of the men would occasionally come into the village, but I cannot recall the children ever mixing with us, either at school or at play.

For us children, that small flock on the outskirts of the village was both a curious novelty and a sign that winter was about to set in. Apart from this bucolic sight lasting but a few weeks in almost total isolation through the cold and dank days of winter, when the land was asleep under a blanket of snow, sheep and shepherd were unknown to me. Then, with the cold rays of sunshine of early springtime, they would disappear just unobtrusively almost overnight, not to be seen again for another twelve months at least. A short stay by strange people, living in a strange manner. An odd curiosity – harbinger of cold winter snow, we thought!

Eventually, I came to this country, where I encountered quite a different scenario, sheep identifying a valuable economic proposition, counted not by units but by thousands. Again, that did nothing to endear me to the idea of being a sheep, even if led by a shepherd-God.

It was only a chance event in my mid-thirties that suddenly and unexpectedly the powerful significance of Jesus' claim as the Good Shepherd exploded into my consciousness, its message linking and surpassing both my cultural presuppositions and the millennial expression of Scripture.

In the course of a visit to Palestine, one day a couple of friends invited me to join them to visit a Bedouin camp, not far from historic Bethlehem. The official tourist guide that met us was very keen to make a serious impression on these "Americans", and enthusiastically set out to illustrate the life around the tent settlement. After walking us through a variety of multi-shaped and multi-purpose tents – all the time the guide proudly enlightening us about their use and purpose – we returned into the sunshine, and immediately he pointed to a small rocky outcrop halfway up a gently sloping hillside. "And there is the shepherd", he declared with conviction. Did he read that "so what" look on our faces? He must have, as he immediately launched into a passionate description of the Palestinian shepherd.

"Things haven't changed in three thousand years, you know", he started, "because the shepherd is a shepherd forever, and that is all he can be", he explained. No, those sheep (about 20 goats, really!), did not belong to him; they were entrusted to him by various families of the clan. He was the trusted guardian of those animals and his whole life was totally enmeshed with their life and welfare, living with his flock and sleeping out in the fields, under a tent perhaps, with the sheep around him for mutual security and company. Yes, he had a name for each of those animals and they would respond to a personal unique pitch of his reed whistle, as they recognised the sound as their personal call. Yes, he would follow the brash one boldly wondering off and gently prod along the track the quiet and feeble. It was then that I found myself hearing again from the mouth of this simple but persuasive man the same expressions that were familiar to me from my years of repeated reading of Scripture, but without ever confronting the pith of the message. With enthusiasm now an unrelenting crescendo, our guide looked at us and declared with conviction, "That man is a shepherd and he can be nothing else. He is born a shepherd, he will die a shepherd, and he cannot be anything else but a shepherd. Take away those sheep from him, and he is nobody; he will no longer exist. His life is with those sheep or he is nothing at all". Then the final commanding revelation, "Take away those sheep, and he has no reason for living, he becomes a "nobody".

Suddenly, I found myself hearing the living voice of the Gospel for the first time with the same imagery, the same tone and, most of all, the obstinate message addressed to me and about me.

> *I am the good shepherd. The good shepherd lays down his life for the sheep. The hired hand, who*

> *is not the shepherd and does not own the sheep... I am the good shepherd. I know my own and my own know me ... And I lay down my life for the sheep. I have other sheep that do not belong to this fold. I must bring them also, and they will listen to my voice. So there will be one flock, one shepherd* (John 10:11-12, 14-16).

For the first time in my life, I understood the meaning and the power of the shepherd-image. Our God is a Shepherd-God, that One who can only be God in relation to us, and we are the reason for God's very existence. That is why God will stop at nothing to search and find me, not matter what I do, or wherever I stray, and rejoices at bringing me back from my straying ways (Luke 15:1-7). I no longer resent being likened to a sheep following a God who wants to share totality of life with me to an extent that my life is God's life and God's life is my life in return. The relationship is total, life-giving, and eternal, and we can only be thankful for such a revelation.

The biblical image of the Good Shepherd

It is a given of history that faith and spirituality revolve around its cultural/social context of daily life and draw expression and energy from that same daily life. The people of Israel were innately a nomadic people, and it was only through the dominant categories of that culture that they understood their personal and national identity in relation to their God, expressed their beliefs, and celebrated their rituals on the rhythm of seasons and place.

Consequently, the image-parable of the shepherd runs unrestrained through the whole of Scripture describing both the nature of God and that obsessive yearning on God's part in reaching out and enmeshing himself into the human story, a divine yearning that Pope Francis calls '*Mercy*'.[6]

The Old Testament is a millennial story of a rural and pastoral people whose very livelihood depended almost exclusively on nurturing and caring for their small but invaluable flocks.

> *I myself will be the shepherd of my sheep, and*
> *I will make them lie down, says the* LORD *God*
> (Ezekiel 34:15).

In the pastoral setting of first century Palestine, more than family heirlooms or expensive goods, the real riches lay outside the bounds of a dwelling, generally in the form of a small flock of sheep and goats, grazing about a rocky outcrop on the very edge of the village. That was the precious treasure for the biblical family, a treasure jealously safeguarded from wild animals and nightly marauders. Encircled by a secure stone enclosure, the shepherd was the one trusted member of the clan, delegated with keeping diligent watch at the gate. Indeed, he would sleep under the stars by that gate, surrounded by his flock.

Here is deep preciousness and a powerful significance at the same time. That flock was much more than an economic security or a means of livelihood. On the contrary, it assumed a sense of cultural identity, expressing the intimate relationship between God and his people. From the very beginning of its millennial history, dying Jacob blessed Joseph and his brothers saying,

---

6 [2] Pope Francis, *The Name of God is Mercy*, Bluebird Books for Life, 2016.

> *The God before whom my ancestors Abraham and Isaac walked, the God who has been my shepherd all my life to this day* (Genesis 48:15).

This reminder of Israel's unique identity and of God's commitment to his promises became the mantra of the entire prophetic tradition. Reflecting on the national tragedy of the exile and the total destruction of Israel's very identity, Isaiah would remind the people of God's unfailing fidelity by likening the return from Babylon and the reconstruction of Israel to a coming home in the evening when

> *Yahweh will feed his flock like a shepherd, he will gather the lambs in his arms and carry them in his bosom, and gently lead the mother sheep* (Isaiah 40:11).

With Ezekiel, Isaiah, and Jeremiah, we have a personification of the relationship between Israel as God's flock and Yahweh as the ever-nurturing and protecting Shepherd. Such was the relationship between shepherds and sheep that the flock became the symbol of Israel's lifestyle and the expression of its social, political and religious culture. Indeed, so intense was the power of the image that Yahweh himself identified with *the Shepherd of Israel*, totally given over to the care and welfare of his chosen flock. The identification was thus sanctioned, complete and eternal. The Shepherd-God was the guarantor of safety and preciousness for Israel, and Israel was Yahweh's uniquely precious flock. Sung in the psalms and proclaimed by the prophets, through the oracle of Ezekiel, Yahweh declares,

> *I myself will be the shepherd of my sheep, and
> I will make them lie down, says the Lord God'*
> (Ezekiel 34:15).

Psalm 23 (*The Lord is my shepherd*) has almost a bucolic feeling about it, as the pray-er stands in amazement, contemplating a peaceful and peace-filling scene of a shepherd gazing on a flock grazing by a flowing stream in absolute security and abundant nourishment.

The prophetic literature leaves no doubt that God is not only *The Shepherd* who leads and protects his flock, but also delegates this precious task to the leaders of the people. In a way, the image of a Shepherd-God flows instinctively down to those who have been entrusted with the responsibility *to be shepherd* and to secure care of the flock. It is up to these leaders to ensure that the human response to the relationship with God is fostered and the sheep are fed and looked after. The flock is too precious a treasure to be abandoned. Hence, the same prophetic culture becomes unforgiving in denouncing those leaders who, called to be shepherds, fail to care for the God's precious possession.

> *Woe to the shepherds who destroy and scatter
> the sheep of my pasture, says the Lord. Therefore,
> thus says the Lord, the God of Israel, concerning
> the shepherds who shepherd my people. It is you
> who have scattered my flock, and have driven
> them away, and you have not attended to them.
> So I will attend to you for your evil doing . . . I
> myself will gather the remnant of my flock out
> of all the lands where I have driven them. I will*

bring them back to their fold and they shall be fruitful and multiply. I will raise up shepherds over them who will shepherd them, and they shall not fear any longer, or be dismayed, nor shall any be missing (Jeremiah 23:1-4).

Likewise, Ezekiel is fierce against the shepherds who have betrayed their call and abuse the treasured flock entrusted to them.

As I live, says the Lord GOD, because my sheep have become a prey, and my sheep have become food for all the wild animals, since there was no shepherd; and because my shepherds have not searched for my sheep, but the shepherds have fed themselves, and have not fed my sheep; therefore, you shepherds, hear the word of the LORD: Thus says the Lord GOD, I am against the shepherds; and I will demand my sheep at their hand, and put a stop to their feeding the sheep; no longer shall the shepherds feed themselves. I will rescue my sheep from their mouths, so that they may not be food for them (Ezekiel 34:8-11).

Clearly, the image parable of the shepherd in the Old Testament carries a double dimension: the *mutual relationship* between us and God, and the *mission* of the people of God, with the leaders entrusted with the responsibility of nourishing and ensuring safety and growth for the whole flock. A *personal* dimension and a *community* commitment.

As Michael Winstanley puts it,

> The Scriptural image of the shepherd is certainly a window into the mystery of God and God's dealings with us. It illustrates God's provident care and healing love. It is also a symbol which captures so expressively the reality and role of Jesus. It captures his compassion, his teaching and revealing, his healing and solicitude, the life-giving and liberating intimacy of his relating, his faith protecting, and his commitment to us to the extent of dying for us. It is an image, which beckons us to reflection and contemplation, and to a response of trusting love.[7]

True to his Old Testament socio-religious culture, Jesus readily taps into the same symbolism, and the dominant language of the shepherd who gives his life for the flock becomes a catechesis and the central underlying theme of his earthly life and mission. Fullness of life is what God wants for us, and this gift is ours because Jesus, in total obedience to the Father, is the Shepherd who does not find laying down his life for humanity too great a price to pay, so that we may have life.

> *I came that they may have life, and have it abundantly* (John 10:10).

By contra-posing a series of opposites, such as the gate versus the wall of the sheepfold, the shepherd versus the stranger, and the authentic shepherd versus the hireling, Jesus highlights the

---

[7] Michael T. Winstanley, *Don Bosco's Gospel Way*, Bolton: Don Bosco Publications 2002, 40.

transformation that faith and abandonment into our Shepherd-God can bring about in our life. The Shepherd God is the God who knows us with a deep and personal knowing of the heart, offers us security if we but trust in him. This Shepherd-God yearns to enter at all costs into a relationship so personal, so deep that is all embracing, and life-giving; and nothing will frustrate this yearning, not even death itself.

> *I am the good shepherd. I know my own and my own know me, just as the Father knows me and I know the Father. And I lay down my life for the sheep* (John 10:14-15).

Each person ever created is worth more than the entire world, and God is prepared to risk the whole world for each one of us. When it comes to the relationship between God and us, our God is reckless, and he will do anything to bring us home from our wayward wonderings, seeking, pursuing, and wasting energy for each one of us. The parable of the lost sheep is a classic example, illustrating this divine recklessness, expressed once again in terms of sheep and shepherds.

> *Which one of you, having a hundred sheep and losing one of them, does not leave the ninety-nine in the wilderness and go after the one that is lost until he finds it? When he has found it, he lays it on his shoulders and rejoices. And when he comes home, he calls together his friends and neighbours, saying to them, "Rejoice with me, for I have found my sheep that was lost* (Luke 15:4-7).

Here we have a preposterous situation deliberately told in hyperbolic terms, aimed at shocking his audience directly into a personal challenge. It must have sounded shocking and absurd to Jesus' contemporaries. No one in Israel could claim possession to more than twenty or so sheep or goats, and these were entrusted to the care of the shepherd, who would look after them even at the risk of his own life. A flock of one hundred sheep was an unimaginable and unattainable fortune that only an unbelievably rich man could dream to possess. Yet, very bluntly, Jesus tells his hearers and us that this shepherd was prepared to risk everything, his reputation, his livelihood, and indeed his very life, and do the unthinkable for the sake of just that one sheep, who after all had decided to go astray and leave the flock.

We can only surmise the response of Jesus' hearers to such an outrageous story, but to us, two millennia later, the pith of the story is unquestionable. The parable of the reckless God abandoning everything to search for me demands a conversion of both heart and mind. The parable invites us to contra-pose positive attitudes to negative experiences, expressed through joy even in a situation of loss and fear.

> *Rejoice with me, for I have found my sheep that was lost* (Luke 15:6).

Is such a revelation too good to be true? Well, Jesus persists in reassuring us that we are entrusted into his hands by the Father himself, because God thinks that we are individually worth more than anything in creation and, *"no one can steal me from the Father"* (John 10:29).

A spirituality of "The Good Shepherd"

The message is clear. As Pope Francis has been shouting to the whole world since the Jubilee Year (2016), the God of mercy and compassion is prepared to lose everything just for me, to meet all my needs, whatever my needs or my faults may be.[8] Can I accept such a challenge and live accordingly, or is the news too good to be true, and so I prefer to wallow in self-pity, rather than accepting that God thinks that I am worth risking everything, and comes after me precisely when I prefer to wander away and live by my personal agenda?

The image of the Good Shepherd assures me that when I am lost in confusion and anxiety, imprisoned by loneliness, fear and guilt; or I feel trapped by weakness, mistakes and sinfulness, I can only respond through hope, courage, and trust. In the topsy-turvy of my life, I can rest assured that my Shepherd God will come after me, embrace me in my uncleanliness and fears, put me on his shoulders and take me home rejoicing. Whatever I think I am, or my conscience may reproach me of, though often the unwilling sheep, I am God's most treasured possession and the reason for God being God. God's life is enmeshed integrally with mine, and God's care, concern, presence, healing and affection is completely focused on me. This God knows me by my name; indeed, he has given me a name, and even if I do tend to be a wanderer, seeking personal interest and agenda, somehow I can never escape God's watchful eye calling me to safety, or his searching presence bestowing safety, healing and security.

---

8   Pope Francis, *The Name of God is Mercy*, 2016. Also, *The Infinite Tenderness of God. Meditations on the Gospels*. The Word among Us Press, 2016.

> *Very truly, I tell you, I am the gate for the sheep... Whoever enters by me will be saved, and will come in and go out and find pasture.... I came that they may have life, and have it abundantly.... I am the good shepherd. The good shepherd lays down his life for the sheep... I am the good shepherd. I know my own and my own know me, just as the Father knows me and I know the Father. And I lay down my life for the sheep* (John 10:11-15).

Gates and doors are meant to give security and safety, preventing intruders and marauders from entering, and safeguarding the people and the property inside the house. Anybody who has been the victim of a housebreaking or of any unauthorised entry will know that nothing is more disturbing and disquieting than finding an unknown intruder in one's private dwelling, or discovering the horror of a ransacked home. Yes, our life can be full of intruders disturbing our peace and creating anxiety for our future. Beyond the pain of loss and damage of personal and precious property, one feels violated deep inside one's psyche where the trauma can leave lifelong scars with psychological syndromes of insecurity, anxiety and suspicion. Yet, even in this kind of turmoil or upheaval, the disciple can be at peace, protected inside the wall of God's love, and safe with our God at the gate.

As human beings, we must be worth a great deal if our Shepherd-God commits himself to stand by us in order to secure our comings and goings, and to safeguard our wellbeing, not only as a faithful guard, but also as the very gate into life itself. In this powerful rural image, Jesus identifies himself as the instrumental presence and energy that will give us fullness of life and make us who we are meant to be and to become. All too often, we waste a great deal of psychological and emotional energy in breast beating and wallowing in self-pity, nourishing that deep but unspoken sense of unworthiness and of being unloved, while all the time our God is there at the gate of our hearts, calling us into awareness that we are precious in God's eyes and loved as we are. Too often we curse the darkness of the night, while not realising that our God is there as our security right through that night.

Personifying God as Mercy, Pope Francis reminds us that

> There are no situations in life we cannot get out of, we are not condemned to sink into the quicksand, in which the more we move the deeper we sink. Jesus is there, his hand extended, ready to reach out to us and pull us out of the mud, out of sin, out of the abyss of evil into which we may have fallen. We need only be conscious of ourselves, and not lick our wounds.[9]

The all-pervading sense of unworthiness often breeds an equivalent and even more dangerous sense of fear, insecurity and hopelessness, which we try to exorcise through compulsions, abuse or escapes into palliatives. However, palliatives do not heal, they only pretend and disguise, distorting our perceptions, easing the pain and generating a twisted sense of reality through loss of life meaning and of personal identity. For the believing disciple, the only security that will heal and generate life is the acceptance of

---

9   Ibid. 85.

our God, which is integral both to the exhilaration of full daylight, as well as to the darker experiences of our lives. Ultimately, our claim to faith rests or falls on our trust in this unconditional God-presence at every turn and twist of our story, and on our readiness to draw energy for individual and cosmic fulfilment by the awareness and acceptance of this life-giving presence.

Significantly, Jesus did not say 'I am *like* a shepherd', but used an expression of ultimate authority and identification, *I am*, projecting us immediately into God's very self-disclosure to Moses and the people of Israel. '*I am who I am*' is the name of God in the Old Testament, bringing into play life as much as the deeply personal and freeing life-relationship between Yahweh and his people. Later, Jesus will use the same expression, *I am*, to identify himself with energy for life (bread), oneness of life between God and us (vine), total and absolute care even at the cost of one's life (shepherd), as well as personal intimate relationship (friend).

Perhaps such a revelation sounds too good to be true, and we may even wonder if we are ever worth or capable to receive such care from our God. Perhaps, like the shepherds of my childhood, God can occasionally be the strange one just drifting on the outskirts of our daily reality. Yet whatever the straying on the rocky outcrop of our existence, God's choice is to be the shepherd-God, and God's name will never change. *I AM* the good shepherd who is prepared to lay down his life for you, and has no reason for existing except for you and me.

Besides making a statement of self-revelation and pointing to the fundamental rationale of Jesus' life and mission, these words carry a triple intent. First, by identifying himself with the shepherd keeping watch at the gate of the sheepfold, he calls forth in the disciples a new awareness of their preciousness in the eyes of God. Secondly, by making himself the guarantor of life-giving Good News, Jesus offers reassurance and peace, allaying fears and undue anxiety in the face of struggle and personal or collective negativity. Thirdly, Jesus entrusts his mission of peace and of guardianship to the believing disciples, wounded to become healers, and called to be messengers and instruments of peace, joy and security for the whole world. Secured by the Good Shepherd guiding our comings and goings through the various gates of our lives, now we believers must in turn become shepherds to each other and to the whole world.

Conclusion

With God as the living presence in our lives, and with Jesus as the Shepherd securing our pathway to personal fulfilment, we know that at every heartbeat of our existence we are wrapped by the loving care and compassion of our God. Then, we can truly face life with hope in uncertainty, courage in our setbacks, and joy in our struggles. As we wonder through the rocky outcrops of our stories and the uncertainties and darkness that may at times surround us, we can claim with the Apostle Paul,

> *If God is for us... neither death, nor life... nor anything else in all creation, will be able to separate us from the love of God in Christ Jesus our Lord*(Romans 8:31.38-39).

As I look back at the shepherds of my younger years at the foot of the Alps, I will never again see strange people living a strange life, aloof from everybody, suddenly disappearing into the dead of winter. Now the shepherd is the harbinger of deep and precious relationship, of overwhelming care and of eternal life-giving presence. Moreover, all this is lavished on me. Though at times I may be an unwilling sheep, a wanderer often seeking personal adventures of my own, I am God's most treasured possession and the raison d'être for God being God. Totally and integrally enmeshed with my life, God's concern, presence, and affection are focused completely on me. The drifter in me is forever searching for personal interests that take me away from the path set out by the Shepherd-God, or I may be lost among the briars deep in the crevasses of sinfulness and personal mistakes. Yet, I can never escape God's watchful eye calling me to safety, or his searching presence carrying me on his shoulders, bestowing on me unconditional care, compassion, healing, and security, and all the time rejoicing at finding me in spite of myself.

> *If God is for us . . . neither death, nor life . . . nor anything else in all creation, will be able to separate us from the love of God in Christ Jesus our Lord*(Romans 8:31.38-39).

Spirit

The Energy of the Kingdom
Acts 2:1-12

When the day of Pentecost had come, they were all together in one place. And suddenly from heaven there came a sound like the rush of a violent wind, and it filled the entire house where they were sitting. Divided tongues, as of fire, appeared among them, and a tongue rested on each of them. All of them were filled with the Holy Spirit and began to speak in other languages, as the Spirit gave them ability.

Now there were devout Jews from every nation under heaven living in Jerusalem. And at this sound the crowd gathered and was bewildered, because each one heard them speaking in the native language of each. Amazed and astonished, they asked, 'Are not all these who are speaking Galileans? And how is it that we hear, each of us, in our own native language? Parthians, Medes, Elamites, and residents of Mesopotamia, Judea and Cappadocia, Pontus and Asia, Phrygia and Pamphylia, Egypt and the parts of Libya belonging to Cyrene, and visitors from Rome, both Jews and proselytes, Cretans and Arabs—in our own languages we hear them speaking

> about God's deeds of power.' All were amazed
> and perplexed, saying to one another, 'What
> does this mean? (Acts 2:1-12).

At the break of morning

All of us have our little pet hates, small, trivial little things that annoy and irritate us: food that we avoid because of their colour, positioning of papers and clips on our desks, people exhibiting certain mannerisms. Nevertheless, while such pet hates undoubtedly irritate us, they also raise our awareness of differences and diverse reactions to beauty and richness in us and around us. Indeed, those very annoying peculiarities can sometime be the source of rich and deep insights, and occasionally of dramatic awareness stimulating change and transformations. That is what happened to me one early morning.

I dislike the wind intensely. It makes me particularly uptight, unbearable to myself and others; and that had been a particularly wild night: swishing, howling, creaking of boards, and rattling of windows, crashing of branches, and swirling of dead autumn leaves against my door.

I had slept in fits and starts as the haphazard yet unrelenting upsurge of that invisible fury swung me on a rollercoaster of half sleep and wakefulness all night, thus adding to my frustration and tiredness. How foolish to be angry at the wind, but I did feel a strong surge of anger spurred on by that subconscious certainty that I had absolutely no control either over the elements or over my unreasonable, though self-justified, reactions.

The flickering electric clock said 6.00 am and I peered through the curtains, unconvinced that the new day would somehow relieve the restlessness of a sleepless night. It was so intensely dark out there, and I double-checked the time.

Then, suddenly and most unexplainably, heavy boots on my feet and the thick coat wrapped tightly round my body, I was halfway up that track, winding through sparse clumps of trees and green pastures dotted with cattle, grazing unconcerned by the vagaries of the wind or the moodiness of the unusual morning visitor. I had been up that mountain, affectionately – but for no reason at all – labelled Mount Tabor, many times before, when the sun was warm, and the three-hundred-and-sixty-degrees vista was breathtaking. But never before had I trudged my way up that rocky outcrop shielding our rural retreat enclave from the busy thoroughfare of the high intensity roadway at six in the morning, challenging a fierce early winter storm. This was a unique climb, strange in its unplanned timing and spontaneity. "Sheer madness brought on by the frustrations of a sleepless night and a howling wind!", I thought, not finding any other self-justification for my uncharacteristic and deep-down unwanted hike up that track at that time of morning.

It was then that I saw it, and the moodiness of my thoughts was suddenly snapped into awareness. I stopped short, just before the brow of Tabor, my eyes transfixed on the dark outline of the nearby hills to the East. A bright red and orange sheath of light was tearing the black sky apart, ripping away large chunks of clouds in a spectacular and awesome dance of colours, shapes and life, bursting forth from the dark womb of a stormy night. Even the howling wind had taken on a new role, rising and falling in unison and creative harmony with the symphony of a new day exploding in the morning sky. Reds, orange, yellow and blue spread and danced across the sky, as the darker fragments of the heavy night clouds raced recklessly into some magic dissolution point towards northeast.

As I reached the top of the hill, the explosion of light and colour had overtaken me and now it embraced me, bathing the valley below, and spreading a myriad of hues on the vast expanse of the city twenty kilometres away. Distant Mount Macedon, a soft, bluish outline marking the western horizon, seen but mostly unnoticed over many years, now sparkled clear...

Day had broken through, and the onrush of light and warmth had overcome the wildness of the night wind. A new sense of life and peace and harmony seemed to take over, soothing my moods and my limbs, and bringing into sharp relief objects and details seen a thousand times yet never noticed before. As I gazed into the distant horizon, now swept clean, washed by the fury of the night and brought to life by the warmth of the new light, I felt a new vision awakening and a new perspective come into relief. Distant and faint objects came into focus with astonishing sharpness and clarity, as if they were now at arm's length. The dullness of the city sky, shrouded in weeks-long smog, was now crystal clear, revealing a unique richness of shapes and forms. The autumn colours of the nearby hills at my back breathed a sense of wonder and of growth that no Michelangelo will ever portray.

Suddenly, the wind stood still. And the kookaburra laughed. And the hawk hovered silently overhead. All brought on as the triumphant finale of that irritating and stormy night. At that point, an awesome all-transforming explosion of light and life exploded into my consciousness and a sudden realisation overwhelmed me: it was Pentecost Sunday morning. Any wonder then that the early Christians, in trying to express the experience of what happened to them on that first Pentecost morning, used precisely the imagery of wind and fire (Acts 2:1-12)? Re-echoing the creation story, the event of Pentecost proved of such cosmic dimensions that only images and the language of metaphors could adequately express its manifestations and consequences.

> *When Pentecost day came round, they had all met in one room, when suddenly they heard what sounded like a powerful wind from heaven, the noise of which filled the entire house in which they were sitting; and something appeared to them that seemed like tongues of fire; these separated and came to rest on the head of each of them. They were all filled with the Holy Spirit, and began to speak foreign languages as the Spirit gave them the gift of speech. Now there were devout men living in Jerusalem from every nation under heaven, and at this sound they all assembled, each one bewildered to hear these men speaking his own language. They were amazed and astonished. . . . Everyone was amazed and unable to explain it.* (Acts 2:1-12)

Pentecost: death and re-birth

The narrative of the Pentecost event carries a strong sense of deja vu, immersing the reader into the powerful cosmic events of God's creative act of Genesis 1, when

> *the earth was a formless void, there was darkness over the deep, and God's spirit hovered over the water* (Genesis 1:2).

Because of this *breath of God*, life exploded into being and chaos was redeemed. The primordial elements of fire and wind speak of total transformation not only for the cosmic world, but also affecting in a radical way the lives, and indeed the very being of those who live through it for all ages. For the disciples gathered in the Upper Room, grieving the loss of Jesus of Nazareth and all that this loss meant for their lives, Pentecost re-interprets and reincarnates a moment of radical transformation of their life story and a new beginning, totally unexpected, unplanned, and unexplainable. It was as if an irresistible energy had invested those people, upturning every dimension of their life, and propelling them into a totally new and unexpected level of reality and state of being. Pentecost recalls both the saving historical event of Jesus' Resurrection and, most importantly, the personal and communal experience of Resurrection for the disciples and for us.

Taking a chronological view of the events, John Shea makes the point that the disciples experienced the loss of Jesus twice, each time engendering a powerful alternate current of high energy, from hopeless dejection and to explosive elation and dynamic commitment. The first time occurred when Jesus walked out of the Upper Room into the darkness of the night, and eventually into his death and burial. The second time, when they were left staring into the sky, as he finally went to the Father. In between these two events stands the incredible experience of Resurrection, apparently shattering fear and death itself, only to be shattered in return by the final going away.

From a literal perspective, one cannot but notice the strong parallelism between the Easter stories of the gospel narratives on the one hand, and the Pentecost narrative of Acts 2 on the other. In both cases, the disciples are in a state of shock, withdrawal, and denial, searching for a meaning in the world-shattering upheaval that has overtaken them. In both cases, the scenario is one of loss of immeasurable consequence, of emptiness, and of hopeless waiting for the furore to simmer down, before returning each to their fields and their nets, in the hope of forgetting the tragic and ill-conceived events that brought them to this point.

However, in both events there is a definitive turning point that has neither rhyme nor reason in human terms; an experience of such magnitude and power that only a direct intervention of God in human history could have brought it about. In both events, the deep sense of loss somehow explodes into an intense sense of wonder and joy that defy human words and propel those who lived through it not only to proclaim a revolutionary message, but also to live in a totally new way. Diarmuid McGann comments

> Absence and presence seem to be a rhythm all through the Gospel... Each moment of absence seems to be followed by a more intense moment of presence. When he has been with them for a while, they begin to take him for granted and create an illusion about themselves. They elevate their status, position and importance. Their identity becomes inflated. In the moment of darkness there is a reversal, and in the

experience of absence they are invited into a new awareness.[10]

Jesus' reassurance to his disciples at the Last Supper that he *would not leave them orphans*, because the *Father would send another advocate to be with them forever* (John 14:15-20) must have sounded hollow and quite incomprehensible on that tragic day of execution and burial, or as they stood staring into the sky where the Lord seemed to have disappeared. However, as they cowered once again in the Upper Room, gripped by fear and incomprehensibility, waiting for the furore to calm down, suddenly it all made sense. Indeed, the energy released by that "strong wind" and that wild "fire that filled the place", not only reminded them of the promise he had left them, but it touched their heart and soul, transforming them into entirely new creatures. Then, and only then, they understood the words now spoken to them in wind and fire:

> *Do not be afraid... You shall receive power when the Holy Spirit has comes upon you; and you shall be my witnesses,,, and I will be with you until the end of time!* (Acts 1:8).

Then they remembered. The experience of Jesus is foundational for the Christian believer of all times. Historically, however, that physical experience of Jesus' presence is short-lived, limited in time to a few individuals and, from a human perspective, unbelievably tragic in its ultimate solution. Once Jesus of Nazareth was no longer with them, the early Christians had only the memory of Jesus, of what he did and of what he said. However, the

---

10 Diarmuid McGann, *The Journeying Self. The Gospel of Mark through a Jungian Perspective*, New York NJ: Paulist Press, 1985, 159.

memory could not just remain a nostalgic recall of past events, an empty ritual to be performed, or a sentimental and arrogant claim denying the stormy night. The memory of Jesus in the Church of all time can only be real to the extent that it becomes a lived and critical evaluation of the present reality in the light of Jesus' life and death, without sweeteners or alibis, possessiveness or exclusivity. From the very beginning of the story, that *memory* celebrated in word and table fellowship became a celebration of the radical and dramatic transformation from death to life, pre-figuring in Jesus' very life and mission. That memory engendered in them by the onrush of the power promised to them by Jesus as his last will and testament and as his parting gift on the night before he left them and died.

Those parting words of reassurance, of promise of the Spirit, and of missioning to witness, are not just nice platitudes from some ancient text, at best recalling an event of the distant past, probably irrelevant to our life and in our history. The believer of all time is nothing but the reincarnation of the disciples of Jesus in real terms in their own time. For the disciples of long ago, the Resurrection was only subsequent to Good Friday, and the early Christians had to come to terms with the absence of Jesus before they could proclaim him in faith as "Jesus the Lord". They had to experience death before they could announce resurrection. They had to go through the eye of the storm before they came to the full self-realisation of being intimately linked with Jesus through the power of the Advocate whom Jesus would send from the Father (John 16:5-15).

They had to go through the painful, but cleansing and transforming power of fire and storm so that the new life they proclaimed could be really seen as the power of God's Spirit at work in the lives of real men and women. Just as the Resurrection event proclaimed what God worked in Jesus through the power of the Spirit, the Pentecost event proclaimed the presence and the action of the same divine Spirit in the life of people throughout the whole of human history. The one firm conviction of the early Christians was the certainty of the active presence of Jesus in their midst in a unique and all-transforming manner, a presence so powerful and so real that it could only be described in metaphors of fire and wind.

Pentecost is precisely the celebration of this God-empowered transformation from death to life, from fear to hope, from sadness to joy, and from absence to presence, not just for a handful of people hiding in a house "*for fear of the Jews*" (John 20:19), but for all believers and for all times.

The Spirit: presence and destiny

As I came down from the mountain, now aglow in the morning sun, I became distinctly aware of being caught up in a process of transformation, far beyond my powers of comprehension or my ability of expression. Light-footed and boisterous of mind and body, now I was no longer a mere spectator of a meteorological spectacle on the cusp of changing seasons. I knew that, by my standing there on that mountain, I had become an integral part of a re-creation that no human power could ever call into being. This was no mere passage of time from night to day, heralded by a spectacular sunrise. Here was much more than the beginning of a new day. This was a moment of passage from the warm apathy of a long summer to the wild but pregnant fruitfulness of autumn.

The fury of the nightly elements had ushered in a new season. The hot dry summer was coming to an end and the symphony of colour and sounds around me spoke of calm and gathering time just around the corner.

A new presence impregnated the cosmos, and all around me a new energy was stirring. New gifts were in store, new energies groaned and waited to be released (Romans 8:22-24). New perspectives pushed beyond a horizon, so clear now but probably soon to be dulled by forgetfulness and self-interest. New visions and dreams gave meaning and worth both to the storm and to the untimely mountain climb. This was truly a transforming moment, and now, energised by the memory of wind and fire, it was my turn to tell the story. My life had to tell that story.

The seasonal transformation and the natural rites of passage are inexorable and teeming with possibilities. Likewise, our liturgical cycle is calling us out of Easter and into Pentecost, the season of fire and wind, of transformation and new beginnings, of energy and renewed sense of presence. Are we such people of transformation, of new beginnings, of renewed energy, and of fresh awareness? On the other hand, are we just gazing at an event of the past with no significance and even less bearing on our daily life?

At the Ascension of Jesus, the disciples stood gazing into the heavens, worrying about the destiny of Jesus, and wondering, once again, about the absurdity of another good-bye, of more unanswered questions, and of further loss and loneliness. The sense of loss is so all pervading at times, that even idle wondering and speculation seems to relieve the boredom of questioning where God is. However, the message of Easter and Pentecost is not about speculations. It cuts deeply into the sameness and practicality of our lives and, like a fiery sword of light, it must reshape our perspective and our praxis. There is a strong sense of earthiness in words spoken to the disciples by God's messenger. The presence of Jesus in the Spirit is not an otherworldly pie-in-the-sky, but an energy in our life and in our hands, enabling a new self-awareness of who we are, and a new vision of what we do, both as individual believers and as a Church community.

> *Why are you men from Galilee standing here looking into the sky? Jesus who has been taken up from you into heaven, this same Jesus will come back in the same way as you have seen him go there* (Acts 1:11).

Pentecost is a celebration both of God's ongoing presence and of our own personal destiny as disciples. The sense of *presence* calls us to accept that the power of God's Spirit is forever at work in our life, whatever the vagaries of our human story. On the other hand, the sense of *destiny* challenges us to nourish our awareness that this active power of God at work is a power for *transformation* with a precise, uniquely personal, and eternal intentionality expressed by the author of Ephesians as intimacy with God from all eternity and for all eternity (Ephesians 1:3-12). There is no doubt in Paul's mind as to who we are, once we accept the "breath (*ruah*) of God" in our life. The Spirit promised by Jesus and sent by the Father establishes a total and intimate relationship between God, the relationship of child and life-giver and us (Romans 8:14-17). The believing disciple is forever a child of God, and God is forever our 'Abba'. The Spirit is the spirit of wholeness within us, with each other, and with our God.

> *For all who are led by the Spirit of God are children of God. For you did not receive the spirit of slavery to fall back into fear, but you have received the spirit of adoption. When we cry, "Abba! Father!" it is the Spirit himself bearing witness with our spirit that we are children of God, and if children, then heirs, heirs of God and fellow heirs with Christ, provided we suffer with him in order that we may also be glorified with him*(Romans 8:14-17).

Are we people who have grown and been transformed, or have we been more concerned with maintaining our own perspectives and our securities? Are we people who have the courage to climb the mountain of self-discovery, and allow ourselves to change our perspective on God, on ourselves and on others; or are we people who lock themselves in their own private spirituality, cursing the wind of change and of insecurity? In the words of Richard Rohr, "Authentic and mature religion is always about *your transformation*".[11] Are we truly convinced of such a human-divine identity beyond some shallow sentimentality, ritual correctness, or academic assent? When the unexpected, the unplanned and the unwanted shatters all our well laid plans, do we wallow in self-pity, or do we become *people of silent joy, of active hope, and of down-to-earth commitment*?

Hope is never waiting for things to happen to us. The disciples had to stop looking up to the heavens, and start focusing on the earth where they stood and where they had been sent by the Lord.

---

11 Richard Rohr, *A Spring Within Us. A Year of Daily Meditations*, SPCK, 2018, 126.

Hope is making things happen in spite of ourselves, and allowing God to make things happen through us, on the one surety that the Spirit-Advocate groans within us and walks the darkness with us. Hope is seeing the smile of God in the smile of the child and the pain of God in the loneliness of the aged and/or abandoned person. As the good sister said to her younger sibling when she realised that her incurable disease was progressing rapidly and that soon she would no longer be able to do or speak, to walk or to communicate in any way, "I know that everything will be taken away from me. But nobody will ever be able to take away my ability to smile". And that was the way she lived and died: smiling. Hope is remaining open to the revelation of God, wherever and however God reveals himself in our daily commonality and drudgery, in our success and laughter, in our living and in our dying (Galatians 5:16-25).

This is the kind of transformation that we celebrate at Pentecost and to which we re-commit ourselves each time we say we believe in God-with-us. However, unless this transformation becomes incarnated in every fibre of our being, we may hold on to the memory of a distant and unintelligible event for the sake of human traditions, but we will never celebrate the memory of Jesus, the Risen Lord who left us with the assurance that he *is* with us always, yes, "*to the end of time*" (Matthew 28:20). As Ronald Rolheiser put it,

> Pentecost is not an abstract mystery. We are asked to accept the spirit of our actual lives. When we do this, then we no longer belittle our own lives but know that even with all our

inferiorities and frustrations, just by ourselves, we are something.[12]

Pentecost proclaims both presence and destiny. Presence, in so far as to believe is to accept that the power of God's Spirit is forever at work in our life, whatever the vagaries of our human story. Destiny, because the believing disciple knows that this active power of God at work is a power for transformation toward a unique and personal intimacy with God, from all eternity and for all eternity. A person who has been touched and transformed by the power of God can no longer be satisfied with an individualistic, me-and-God-alone type of faith expression or relationship. The family business has to be carried on, and I, who profess belief, must now shout my newly discovered Good News to all I meet. Touched and transformed by the power of the Spirit, the disciples cannot hide the secret any longer. The Spirit is the spirit of wholeness stirring deep within the very spiritual DNA of each of us, urging us to each other, and to our God. As if impelled by a force beyond their control, immediately following the storm of fire and wind, the disciples became reckless and fearless proclaimers of hope, and bearers of joy to the whole world.

Let us also allow ourselves to be challenged and questioned by this presence. What happened to the apostles as a community gathered and enlightened by the Spirit, struggling against all odds and in spite of human incompleteness and limitations, must take place again today in our ecclesial assemblies, in our classrooms, parishes, youth centres, playgrounds, in our tenement houses and just down the main street. The self-awareness of the Good News of

---

12 Ronald Rolheiser, *Forgotten Among the Lilies. Learning to Love Beyond Our Fears*, New York NY: Doubleday, 2005, 195

a God, whom we know as life-giver and energiser, has to transform the world and radically change people in the way they think, they speak, and they act; indeed, in their very self-consciousness, or it is not good news at all. Witness and commitment to joy, hope, peace, and unity are not optional extras for the believer, but the unstoppable outpouring exuding from faith in the power of God in our hands. Then we can honestly pray, *'may your kingdom come'*, as we will be the instruments of this kingdom. Then people will take notice, and wonder, and be transformed. Then the world will know the peace and love that the human heart yearns for, and that Jesus left us as his Spirit-powered, parting gift and last will and testament.

Calling

Called by Name into the Kingdom
Matthew 9:36 to 10:8

When he saw the crowds, he had compassion for them, because they were harassed and helpless, like sheep without a shepherd. Then he said to his disciples, 'The harvest is plentiful, but the labourers are few; therefore ask the Lord of the harvest to send out labourers into his harvest.'

Then Jesus summoned his twelve disciples and gave them authority over unclean spirits, to cast them out, and to cure every disease and every sickness. These are the names of the twelve apostles: first, Simon, also known as Peter, and his brother Andrew; James son of Zebedee, and his brother John; Philip and Bartholomew; Thomas and Matthew the tax-collector; James son of Alphaeus, and Thaddaeus; Simon the Cananaean, and Judas Iscariot, the one who betrayed him.

These twelve Jesus sent out with the following instructions: 'Go nowhere among the Gentiles, and enter no town of the Samaritans, but go rather to the lost sheep of the house of Israel. As you go, proclaim the good news, "The kingdom of heaven has come near". Cure the sick, raise

> *the dead, cleanse the lepers, cast out demons. You received without payment; give without payment'* (Matthew 9:36 to 10:8)

The human experience of naming

We have all encountered some embarrassing situations in life; moments when we knew that we said the wrong thing, or maybe when we had to confront an unexpected turn of events. Sometimes, however, these awkward experiences teach us a great deal about human nature, as it happened to me that night when I decided to call in, unexpectedly, at a friend's house. There was an unusual car in the driveway but, given the long friendship that bonded me to that family, it did not prevent me from ringing the front door bell. Yes, my friends had visitors: a middle-aged couple displaying clearly a very professional deportment. On welcoming, I was promptly introduced as Peter, and the unknown gentleman was warm in extending his hand. "Paul", he said easily. However, as I turned to his companion, I detected a strange coldness, though nothing had prepared me for the iceberg that I slammed against. To my "pleased to meet you", she barely moved her lips, let alone any facial muscle, as she simply declared, "And I am Paul's partner, a psychologist".

Coldness, distance, personal safety-first, rejection, do not come any closer, go away, were blatantly visible all rolled into one, and I readily accommodated by quickly mumbling some excuse, if there was any need of one, about having to leave early. I terminated sipping my coffee, greeted my friends, and made a quick exit. To this day, I still do not know the name of the lady, and honestly, I have no desire to know it. Her attitude said it all, and I wish to respect her choice of no-relationship. I had no part in her life, nor was she prepared to have any part of mine either, though I never felt so much a stranger to myself, and so unwanted in my whole life.

By contrast, have you ever seen the look of sheer excitement of the little child when you address her for the first time with her proper name? Of course, she is not to know that you have just heard somebody else address her by that name! "How do you know my name?" she will immediately enquire; and the chances are that she will ask you your name in return.

I remember when, following Vatican II, we religious were allowed and encouraged to relinquishing religious names and return to our baptismal names. I wonder if we still remember what it felt like when, for the first time since entering religious life, one of our sisters or brothers addressed us by our first name. For some, this gave rise to sheer exhilaration and freedom. For others, it turned out to be a real trauma, strongly resisting such innovations that appeared an attack to the very roots of one's personal identity, and defying the very ethos of religious life. In both cases, the underlying motivation for either joy or the pain elicited was the same, insinuating a radical revelation of who we were. For some of us being called by our baptismal name meant recognition of who we were for our parents and family, and it became a source of great joy and almost a re-discovery of our identity. For others, instead, it was just the opposite, namely a loss of their religious identity as the only identity they had ever known, and they had vowed their life to.

Our name impinges deeply on our psyche, saying something about us, and affecting deeply our very self-image. That is the power of the name. To call someone by name is to invite her or him into a very personal relationship with us, to break down the barriers and the masks that we carry – ('I am a psychologist', qualified my unknown friend) – and to remain open and transparent to the other, as he or she chooses to enter our life.

A biblical perspective

In this context, I would like to reflect on a Gospel event that to me is foundational to the meaning and nature of discipleship, both from an individual and personal perspective as well as at a community and ecclesial level.

To the Semitic mind, to know a person's name means to enter so deeply into that person's life as to possess that life totally and to have control over that person. Have we ever stopped and reflected on the words of the prophet Isaiah that we pray so often, *"I have called you by your name; you are mine"* (Isaiah 43:1)? From a reversed perspective, the Israelites always refused to pronounce the name of Yahweh, expressing it with the Tetragrammaton YHWH, and translating it as "Lord" (Adoni), precisely in order to avoid any misunderstanding that human being can possess and control God in any way.

I would like to focus on a Gospel event that to me represents a foundational element towards understanding our personal ID as disciples and as a Christian community.

> *When he saw the crowds, he had compassion for them, because they were harassed and helpless, like sheep without a shepherd... And he called to him his twelve disciples and gave them authority*

> *over unclean spirits, to cast them out, and to heal every disease and every infirmity. The names of the twelve apostles are these: first, Simon, who is called Peter, and Andrew his brother; James the son of Zebedee, and John his brother; Philip and Bartholomew; Thomas and Matthew the tax collector; James the son of Alphaeus, and Thaddaeus; Simon the Cananaean, and Judas Iscariot, who betrayed him . . . These twelve Jesus sent out, charging them . . . "Preach as you go, saying, 'The kingdom of heaven is at hand.' Heal the sick, raise the dead, cleanse lepers, cast out demons. You received without paying, give without pay"* (Matthew 9:36-10.8).

In this apparent who-is-who of Jesus' early followers, a number of significant elements stand out. First, unlike some events and narratives reported by only one or two evangelists, all the three Synoptics carry the narrative of the call of the disciples, thus suggesting the significance of this event in the memory of the early Christian communities within their diverse cultural understanding and experience of being called (Matthew 10:1-4; Mark 3:13-19; Luke 6:12-16).

Secondly, in many aspects, there is a noticeable diversity between the three Synoptic narratives, which highlights an important dimension of complementarity within the call of Jesus to follow him. A literal comparison of the three narratives may suggest an evident diversity of understanding and expression of discipleship proposed by the early Christian communities. In his understanding of Jesus as the fulfilment of the Jewish promise of

Messiah, Matthew is outward looking, proposing the call to follow him as an injunction to a mission of healing and compassion. Thus, he inserts this call story within a context of healings events, prefacing the call of the disciples by telling us that Jesus felt compassion on the crowds, *"because they were harassed and helpless, like sheep without a shepherd"*. For the Synoptics, healings are not just the work of a wonder worker, but also the sure sign of that living and active presence of God that Jesus calls the kingdom in our world (Matthew 11:2-19). In this way, Matthew links the calling to discipleship with becoming instruments of divine compassion and healing presence in the reality of one's situation.

On the other hand, both Mark (3:1-6) and Luke (6:1-16) are much more focused on the identity of the disciples themselves, and they highlight this dimension by having Jesus going *"out on the mountain to pray"*, and spending *"the night in prayer"*. In the overall gospel narrative, the withdrawal of Jesus "on the mountain to spend the night in prayer" is always a prelude to a major turning point in the narrative. In this way, Luke and Mark tell us that the disciples, called by Jesus in their full humanity, are challenged in their own identity and invited to enter into a special relationship with him. While Matthew is clearly mission oriented, Luke and Mark put more stress on the identity of the caller who is invited *to be and to walk with Jesus*.

These two diverse perceptions are foundational to understand the Gospel call to discipleship, not in terms of contradiction but of essential complementarity. Here we do not have a contraposition between ministry and identity but two critical dimensions balancing each other and constituting the very nature of discipleship. The call is an invitation *to be with Jesus*, so that, on the *energy* of that personal relationship, the disciple can then take up *the mission of healing and compassion* in the situation where he/she is at any one moment. The call of the disciples becomes a divine invitation to enter a special relationship with God, to be God's active instruments of healing and salvation in that kingdom, here and now. In that call, we, as disciples, have both identity and mission expressed as one. Our personal identity as disciples is linked with our mission of healing and compassion and our claim to discipleship must find its expression through our relationship with those who surround us. We have to be active instruments of a human/divine presence in the world, or the Word is dead and our claim to discipleship is ephemeral or void.

Thirdly, we are told that Jesus spent the night in prayer, before coming down from the mountain and choosing twelve from among the many that were by now following him. Here we do not have a casual trialling by a number of people fascinated by Jesus. On the contrary, this is a deliberate call by Jesus to those twelve to become his disciples. He chooses them, and he will remind them precisely of this at the last supper.

> *You did not choose me but I chose you. And I appointed you to go and bear fruit, fruit that will last, so that the Father will give you whatever you ask him in my name. I am giving you these commands so that you may love one another* (John 15:16-17).

Clearly, from the very beginning, we are told that our following of Jesus, in whatever walk of life, is primarily a considered divine decision, a call whereby God takes the initiative and invites us into his own company, for his own good reasons, in order to make us his friends, and send us on his mission of healing and compassion (Ephesians 1:3-14).

A fourth significant characteristic of these list of names is the *very personal and personalised call* addressed by Jesus to specific individuals, each with his own character and distinctive nature. These followers are called by their personal names, but a name that is far more than some anonymous electronic impulse hidden in some cyber cloud in space, or a blip in a complex computer system in some obscure government department. These followers are people, real and ordinary people called by name out of their ordinary life, and they are called as they are, gratuitously, into a relationship with Jesus that is deeply personal and powerfully intimate. As if to remind the reader that some of these first followers had no claim at all on the call, and to highlight the gratuitousness of it all, the evangelists qualify people by their family network (*"James, son of Alphaeus", "Sons of Zebedee)"*), by their profession (*"Matthew, the tax collector"*), and even by their political and social affiliations (*"Simon called the Zealot"*), or like Judas Iscariot as the one *"who betrayed him"*.

Of course, as the story unfolds, we know that eventually Peter openly betrayed Jesus to his face, and in the end *"they all deserted him and all run away"* (Mark 14:51), abandoning him to the ignominious death of a criminal. Yet, the call by name stands, gratuitous, undeserved and personal, and to the end Jesus will address these same broken and whimsical people as his "friends" and his "little children" (John 15:12-17). In spite of who they are or of what they do, it is clear that for Jesus the disciples are not anonymous or an impersonal bunch of individuals, but people with a unique and precious identity that has to be acknowledged by their individual names. God is not in the habit of addressing us impersonally. Created unique and precious, we are the work of God's hands; he calls us each by name into his own life to be disciples.

This is the reassuring and affirming message of the Gospel. To claim to be followers of Jesus in discipleship means to accept that we are called by name into a personal relationship with our God, just as we are, not because of any personal achievement or faith claim; simply because this is the way God wants it to be for each of us personally. Can I accept that God yearns to enter into a relationship with me as intense as the relationship between two people who know each other by name? Have we ever stopped to reflect and to thank God as we pray the words of the prophet, *'I have called you by your name; you are mine'* (Isaiah 43:1)? Whoever we may think we are and whatever our heart may hold or our memory may bring to consciousness, as believers we are people who are loved intensely by our God, simply because God thinks we are loveable as we are. God knows our names, and calls us by our name.

St Gregory the Great, writing about the encounter between Jesus and Mary Magdalene by the empty tomb, makes the point that when Jesus addresses her by the generic appellative of "woman" common to all her gender, she fails to recognise him. It is only when Jesus calls out to her as "Mary" that she recognises the one who is standing right there beside her as the one she longs for and who gives meaning to her life and to her own broken identity. And immediately the response is *"'Rabbouni', that is, 'Teacher'"* (John 20:11-18), a cry of recognition, of yearning, and of deep love by Mary of Magdala.[13] The love relationship is immediately re-established.

A revelation of who we are

The calling of the disciples by name then becomes a revelation of who we are. For Richard Rohr, we are "people on a gradual, lifelong journey of discovering and living our authentic identity as a unique, one-of a kind *beloved*.[14]

Fundamentally, we are ordinary people loved intensely by our God in the midst of our ordinary lives, as much as in death, loss and emptiness. We are loved even and in spite of sinfulness and betrayal, as the Gospel story so often reveals in so many ways. We are loved simply because God thinks we are loveable as we are, and in this love relationship, Jesus calls us each by name to be his disciples. However, in order to recognise the call, each of us has to look deeply into their hearts and there discern God speaking to us. In addition, once we have heard God's voice, we need to respond as Samuel did, '*Here I am, Lord; your servant is listening. I come to do your will*' (1 Samuel 3:8-9).

I always remember the lesson taught to me by a friend of mine many years ago, during a particularly challenging time of my life journey. As I was grieving over a very uncertain future and the stark reality of a radical change in lifestyle and ministry, with the transparency and honesty of a true friend, he said to me, "What do you think? God does not want your work, or even your priesthood.

---

13 "A Reading from the Homilies of Pope Gregory the Great on the Gospels", in *The Divine Office: The Office of Readings* on the Feast of St Mary Magdalene (22 July).
14 Richard Rohr, *A Spring Within Us. A Year of Daily Meditations*, London: SPCK, 2018, 11.

God wants you!" I will treasure that revelation for the rest of my days, not only because of its honest truthfulness, but especially because of its power to energise me and give me hope into the future. While I was assessing my whole life exclusively from the perspective of what I could do, I was alerted to the much deeper and more challenging truth that my future was entirely shaped and fulfilled by what God would and could do with me.

Because God wants me, and calls me on first name terms, I can say that my future is secure, not because of my puny efforts, but because God wants me and will always want me with the same desire that only two people in love with each other can understand and express.

Because God calls me by name, it means that God will reveal himself in the midst of the most ordinary and most unexpected events, people and situation. In turn, he will make me an instrument of his love to the world on his terms. The disciples were simple folk, fishermen, ordinary men and women, neither wealthy, nor powerful, or influential. On the contrary, they were illiterate, ignorant, powerless, and very, very fragile. Yet to them Jesus entrusted the task of carrying on his life-and-love mission, exactly where and as they are. That is what is happening to us and to every believer who is prepared to accept that God loves them deeply and personally... In my fragility and destitution of means, I must become an instrument of God's very life and love, where I am, and in spite of myself.

Because God calls me by name, I can truly address him as my Life-Giver, and pray to this God as Father and Life-Giver. Naming carries a unique power of closeness and of transparency, and in that case I can truly call upon God no longer as the dispenser of my personal whims or the energy of my own agenda, but as the one who sits with me in silence and journeys with me in my tiredness. Then I can truly pray to God, rather than just say many words that make me feel good, or remind him of what I want, now, all of it. Then truly, the heart of prayer is the prayer of the heart, that very hidden and personal depth where God speaks to me individually and personally.

God calls us by name, loving us unconditionally, and enriching us abundantly with his friendship and presence, not because of what we can achieve, but simply and solely because God wants it to be so. Calling us by name enriches us into the fullness of who we are.

Loving oneself

Concerned with a spirituality of self-denial, we spend a lifetime denying our God-given icon of the first chapter of Genesis, wallowing in self-pity, trying to pull ourselves up by our own bootstraps, and wasting psychic and spiritual energy in trying to keep God as far away from us as possible. This achievement-oriented spirituality only breeds the conviction that that we are not good enough for him, and consequently our whole life becomes a matter of survival through a twisted persuasion that makes us feel good about feeling bad and feeling bad about feeling good.

The early Christians sang about being the chosen ones, called into an eternal and everlasting love-plan of God.

> *He chose us in him, before the foundation of the world, to be holy and without blemish before him. In love he destined us for adoption*

> to himself through Jesus Christ, in accord with the favour of his will for the praise of the glory of his grace that he granted us in the beloved (Ephesians 1:4-6).

Likewise, reflecting on these same sentiments, St Francis de Sales waxes lyrical about God's attitude towards each of us.

> When did his love for you begin? It began even when he began to be God... without beginning and without end... He has always loved you from all eternity... God has placed you in this world not because he needs you in any way – you are altogether useless to him – but only to exercise his goodness in you by giving you his grace and glory.[15]

We need to remind ourselves that the yardstick of Jesus' all-embracing commandment of love is not outside of us, but deep within our own very self. *"Love your neighbour as yourself"*, said Jesus, and not "Love your neighbour as you hate yourself". Such an admission carries a fundamental bearing in relation to our mission as an expression of identity. How can we claim that we touch the lives of others, leading them to discover that they are loved unconditionally and eternally by their God, if we despise our own very self?

Reflecting on a long tradition of the Western Church, Richard Rohr laments on our spiritual journey:

---

15   St Francis de Sales, *Introduction to the Devout Life.* See also Vincenzo Mercadante, "Meekness in St Francis de Sales", (Trans. Germano Baiguini), 11.

> Our True Self remains untouched for most of us because any direct experience of God or explicit union with God was blocked, denied, and largely declared impossible. . . It always had to be mediated by a Bible, priest, minister, church, or sacrament, and very often the mediators, and the defending of their mediations, became the primary message itself. Most sermons reminded us quickly of our unworthiness before first telling us of our worthiness. Many were then so deep in a black hole of low self-image that they had no way to climb back out. There was no foundation to build on, and all they could see was their weakness and incapacity. We have had no solid or objective foundation upon which to build human personhood, and everybody was sent on their own – in total free fall. It did not need to be this way.[16]

When we accept our true self as people loved unconditionally by God, then such a belief in the goodness of God overflows naturally into the belief in an intrinsic goodness of human beings. However, we will never see the goodness of God in those around us or in those we work for, unless we are personally and deeply convinced that we are both loved and loveable in the eyes of God, regardless of our conditions, history, or circumstances.

The self-perception of being unloved can lead us to fear and discouragement at our own brokenness. Hence, it is vital that we

---

16 Richard Rohr, *Immortal Diamond*, London: SPCK, 2013, 125.

nourish an awareness that God knows our name and that even our brokenness is an inherent element of the masterpiece that we are, shaped by God's very hands out of amorphous and fragile clay and enlivened by God's very breath of life. Again, Richard Rohr very insightfully comments,

> How you love yourself is how you love the world, and how you love the world is the only way you will know how to love yourself. Our loving is of one piece. That is why we need to emphasise our inherent human identity as good and more than adequate, instead of always creating ever new contests for success and importance. This is the secret gift of any spirituality.[17]

Through the image of the potter and the clay, the prophet Jeremiah offers us a powerful parable in action and a deep insight into God's perception of human fragility as an inherent part of a divine masterpiece (Jeremiah 18:1-6). We need to believe in love of self as God's handiwork. Indeed, the preciousness lies precisely in that smallness and fragility, a fragility that may break and shatter, but paradoxically is strengthened further by every attempt to knit the pieces together (2 Corinthians 4:7-15).

Such ownership of the imagery, however, demands on our part self-forgiveness and reconciliation. A spirituality by which brokenness and fragility become a source of wallowing in self-pity and self-rejection, ultimately denies all possibility of God's healing intervention. On the contrary, from the perspective of the

---

17 Richard Rohr *A Spring within Us*, 18.

Potter-God, the fragility that we experience in our life is ultimately what makes us uniquely precious. My frailty is his delight and I am precious in his eyes (Isaiah 43:1-5). I am clayish, paper-thin, fragile, and yet precious and secure, because I am God's very own creation, his handiwork. This is the focus of Jesus' whole life and mission, witnessed, and proclaimed through his Abba experience: unconditional and unbounded love for each individual as a precious child. If God is the bountiful Abba who calls me by my name, then this involves an intrinsic sense of self as the recipient of Abba's love and life, and the first step in discipleship needs to be a conversion from a spirituality of brokenness to one of calling into life and love.

Befriending the shadow

However, to achieve this conversion, we need to befriend that shadow side that we all carry, and acknowledge as ours the negative feelings arising from memories of hurts and mistakes of the past, real or imaginary, that may continue to haunt us for a whole lifetime. When we learn to make friend with our negative feelings and to see beyond them to our true selves, then we discover that at the core of our being we are loveable. Then we begin to recognise more and more that God loves us intensely and calls us into life and love.

We need not suppress or exorcise our shadow side, but learn to hear the voice of our God calling us in the depth of our heart and through the shadows of our life. We need to become aware that the darkest recesses of the forest are teeming with life and growth and beauty, a life and growth that can only burst forth precisely because of the darkness and coldness of the environment. As I stand in the middle of the clearing half way up the hillside, gazing at the rain drifting away in the distance, I become suddenly aware that the power and beauty of the world around me is only enhanced by the interplay of darkness and light, by the storm rumbling in the distance, and by the shafts of sun-rays cascading through the blackest clouds onto the myriad of hues of the trees glistening with rain.

Jesus never once condemned sin and darkness. On the contrary, he not only confronted darkness but physically touched death, risking defilement and accepting the condemnation of uncleanliness on the part of those who considered themselves ritually pure. Jesus was not about pharisaic ritual purity or moral judgment, but about healing, affirmation, and revelation of a loving Abba. Consequently, he touches the bier of a dead person, and restores life to the only son of a widow (Luke 7:11-17). While pressed by crowds, just a simple touch of his cloak brings healing to the haemorrhaging woman (Mark 5:21-34). He calls the man who has never met him because he is blind, and he gives him back his sight (Luke 9:1-12). He orders dead Lazarus out of the tomb, and restores him to life (John 11:38-44). And, with the most exquisite touch of all, Jesus holds the hand of a little girl whom everybody bewails as dead, and calls her to life by naming her with a name of endearment, "Talitha Kum" (Luke 8:54). Where there is brokenness and death, Jesus seems to repeat always the same mantra: *"Stand up, do not be afraid"* (Matthew 17:7-9).

In all these situations, here was someone who was uniquely precious and fragile, and by touching and embracing that human fragility, besides healing the brokenness engendered by the darkness of their fears and self-condemnation, Jesus declared the preciousness of those people in the eyes of God. However, to do that, he had physically to touch death and darkness. Indeed, the resurrected Jesus carried the wounds of his own broken body, as a proclamation for all time that woundedness and brokenness are part of our reality as the beloved of Abba, never diminishing our relationship with God. The victorious resurrected Christ is a wounded Christ, who gives life to wounded but trusting disciples.

Our very nature as human beings as much as our commitment to follow the Master Craftsman in discipleship demands that we have the courage to admit to being called by God into a relationship so deep and so life-giving that it can only be expressed through being addressed on first name terms by the one who knows us deeply and loves us dearly. And when such human frailty makes heavy demands on our joy and hopefulness, let us pray for the courage and wisdom to listen with the heart. Then we will hear our God call us by name, and we will discover him holding us in the palm of his hand, a fragile but precious masterpiece, smiling at us with approval and love.

Relationship

Vines and Branches – Oneness of Life in the Kingdom
John 15:3-16

Abide in me as I abide in you. Just as the branch cannot bear fruit by itself unless it abides in the vine, neither can you unless you abide in me. I am the vine, you are the branches. Those who abide in me and I in them bear much fruit, because apart from me you can do nothing. Whoever does not abide in me is thrown away like a branch and withers; such branches are gathered, thrown into the fire, and burned. If you abide in me, and my words abide in you, ask for whatever you wish, and it will be done for you. My Father is glorified by this, that you bear much fruit and become my disciples. As the Father has loved me, so I have loved you; abide in my love. If you keep my commandments, you will abide in my love, just as I have kept my Father's commandments and abide in his love. I have said these things to you so that my joy may be in you, and that your joy may be complete.

This is my commandment, that you love one another as I have loved you. No one has greater love than this, to lay down one's life for one's friends. You are my friends if you do what I command you. I do not call you servants any longer, because the servant does not know what the master is doing; but I have called you friends, because I have made known to you everything that I have heard from my Father. You did not choose me but I chose you. And I appointed you to go and bear fruit, fruit that will last, so that the Father will give you whatever you ask him in my name (John 15:3-16).

Across the four Gospel narratives, few incidents carry more significance and energy than the Last Supper. On that last evening of his earthly life, Jesus gathered those who were his own, and in the intimacy of a family meal, he opened his heart and poured out his soul to his disciples in an explosion of unconditional love and deep trust, as one does with intimate and trusted friends.

However, while the three Synoptics focus primarily on Jesus' Eucharistic institution, as the sign and declaration of ultimate self-giving to his disciples for all time, the Fourth evangelist does not mention the Eucharist at all in the Upper Room. On the other hand, one of the highlights of John's Gospel is his strong emphasis on the Last Supper, dedicating to it a quarter of the whole Gospel, over five chapters out of twenty-one. Having already dealt at length and in depth with the Eucharist in chapter 6, following one of the six gospel versions of the multiplication of the loaves and fishes, John substitutes the gesture of Eucharistic institution with the parable in action of the washing of the feet. For John that good-bye meal embracing both life and death is an experience of deep emotions and a powerful revelation at the same time.

In a long conversation mingling strong symbolic gestures, like washing the disciples' feet, Jesus hands over to them his last will and testament, and in that one word "*love*' he reveals to his disciples and to believers of all time who God is for us and who we are for God. On his last earthly night, as he tries to convey his message and attempts to express the deep feelings of love that he harbours for those he calls his *friends*, Jesus seems to struggle for words, resorting to speak in images and metaphors. In an attempt at giving expression to this inexpressible reality of God in human terms, and drawing heavily on the agricultural and pastoral tradition of his contemporaries, alongside the imagery of the shepherd, biblical language is rich in images of vines and vineyards, articulating the symbiosis of elements that undergirds our relationship with God and with each other.

Shepherds, sheep and sheepfold, vines and branches, women in labour, they all concur to express the fundamental truth that he wants to impress in our hearts and minds as his last will and testament. Mingling together past memories, present emotions and a hopeful future, his goodbyes are couched in a powerful outflow of figurative and imaginative language.

In particular, two metaphors carry a unique and powerful significance as expressions of that *love* which he left us as his parting gift; the metaphor of the vine and branches (John 15:1-8), and the parable in action of the washing of the disciples' feet (John 13:1-17). In his last will and testament, Jesus is at pains to express the deep relationship that God longs to establish with each of us individually and all of us collectively, and he draws our attention to the dynamics of the life-giving sap enlivening the whole of the vine to its tiniest tendril.

Abiding or rejection

In the Old Testament, vines and vineyards came to be identified as the fulfilment of God's promises to his people, a symbol of the new reality where Yahweh would be Israel's God, and Israel would belong entirely to Yahweh (Isaiah 5:1-10), a mutuality of life and relationship promised and anticipated for centuries (Jeremiah 2:21; Ezekiel 28:26; Hosea 10:1).

By reflecting on daily experiences, Jesus pushes our consciousness beyond the narrow limits of the daily and the personal, into a kingdom view of reality, where God is at work and the disciples are to bring to fruitfulness the message of Good News. Therefore, true to his own cultural tradition, Jesus repeatedly likened the vineyard to the kingdom, and some of his most dramatic parables are set precisely within this agricultural context.

In Matthew 20:1-16, we encounter a generous but controversial landowner who invites labourers to work in his vineyard, and then rewards them not out of their personal merits or the hours they have laboured, but out of his gratuitous generosity, paying the last arrival the same wage as the first. Questionable as it may seem to our categories of retributive justice, Jesus is not about industrial relations or labour laws. He is about the kingdom, a reality that is not the result of conquest, personal achievements, or merits, but exclusively a gift offered to us by our God, inviting us into his life out of his love for us, as we are, and exclusively on his generous terms.

A gift carries a strong connotation of mutual relationship between giver and receiver, and it can only be an expression of love between people when accepted with gratitude by the receiver.

Conversely, refused or ignored, the gift becomes a statement of rejection of the relationship, and an insult towards the giver. That is the only human condition attached to the kingdom: God invites us into his life and love, but we must say yes to the offer. This tension between God's unconditional invitation on the one hand, and on the other the human tendency to seek and adopt a personally satisfying and self-styled relationship by asserting one's own freedom of decision, is exemplified by a number of synoptic narratives unified under the one title of '*The Wicked Tenants*', joined together by one single theme (Matthew 21:33-46; Mark 12:1-11; Luke 20:9-17).

God will do anything to draw us into his loving relationship, but he seems impotent against the human decision to refuse his advances. Matthew clearly stresses the love relationship between God and his people, by placing the parable within the context of a discussion between Jesus and the leaders of the people, in which Jesus sternly points out that prostitutes and tax collectors can claim priority in the kingdom ahead of God's chosen ones (Matthew 21:31). This is because, unlike those who should know better but refused to accept the presence of God in their lives, prostitutes and tax collectors, regardless of their moral or religious situation, have unconditionally accepted this presence and love.

God is driven to call each of us into his own and as his own, drawing us to himself, and energising us by his own life-energy, but we must be prepared to say yes to this invitation, to accept his love, to let the current of life-energy course through us, and so become active instruments in his vineyard. By contrast, any refusal to accept the flow of love between God and us will result in self-destruction, as the parables tell us. Any attempt at asserting one's individuality by refusing to be instruments of fruitfulness and goodness in the kingdom blocks the flow of God-enriched love and energy, and leads to total death. Conversely, when we accept the invitation into God's kingdom and abide in his presence, then there is no stopping the vitality and energy for goodness that is unleashed in our life and our world. Then God will be fully at work in us and our life will be truly source of fruitfulness and goodness for the whole world (John 15:1-8).

Oneness of life and love

This concept of allowing God's love to flow in us and energise us into life, is repeatedly expressed in the Fourth Gospel by that emblematic word *abide* which, mantra-like, runs through John's narrative from the very beginning, and is repeated several times on the night of good-byes during that long conversation of Jesus in the Upper Room. Following Jesus in discipleship means *to abide in his love* (John 15:4-16), to be caught passionately and obsessively in a love affair so intense that often defies any human attempt at verbal expression; a love affair that can only be understood and experienced by two people madly in love with each other.

The relationship between God and each one of us is so intense and so life-giving that it finds full expression in the life-giving sap that, life-blood-like, floods every fibre of the vine, roots, trunks, canes and branches, seeping deep into the leaves and up into the tiniest shoots and tendrils, to bring life and abundant fruitfulness.

Like in a network of interconnected channels each dependent on the other for a constant rush of energy, all the elements need to ensure an uninterrupted flow, and even a single blockage paralyses the whole system of life-flow. In the same manner, in the kingdom the life-energy that binds Jesus with the Father, flowing through both of them as one life-sap, also binds Jesus to his disciples. In turn, the same life-giving sap is shared totally and equally by all the disciples, binding them to one another. The same one vital sap flows through God, each of us individually, and all of us collectively, all sharing the same Spirit-DNA. Any other dynamics brings only death and destruction.

To be a disciple, then, is to live the very life Jesus lived, as he himself assures us. *'Because I live and you will live also'* (John 14:19). The sap-energy that enlivens God, gives life to the disciples, and the love with which the Father loves Jesus, is the same love that the Father has for the disciples. *'The Father himself loves you, because you have loved me'* (John 16:27). The rationale for this fundamental and yet almost inexpressible bond between God and us lies in the powerful dynamism of shared life and love expressed precisely through the metaphor of the vine, a metaphor that speaks of vigorous vitality, of shared oneness of life, as much as of dramatic and painful stripping, all at once.

Let us go down into the vineyard then, and let that landscape speak to us, about us, and about God-with-us. Indeed, the image of the vine, speaks to me of something greater than richness of life and abundance of fruitfulness. It speaks of personal identity and of abundance born out of stripping, and cutting, and pruning.

Obsessive possessiveness

The image-memory of vines and vineyards and vinedressers brings me back to my roots and to my childhood days in a small corner of the world tucked away between Italy, France and Switzerland; and it speaks to me of obsessive love. I grew up in one of the main vine-producing area of Northern Italy, a land teeming with exclusively luscious green and gold as far as the eye can stretch, and vines are a primordial element etched in my memory. I remember that, as a child, I was convinced that the whole world was made up of hills covered with vines, and to my younger brother the big industrial city of Turin, barely fifty kilometres away, was "the place where there are no vineyards". With amusing and child-like honesty, he would ask my father how those people could live, and what they were doing all day, if they had no vineyards to till and no vines to tend.

To own a plot of land planted with vines, carefully manicured in neat rows, meant far more than an economic proposition. It was part of the very identity of the old farmer of Piedmont, as even his parlance would reveal. Whenever a new family moved into the district in search of a future or some casual work, these new arrivals were known as "those without even two vines to bless themselves with". People were identified by the location of their vineyard more than by their home address, and bankruptcy was called "losing that last piece of vine off your back". Vines and vignerons seemed to be linked by a living relationship, such that they specified the very identity of their owners, and qualified their peasant socio-economic status.

Over the years, occasionally I have had the opportunity of revisiting those recollections by tramping through those perfectly manicured rows of freshness and vitality, and breathing in deep gulps the richness of reminiscence and of goodness. It was during one of these strolls that I suddenly remembered one of those once-in-a-life-time experiences that open up a whole new vision of reality, a moment-revelation that for the first time awakened my awareness to the full power of Jesus' words, *"I am the true vine, and my Father is the vine-grower"* (John 15:1).

I was in my late middle age years when, trying to play the concerned son, I hurt my mother and I hurt her deeply. Our family too had the mandatory small plot of land behind the old house where mum and dad tended a few vines, more as a hobby and a cultural expression than for any economic returns they may have engendered. Actually, those vines alongside the old family home had long borne the harsh and twisted markings of age. They had been there for as long as I could remember, and by then I had passed my fiftieth birthday. My father had died some years before, but mum kept tending those vines with passion and religious duty. No, it was not easy to climb the hillside to which they clung, but mother would not abandon those small twisted trunks, nor she would stop talking about them to anyone who happened to pass by. It was then that in my ignorance I tried to play the dutiful and concerned son by suggesting to mother that maybe, just maybe, it was time to let go of those old vines, to rip them up and to recoup time and energy.

The reaction was immediate, shockingly passionate, and unforgettably emotional. Mother looked at me sternly, her eyes bulging with reproach and tears. "So long as I live, those vines will remain there", she sentenced with conviction. "Don't you know that those were our first vines, our first possession? Your father and I planted them one by one, carefully sowing the dreams of our life, when you were barely two years old, and I was carrying your brother yet unborn?" She caught her breath and wiped a tear, but the passion did not subside. "Every one of those vines carries a million memories, laughter, anxiety, plans, and experiences of intense togetherness with your father and with us all?" Then the final plea: "No, please don't deprive me of those memories! My life is there! Our life is there!" In my efficiency-focused narrow-mindedness, I suddenly felt a deep sense of guilt. No, I never mentioned those vines again, and one of my most enduring memories is that of mum standing in the midst of those old vines, just looking at them, still being energised by the memories, even if by then she could no longer tend them.

Mum was obsessively possessive of those vines, and those words of Jesus will never sound the same again to me, "*I am the vine and you are the branches, and my Father is the vine dresser*"(John 15:1).

Love calls for sharing

Ours is a God longing and yearning to enter into intimate and eternal relationship with you and me, sharing my life and your life to the full, transforming our very selves in spite of ourselves. We are the object of an incredible God-empowered love, and our task is simply to accept this unique, personal, and eternal relationship of our God, obsessively possessive of you and me. We are God's fruitfulness, the work of his labours, his memories, and his joys. We are God's possession from all eternity and for all eternity, and the very life-sap of energy flows through us, the branches, as it flowed through Jesus, the sap of life put there and nurtured by the Father. Our God is driven by an obsessive possessiveness, so that we may have life, and have it in abundance (John 10:10).

A mind shattering revelation indeed, but also a challenging demand for us all to live the same relationship of oneness of life and love with each other. Nurtured by the energy of its sap flowing into every fibre and hidden bud, the vine explodes into life bearing fruit, and shelter, and freshness, all around it. Somehow, it cannot contain the vitality with which it is gifted. Paradoxically, unless it bears fruit, the vine will die, choked by its own sap of life. It is the same with the love lavished on the disciple. Unless this love is shared in turn among one another, then love is wasted and dead. *"This is to my Father's glory, that you bear much fruit, showing yourselves to be my disciples"* (John 18:8). Energised by the same divine energy, this powerful dynamism of love becomes the only and unequivocal yardstick of the love the disciples must have for one another. There is absolutely no escaping the two imperatives of *abiding in God's love* and of *loving one another*. We will truly belong to the kingdom and witness to Jesus only if we are prepared to let the love-sap flow fully into our daily life and relationships, in a deeply human and concrete way. If the life we live is the life of love for one another, then people will *know* the God of love who longs to be with them and embrace them in his love (John 14:31; 17:20-24).

Painful fruitfulness

We must bear fruit; we have no choice. But fruitfulness can be painful and seemingly unfathomable. Only by accepting the love of the vinedresser who calls me friend and yet strips me bare, will we truly discover the God of life and freedom, and truly experience fruitfulness beyond belief or any human expectation. This is the stunning revelation that Jesus left us as his parting gift. God loves us with a love beyond all telling, but Jesus was also a great realist, and the image of the vine is as much a stunning disclosure of God's obsession with each of us as it is a challenging prospect.

The explosive power of the vine's richness and abundance of life and fruitfulness are born of stripping, and cutting, and pruning. The whole life cycle of the vine from bud to fruit, is conditional on obsessive tearing and stripping away. Indeed, the greater the expression of vitality the more drastic is the cutting away, to the point that growth seems to be proportional to the savagery at the hands of the vigneron.

> *I am the true vine, and my Father is the gardener. He cuts off every branch in me that bears no fruit, while every branch that does bear fruit he prunes so that it will be even more fruitful* (John 15:1-2).

At the very peak of its explosive potential, right through the summer season and into early autumn, the vine is deprived of its ultimate richness. I have seen it happen so many times. Week after week, and long before the first signs of the fruit appear, scissors, bare hands, secateurs, and powerful clippers attack the vine in a relentless and violent process of stripping off its explosive growth. From late springtime and throughout the full vitality of summer, when the vine is at its most majestic, vigorous branches are cut down and its superb foliage thinned and rarefied, as if some relentless destructive force was trying violently to subdue the power of growth and vitality exploding uncontrollably into life and self-giving. And the process continues, repeatedly many times over the summer period.

Finally, at the very peak of its explosive potential and heavy with turgid abundance, the vine is deprived of its ultimate richness and of the very rationale of that long process of cutting and pruning and stripping. It is vintage time, and the vinedresser rejoices as he gathers the ultimate self-giving of the vine, the gift of its abundance and fruitfulness. Yes, the vinedresser knows the time, and this is the time to strip the vine of its ultimate richness, until there is nothing left on its red and amber coloured branches but tired and crumpled leaves, dying in the fading autumn sun and dulling morning mist. Now, bare and abandoned, the vine is left to die by itself in dank and cold earth, shrouded in mists and winter chill. But it will not die in spite of further pain in store.

I have seen what happens to vines once their rich fruit has been stripped and taken away! At the onset of winter, when cold mist and dense fog are already obliterating the last traces of sunlight, the vinedresser sets to work again. Secateurs, rusty clippers, and sharply filed saws set to work, tearing, cutting, stripping away the remaining tangle of naked branches of a once proud vine, and only recently exploding with richness of life and lavish fruitfulness. That obsessive possessiveness that had nurtured that vine for months now seems to have turned into fearsome ruthlessness once again, as once rich foliage and intricate twines are torn asunder, gathered into bundles on the dank earth before the final annihilation by fire.

The vine will not die, because the vine is too precious a gift to be thrown away. Its very nature is to be a source of life, and so long as the tiniest remnant of cane remains attached to the old and twisted trunk and stock, thus allowing the flow of life sap, the vine will never die. With some strange inner vision, the eye of the artist seems to guide the apparent savage hand of the vinedresser. Yes, the vinedresser knows the single strand that needs to be set free, and then apparently abandoned to the coldness and darkness of the winter. That single strand attached to the old gnarly trunk, and that ten centimetres strand alone, bare, and stripped of all beauty and seemingly of any power, will be the one that will blossom at the first cold rays of the springtime sun.

I have seen the cutting and the stripping, and I have seen the glow of joy and hope on the face of the vinedresser as his keen eye discovers that small dot, the first fragile and almost insignificant bud breaking out of that single strand left abandoned to the rigours of winter. I have heard the vigneron's alleluia-like call of excitement. "They are breaking!" they would proclaim to each other at the first faint and cold glimmer of early springtime sun. The paradox of the vine's life cycle is now complete. The vine stripped of its energy, beauty and most of all of its fruitfulness, is now ready for a new burst of vitality. All that abandonment, struggle, and pain now herald a completely new explosion of life and fruitfulness and deep love, because of and in spite of the rigours of a cold winter.

That clinging to the trunk and roots is the source of life, and that is the power of Jesus' "*I am*" statement. So long as we cling to him, even if tired, twisted or empty, we will experience life in full and never taste death or annihilation, whatever our human story may be. Our life will have its challenges, its stripping and its barrenness, but we will not die. This is the Easter story. This is precisely the story of the vine, life through stripping away and apparent abandonment.

Pruning for life

> *I am the true vine, and my Father is the gardener.*
> *He removes every branch in me that bears no*

fruit. Every branch that bears fruit he prunes to make it bear more fruit (John 15:1-2).

Jesus is very explicit, "*I AM the vine, and my Father is the vinedresser*" and, if we are to live fully, we have no choice but to accept the flow of life and love that binds us to our God and to each other, as well as the pruning that releases God's energy in us. As Christians, we are not about canonising suffering as some good to be pursued and fostered, a springboard into an otherworldly or after-life reward directly proportional to the degree or amount of suffering one has to endure throughout one's earthly experience. God's possessive love truly embraces us across, in, and through the full gamut of human experiences, even throughout the painful pruning of the winter of suffering and of death. On occasions, this flow may have its pains and deprivations, and it may well be that at times pruning and cutting may seem overwhelming, mist and cold enveloping us on all sides, and we feel destitute and abandoned, deprived of all energy and achievements. The winters of the vine invite us to trust, and to let God into our pain, abandoning our false images and our false expectations and securities into God's hands.

When we have the courage and strength to do that, then truly pain becomes redemptive and life-giving, and God's pruning will only revitalise us into new possibilities and release the life sap for more vigorous and more abundant fruitfulness. Then the kingdom will be truly here, because God's energy will truly course in our life, in all seasons, and under every imaginable circumstance. When our life is reduced to an insignificant twig with nothing to hold on to of our own making, only God can then make us into what God has always wanted us to be.

Only in this perspective can we speak of abundant fruitfulness through suffering and death. Then suffering will not be in vain, but it will become a witness of trust in and love of God. Then our life will become a revelation of the God of love, and of trust in God actively present in our human story. The struggle and pain will truly be heralds of more abundant fruitfulness and deeper love. Only by accepting the love of the Vinedresser who calls me friend and yet strips me bare, we will truly discover the God of life and freedom, and will truly experience fruitfulness beyond belief or human expectations.

The Vinedresser knows the time and patiently waits for the smallest bud to break the delicate skin of that short stump left in the snow. Then he rejoices because the vital flow of divine sap will surely and inevitably burst out into a new explosion of life and rich fruitfulness. Then, with the Vinedresser–God, we too can rejoice, because fullness of life is inevitably our destiny, if we but accept that we are the branches that the Father tends with obsession and possessive love.

SELF

The Treasure Within – The Person of the Kingdom
Matthew 13:1-52

He put before them another parable: 'The kingdom of heaven may be compared to someone who sowed good seed in his field; but while everybody was asleep, an enemy came and sowed weeds among the wheat, and then went away. So when the plants came up and bore grain, then the weeds appeared as well. And the slaves of the householder came and said to him, "Master, did you not sow good seed in your field? Where, then, did these weeds come from?" He answered, "An enemy has done this." The slaves said to him, "Then do you want us to go and gather them?" But he replied, "No; for in gathering the weeds you would uproot the wheat along with them. Let both of them grow together until the harvest; and at harvest time I will tell the reapers, Collect the weeds first and bind them in bundles to be burned, but gather the wheat into my barn".

He put before them another parable: 'The kingdom of heaven is like a mustard seed that someone took and sowed in his field; it is the

> smallest of all the seeds, but when it has grown it is the greatest of shrubs and becomes a tree, so that the birds of the air come and make nests in its branches.
>
> He told them another parable: "The kingdom of heaven is like yeast that a woman took and mixed in with three measures of flour until all of it was leavened" (Matthew 13:24-33, 44-45).

God's grace is gratuitous, universal, and always fruitful; but this fruitfulness depends on one's readiness to accept its potency for life within the soil of daily experience. We know that the Lord scatters seeds of goodness with largess into the soil of our human story (Matthew 13:1-9), but are we able to recognise, accept, and nourish this goodness that is ours? Are we prepared to accept that God loves us not because we make ourselves loveable, but because he finds us unconditionally loveable? Are we prepared to accept that we are good? Our daily life is the humus where God's goodness abounds, yes even in the thorny and less savoury moments of our individual and collective story, but are we prepared to clear the ground of all that may silence God's voice or stifle the drive towards growth into fullness of life?

The symphony of creation

Recently, I had the opportunity of soothing soul, mind and body by attending a symphonic concert. Have you ever noticed the chaotic conglomerate of sound, colour and sights that precedes the opening notes? Tuning of instruments, excitement at recognising an acquaintance, small talk, attendants fleeting back and forth. Slowly, the lights begin to dim and the cacophony fades out, ushering a strange hush into the velvet-hung auditorium, until total darkness brings silence and expectancy. A single thread of lights spots the flute, glistening and undefined, calling forth out of the darkness a faint sequence of slow semibreves, imperceptible at first but inviting and pregnant like strengthening breeze before the storm. Slowly the strings join in response, as the light diffuses through the darkness with gentle persuasion, creating a unique blend of sound, light and energy, inviting into a new level of consciousness. Now the tempo picks up with a feeling of urgency and expectation, woodwinds and trumpets stirring the heavy brass into life. The percussion instruments join in, surging with unrelenting power and unrepressed energy until the curtains silently break apart, prelude to the final explosion of light and sound. Suddenly, powerful beams of light reveal a single figure, centre stage. There stands a human silhouette, sculptured out of darkness and cacophony, born out of light and sound. Chaos has been redeemed, darkness is vanquished, and the symphony of creation has begun.

The first chapter of human history in the book of Genesis tells a story of light being called forth to fill up void and emptiness, to shatter darkness, and to redeem chaos. It is an enfolding of cosmic proportion, culminating with the dramatic bursting of Adam onto the scene of life, the apex of creation, the only creature in the image of God (Genesis 1:26), because God has breathed his very breath of life into that human form (Genesis 2:7). From the very beginning of time, the human story is one of cosmic dimensions and of becoming, speaking of redemption and of goodness, not of human making but of God's creative power.

In Genesis 1, God wills the whole of creation into being by calling forth land and sea, day and night, animals and plants through a progressive and compelling outburst of creative power.

"*Let there be!*" God wants creation to be the very outflow of his life-giving spirit (*ruah*), and after each creative intervention, God – pleased with each accomplishment – compliments himself with the refrain, "*God saw that it was good!*" We need to remind ourselves that creation is good, and God is pleased with it.

As we reach the last bars of the symphony (Genesis 1:26-31), however, both the tone and the refrain change dramatically. While previously each creative act was introduced by the explicit command, "*Let there be*", now we can picture God pondering intently as if to ensure that the final stroke is the perfect one:

> *Then God said, 'Let us make humankind in our image, according to our likeness; and let them have dominion over the fish of the sea, and over the birds of the air, and over the cattle, and over all the wild animals of the earth, and over every creeping thing that creeps upon the earth.' So God created humankind in his image, in the image of God he created them; male and female he created them* (Genesis 1:26-27).

The text clearly depicts God pausing in his endeavours, and, absorbed in deep thought, planning his next move. This has to be his masterstroke, the ultimate and most decisive act of all, the masterpiece that bears not only the imprint of the Artist, but, indeed, the very self-portrait, and the breath of life of the Creator himself. "*Let us make humankind in our image, according to our likeness"*. Yes, indeed, every human being for all time is the fruit of a deliberate design and of a personal decision of God, and God's very image throughout the whole of history and of creation. Then, the final satisfied self-appraisal: *"God saw everything that he had made, and indeed, it was very good!"* In the Hebrew Bible, the expression "good (*tov*)" becomes "unbelievably good' (*tov meod*)", and is applied exclusively to the creation of Adam. If creation is good, humanity is "unbelievably good", and there lies the God-sanctioned appraisal of our identity and of our destiny.

We must believe in the innate goodness that is ours, because God put it there in the first place. *"And indeed, it was very good!"* We need to own the conviction that we are the fruit of a deliberate design of explosive love, and our destiny is nothing short of divinity. It is true that the story of creation soon degenerated into the tragedy of Eden (Genesis 3), when humanity, losing sight of the relationship between masterpiece and master artisan, pretended to draw a line in the sand between the two. Yet, even after that apparent disintegration, there was no act of re-creation. There is no need of it because a masterpiece is forever, whatever the tithes of time. "The original '*you*' is perfect, because God does not have bad words", says Francis J. Moloney. Maybe the news is too good to be true, and any attempt at re-appropriating that original masterstroke at a conscious level will always involve a great deal of struggle, as Paul says about himself (Romans 7:14-24). On the other hand, a line in Zeffirelli's *Brother Sun and Sister Moon* is pertinent here. At the climax of the dramatic encounter of Francis of Assisi before the assembled glittering papal court, intent only on dismissal of those shameful and embarrassing beggars, Pope Innocent III poignantly welcomes the pauper from Assisi by remarking: "In our obsession with original sin, we have all too often and for too long forgotten original innocence". In the eyes of God, the human person is always innocent, and will always be his masterstroke, a divine icon.

Treasure in a field

The whole of chapter thirteen of Matthew's Gospel revolves around this tension between the reality of who we are in God's eyes, against that negative and destructive self-image that we may have been fed on for too long and, quagmire-like, we continue to entertain and wallow in with almost sadistic pleasure. As if in a sheaf of agricultural images, the Word of God in Matthew 13 points to the tension existing in the kingdom-presence, mingling together good and evil. At the same time, it highlights the richness, preciousness, abundance, and the joy that comes with the discovery of something very valuable. However, the appropriation of such richness that the Creator has infused into our very nature from the beginning will always demand risky decisions, conversion of perspectives and attitudes, and a radical change of self-image. That is what the kingdom is for Jesus: an experience of joy and love offered to us and possessed by us, so long as we are prepared to seek it and commit ourselves to its attainment and nurture.

As the narrative unfolds, we encounter an enterprising merchant who will do anything in order to gain possession of a field where he knows there is a hidden treasure, or to buy that one precious stone he has discovered. Preciousness, joy and commitment all rolled into one are thus the outcome of discovering and of seeking God in our life.

> *The kingdom of heaven is like a treasure hidden in a field, which someone found and hid; then in*

> *his joy he goes and sells all that he has and buys that field. Again, the kingdom of heaven is like a merchant in search of fine pearls; on finding one pearl of great value, he went and sold all that he had and bought it* (Matthew 13:44-45).

I must confess that, in spite of its affirming connotations, somehow, this parable always sets off the doubting Thomas syndrome in me. I cannot help thinking that here we find quite a foolish merchant. Given the custom at the time of hiding precious things or family heirlooms underground, we can well surmise that the treasure in the field may have been buried there unknown and forgotten for a long time. As precious as the treasure may have been, its hiding place was probably a mini jungle, overgrown with noxious weeds and a wild tangle of vines. Yes, a treasure hidden and disfigured by unwanted and pernicious elements that seem to obliterate the beauty and preciousness below the ground!

Likewise, a certain defensive human prudence will ask the question of its authenticity. What if the treasure buried in that field proved not to be what the merchant first thought it would be, or the pearl turn out to be a fake? The master merchant has now risked everything and lost it all, his efforts turned to waste and all come to nothing. However, in the economy of God, these are irrelevant and idle considerations stemming from a worldview obsessed with security and certainty, while such considerations seems to be foreign to the realm of the kingdom. Yes, our God is foolish by human reckoning, prepared as he is to risk everything, gambling his very credibility, indeed his very existence of being God. Our God is capable not only of seeing the rare treasure buried deep inside unkempt and unwelcome appearance, but he believes in the beauty and richness of that treasure, whatever it may be. We must be valuable in his eyes!

The richness of God's presence and the beauty of God's gifts are not denied by the ugliness and the brokenness that we experience in ourselves and in the world around us. God is not blind to the rough and ugly exterior of sin, suffering and injustice that sometimes seem to overrun our life and our story, and obliterate God's life-giving presence and action. In the end, God is only interested in the goodness and richness that are there – whatever the appearance – or even the risk that it may be false or choked out of existence by other destructive energies. The real issue is that the briars of evil and the noxious weeds of human frailty and mistakes do not deter God from seeking us and possessing us as his very own precious treasure. God does not put any conditions to our belonging to the kingdom. He just wants to possess us, and journey with us. This message imbibes the whole chapter thirteen of Matthew, where Jesus insists on the tension between the richness and power of God's presence in this world and its apparently contradictory manifestations within the reality we experience around us and within ourselves.

Richness in contradiction

If we are to believe our twenty-four hours immersion into any media outlets, our world is becoming less and less like the place to be. Wars, famine, ethnic cleansing, detention centres, natural disasters, family breakdown, dysfunctional personal relationships, street crime, gangland violence, terrorism, substance abuse – that is often our "welcome into a new day" emanating from our 6.00 am news, often to be served up again lavishly in their most unsavoury details around 7.00 pm. This is not Good News as we would want, or understand it. This is not the kind of kingdom that Jesus seems to offer us, or that we would wish to believe in, as it challenges all our certitudes or speculations about God, others and certainly self. If we take the Word of God seriously, then honesty demands that we ask ourselves where God is, and what God is doing in all this mayhem of death and evil.

Confronted with the dilemma of Good News, when all we experience around us is negativity and non-life, rather than denying the reality of evil, Jesus proclaimed unequivocally the life-giving presence of our God right in the midst of destruction, of evil, of inadequacy and of insignificance. There is no comparison between the size of a tiny seed or the insignificance of a handful of leaven, and the explosion of power, beauty and richness that these elements hold in their smallness or unsavoury insignificance (Luke 13:18-21). When comparing the reality of a seed and the potency it holds, the parables clearly declare that it is all a matter of perspective. That alone will give us a glimpse towards understanding the workings of God in a world full of contradictions and apparent negation of life. Our God is not limited by human weakness, and our insufficiency can truly become the humus where God can work wonders in this world. As human beings, we are and we will always be weak, fragile, and sinful. If God wanted a perfect world, he would not have created this one. If he planned to populate this world with incarnated sinless angels, none of us would probably be around to see it. If Jesus wanted the Church to be a sect of perfect people, he would have called upon a host of disembodied angels, rather than on ignorant and misguided fishermen.

In a similar frame of mind, following the parable of the reckless merchant, Matthew has Jesus drawing the same message from the immediate experience of his listeners, by telling the parable of the fishermen making a selection of their catch between good and useless fish.

> *Again, the kingdom of heaven is like a net that was thrown into the sea and caught fish of every kind; when it was full, they drew it ashore, sat down, and put the good into baskets but threw out the bad* (Matthew 13:47-48).

In their hard work of catching fish, the fishermen think nothing of having to make a selection of their catch once they are on shore. They know that every catch hauled in always contains some unsuitable or unsavoury fish that would need to be disposed of. However, that does not stop those same fishermen from braving the elements and their physical strength again, and go out repeatedly to look for an even bigger catch.

As believers, we can be neither blind to human weakness nor overdosed with idealism. We have to be honest and acknowledge sinfulness and even contradiction. At the same time, we need also to recognise, affirm and nourish the certainty that our God is so totally given over to goodness, love and life, that he does not shun drawing such gifts out of those same situations that seem to negate his very presence.

A patient landowner amidst wheat and weeds

Immediately before the parable of the merchant seeking precious pearls, Jesus sets yet another agricultural scene by pointing to a field of wheat apparently choked to death by obnoxious weeds.

> *He put before them another parable: 'The kingdom of heaven may be compared to someone who sowed good seed in his field; but while everybody was asleep, an enemy came and sowed weeds among the wheat, and then went away. So when the plants came up and bore grain, then the weeds appeared as well. And the slaves of the householder came and said to him, 'Master, did you not sow good seed in your field? Where, then, did these weeds come from?' He answered, 'An enemy has done this'. The slaves said to him, 'Then do you want us to go and gather them?' But he replied, 'No; for in gathering the weeds you would uproot the wheat along with them. Let both of them grow together until the harvest; and at harvest time I will tell the reapers, Collect the weeds first and bind them in bundles to be burned, but gather the wheat into my barn'* (Matthew 13:24-30).

It is interesting to compare the reaction of the various stakeholders. The landowner knows that he has put good and wholesome seed in his field, and he concentrates on that. He seeks and sees only goodness in all he does and plans, even if the appearance of unwanted and dangerous weeds seems to nullify and frustrate his efforts and expectations. The servants, on the other hand, in their impulsive but less than wise zeal, look only at the weeds of evil and they are only interested in removing them immediately, and at all costs. In their eagerness, they do not seem to see or care about the goodness present there and, for the sake of puritanical self-righteousness, they are quite prepared to remove wrongdoing and destroy the very goodness of the whole crop.

On the other hand, the wise property owner seems almost unconcerned by the apparent destruction of his crop. He is not blind to the presence of weeds, and he frankly acknowledges that *"an enemy has done this"*. However, he focuses on the good seed that he knows to be there, because he put it there in the first place, and he is only interested in nurturing that goodness and that fruitfulness. By allowing *"both of them to grow together until the harvest"*, in the end goodness becomes a rich harvest while the weeds of evil have no future but self-destruction.

Often the experience of finding God in our life is at least ambiguous, if not downright painful or negative. Sometimes our best efforts seem to come to nothing and we wonder where the God of joy and of rich abundance is hiding. We experience loneliness, disappointment, emotional drain, low self-esteem, moral failure, and physical or mental suffering. In all these, where are we to find that idyllic setting and source of God-engendered joy and preciousness of the kingdom that Jesus talks about? Where is God when our guard is down and our life is a never-ending struggle?

As Jesus showed us in his own earthly life, our God is the wise and patient landowner, neither blind nor blasé about the tragedies of life and the pain and suffering of humanity. What the parable is saying, however, is that evil and brokenness, and pain and sin are not the end of the story or the only reality of our world. God invites us to remember that, at the very dawn of time, after breathing life into Adam, he looked at his creation with satisfied appraisal and approval, commenting that "it was unbelievably good". Humanity may be frail and broken, but we are not bad, as sometimes we may be tempted to admit to ourselves. On the contrary, humanity is meant for fruitfulness and the joy of rich harvest. That is why Pope Francis is fond of repeating, "We are weak and even sinful, but none of us is bad".

In the end, life is quite simple really. We either have confidence that God is totally caught up with us – yes even in extreme pain and isolation, and in the most excruciating death – or we focus exclusively on the negativity, and we will never find hope and even less God. By accepting the weeds among the wheat, and being reassured that God has placed the good seed there, life's hardships are not so overwhelming. Indeed, we can still achieve a full and fulfilled life, we can still rejoice and love and be grateful, because, with Julian of Norwich we know that "all will be well, and all will be well, and all manner of thing will be well". Without this appreciation of goodness in ourselves and of a God who upholds and nurtures goodness, life becomes more unbearable every day, crushed by loneliness, anger, and despair. Without hope, we will only see ourselves as a victim, and the world as the enemy.

Loving oneself

Are we perhaps afraid to admit to ourselves, with all honesty, that we are good? That we are lovable and loved? God finds us lovable, so why should we be so selfish as to refuse to admit it to ourselves and to others? Is it perhaps too big a risk to admit that God finds us worthy of his love? Well, God has certainly taken the risk on us.

A spirituality of self-denial, which has created myriad of saints through the millennia, has nothing to do with wallowing in self-pity that denies God's gifts of life and goodness that are ours. In trying to pull ourselves by our bootstraps out of an imaginary quagmire, we lose sight of the dream of God, and sadistically we replace the original icon with our own ego-image, where everything is noxious weeds and the work of an enemy. In a false pretence at incarnating a self-styled escape from a world that we can only imagine steeped in negativity, we deny our true self and waste a great deal of psychic and spiritual energy in trying to feel good about feeling bad and feeling bad about feeling good about ourselves. We have to be honest about ourselves and about our God, under penalty of the complete disintegration at the deepest level of our psyche and, consequently, a distorted and destructive relationship to our God. Often we may feel afraid and disheartened at our own brokenness. Then we must remember the clay in the hands of the potter (Jeremiah 18:1-6), and realise that our brokenness is part of the masterpiece that we are, and the fragility that we experience in our life is ultimately what makes us uniquely precious in the eyes of God.

The sense of being unloved is very much part of our human condition. Yet Jesus' whole life and mission witnessed and proclaimed just the opposite; namely, the possibility and the reality of unbounded love of Abba towards us. The foundational experience of Jesus in the New Testament is a relational experience between God, whom he dared to address as *Abba*, and the human self, as Abba's *Beloved*. If God is the bountiful Abba, then this involves an intrinsic sense of self as the recipient of Abba's love and life.

This self-awareness calls for a conversion from a spirituality of brokenness to a personal ownership of being beloved and lovable. As a disciple, I am called to convert my experience of being broken and unloved into an acceptance of being precious and loved. As we get older, we encounter more and more a sharp split of perspectives among people, either an almost palpable inner peace nourished by grateful memories of what life has given them, or a destructive anger and bitterness gnawing at a heart mired in a pathological concern for lost opportunities and guilt of past mistakes. We either accept the God hidden in human shadows, rejoicing in unexpected life-fruitfulness, or we let the shadows obliterate completely and negate our vision of God, eventually abandoning ourselves to guilt, despair, and death.

The dividing line between these two types of existence is hope. If I have hope, I have a positive and affirming perspective on everything and everybody, and I can rejoice at life as a gift to be lived fully and to be shared. Hope is not just a medicine for the end of one's days, while one bears up stoically through the agony of silent desperation, suffering and destruction. Hope is that energy that comes from the conviction that no matter what negativity our life story may serve up to us, our God is right there underneath and behind the shadows and in spite of personal inadequacy, brokenness, and human tragedy; right there to sustain, nurture and energise us into fullness of life.

Owning the darkness

Jesus never once condemned sin and darkness except in the case of those who thought they had no darkness (John 9:41) and considered themselves pure and 'not like other people', (Luke 18:11). On the contrary, Jesus not only confronted darkness but he physically touched death, facing condemnation and personal defilement, at least in the mind of those who focused only on brokenness and human weakness. Dead bodies (Mark 5:21-23; Luke 7:11-17; John 11:38-44), paralysed and blind people (Mark 2:1-8; John 9:1-12), lepers and public sinners (Luke 17:11-19; 19:1-10) – Jesus could not help but being drawn to these. Here was someone who was uniquely precious and fragile, and by touching and embracing that human fragility, Jesus declared the preciousness of those people in the eyes of God, besides healing the darkness of their fears and self-condemnation.

Belonging in the kingdom and following Jesus in discipleship call for that unqualified honesty in contradiction that acknowledges unconditional personal preciousness and a positive image in ourselves and in others. This kind of attitude is not presumptuous self-centredness. It is honesty, realism and truthfulness, that very truthfulness which educators or parents, role models or mentors, we are called to stimulate and foster in others. In terms of mission, how can we claim that we touch the lives of others, and lead them to discover that they are loved unconditionally and eternally by their God, if we despise our very self? It is deceitful and pretentious to engage in any form of ministry, mission or simple down-to-earth daily Christian witness outside of a Christian anthropology that speaks of each individual as a uniquely precious gift of God, radically embedded in the personal and social experience of each day.

Our personal protestation of faith as well as our presence to others and to the world at large will be credible and growth-producing only when the world will discover us joyful and hopeful in our human frailty and struggle. And when such human frailty will make heavy demands on our joy and hopefulness, let us embrace courage and give thanks, because that will be the moment when we are held in the palm of God's hand (Jeremiah 18:1-5), being moulded by the all-transforming "ruah" of God, all the time smiling at us with approval and love.

Self-image is a vital element of our personality, and we need to accept that –as far as God is concerned – we are good and worthy of his love and care. Often our life seems overrun by non-life, choked by difficulties and strangled by suffering, a clumsy blundering from one crisis to the next. We need to believe in ourselves as that hidden treasure for which the foolish God will risk everything and anything. Memories of the past, as much as helplessness in the present and uncertainty for the future, may trap us into a vortex of guilt and fear, where God is not only the stranger far away, but also very much the judge and executioner in a kingdom of condemnation and rejection. That is the moment calling us to accept that we are the object of God's love and care. Whatever we may think of ourselves, we are citizens of that all-embracing divine presence where God is reckless enough to risk everything in order to draw us into peace and joy, whatever the foibles of life.

Let us rejoice in God's foolishness, and with the psalmist let us give thanks for Jesus' *obsession!*

> *I look up at your heavens, made by your fingers,*
> *at the moon and stars you set in place –*

> *what are we humans that you should spare a*
>   *thought for us,*
> *mortals that you should care for us?*
> *Yet you have made us little less than a god*
> *you have crowned us with glory and splendour,*
> *with authority over the work of your hands,*
> *set all things under our feet,*
> *sheep and oxen, all these,*
> *yes, wild animals too,*
> *birds of the air, fish in the sea*
> *travelling the paths of the ocean.*
> *Yahweh, our Lord,*
> *how great your name throughout the earth!*
>   (Psalm. 8).

And elsewhere,

> *It was you who created my inmost self,*
> *and put me together in my mother's womb;*
> *for all these mysteries I thank you:*
> *for the wonder of myself,*
> *for the wonder of your works.*
> *You know me through and through,*
> *for having watched my bones take shape*
> *when I was being formed in secret,*
> *knitted together in my mother's womb* (Psalm 139:13-15).

BEATITUDES

The Values of the Kingdom
Luke 6:20-26

He came down with them and stood on a level place, with a great crowd of his disciples and a great multitude of people from all Judea, Jerusalem, and the coast of Tyre and Sidon . . . Then he looked up at his disciples and said:

'Blessed are you who are poor, for yours is the kingdom of God.

'Blessed are you who are hungry now, for you will be filled.

'Blessed are you who weep now, for you will laugh.

'Blessed are you when people hate you, and when they exclude you, revile you, and defame you on account of the Son of Man. Rejoice on that day and leap for joy, for surely your reward is great in heaven; for that is what their ancestors did to the prophets.

'But woe to you who are rich, for you have received your consolation.

'Woe to you who are full now, for you will be hungry.

'Woe to you who are laughing now, for you will mourn and weep.

> 'Woe to you when all speak well of you, for that
> is what their ancestors did to the false prophets
> (Luke 6:17, 20-26).

The kingdom is here

Chapter six of Luke's Gospel is pivotal and dramatically perfect (Luke 6:20-49). All the elements are there: the crowds with a mix of curiosity and political expectations, the stage a wide open expanse of water bounded by the hills on the other bank of the lake; some fishing nets lying about with scraggy but meaningful boats as simple props, and the speaker proclaiming a stirring message of blessings and woes. The world is the stage and humanity in its daily reality is the protagonist of the drama being re-enacted and broadcast. Though his words seem to carry a strong political and social undertone, the speaker seems more concerned with the religious leaders than with the policies of Rome and Jerusalem. Here is someone who proclaims a subversive message, driving at the heart of people beyond time and cultures, challenging their accepted categories of faith and life, and reversing radically perceived values and unquestioned standards of human behaviour.

Until this point of Luke's narrative, Jesus has been gradually introducing himself as the "One sent by God", but, with chapter six, Jesus takes on a new and more challenging role (Luke 6:20-49). He becomes the prophet of fiery energy in the tradition of John the Baptist, the lawgiver who speaks with authority (Luke 4:32.36, Mark 1:27). Obsessed with the kingdom, which he identifies as the active, and living presence of God in human history, Jesus unflinchingly proclaims that *'the kingdom is here'* (Luke 17:21, John 18:33-36). In this context then, chapter six of Luke parallels chapter five of Matthew. Though contextually very different, both Luke's proclamation in the plain by the lake (6:17, 20-26) and Matthew's new-Moses-like on the mountain (5:1-48), take on a powerful and primal significance as the Constitution of this kingdom. Here is the Magna Carta for the followers of Jesus, which the two evangelists see from very different perspectives. In Matthew's Jewish tradition, the statements of the Constitution highlight joy and blessedness as the fulfilment of centuries of Messianic expectations, and as the fruits of accepting God's presence in one's life and witnessing it to the world (Matthew 5:1-11). For Luke, instead, while addressing a broader and more Gentile audience, the foundational principles of following Jesus are demanding and subversive in the extreme (Luke 6:20-26). In Luke, posing two sets of four contradictory statements expressed as four *blessings* and four *woes*, Jesus seems to run counter to all the fundamental values that, as human beings, we would consider most fulfilling and life-giving.

There is, however, a fundamental similarity between the two narratives of Matthew and Luke. In both texts, the Beatitudes seem to defy human logic. As if it was not bad enough to follow Jesus' instructions to seasoned fishermen to put down the nets against all fishing sense in a place and time where fish were not supposed to be (Luke 5:1-11), Jesus' solemn proclamation to the assembled crowds fly in the face of all human rationality and fairness (Matthew 5:1-11; Luke 6:20-26). I am not sure how a destitute person would read the injunctions of the Gospel that proclaim poverty, hunger, suffering, sadness and hatred as so many blessings (Luke 6:2-23, Matthew (5:1-11). At the same time, in such a contradiction of blessings and condemnation, it makes little sense to commit one's life to relieving economic poverty and human sufferings from our world, if poverty and sufferings are God-sanctioned blessings.

Can we really rejoice in the face of such claims that sound like the very antithesis of the longings of the human heart and of dedicated endeavour? By contrast, in Luke Jesus sounds a clear warning to those whose honest enterprise in life have brought them achievement, joy, fulfilment and happiness (Luke 6:24-26). These are the longings of the heart but, from Jesus' perspective, they only draw condemnation and warning of dire consequences. What is the value of engaging in any human endeavour or promotion to better oneself and one's life conditions, if they only lead to un-fulfilment, and condemnation?

Nobody wants to be a loser, and on face value the Beatitudes do not make sense, unless, of course we look at these words from the perspective of Jesus, who was not about economics, or social revolutions, or psychological placebos, but about the Reign of God in the world and in each single life. Jesus came to reveal this presence-reign of God within the life and story of every person, and to achieve the universal yearning of the human heart, demanding commitment and trustful reliance on the power of God's presence.

After food and shelter, security is the other fundamental need of all life, and so, as the saying goes, from cradle to grave we are wrapped in insurance policies and economic trusts. We just want to feel secure, and so we rely heavily on work, possessions, achievements, or relationships – sometime at all costs – in order to achieve such things. On the other hand, Jesus has strong words of condemnation against this obsession with material securities, not because they are securities, but because we are obsessed with them (Luke 6:24-25). Once we have everything, all our physical, emotional, psychological, and spiritual needs satisfied, and all our future totally secure – if that were ever possible! – then we have no need of anything or anyone else, least of all of others and of God. When our reliance is totally and obsessively on material satisfaction, then God becomes a threat to our control, and those around us enemies to our grasping. Obsessed with ourselves, we can no longer trust anyone except ourselves in blissful isolation, and certainly, there is no room for God in there.

That is the message of Jesus. The Reign of God has nothing to do with human sovereignty, power or control, but with an unreserved acceptance of God in our world, and an unconditional trust in his active and healing presence in our lives. The poor, the hungry or the suffering of the kingdom are not exclusively those without possessions, or the destitute without food or shelter. The poor of the Beatitudes is every person who is called to confront life without human securities or guarantees, without certainty for tomorrow, or a personally affirming religious practice today. The poor of the Beatitudes is the person who relies entirely and exclusively on God.

After the small remnant of a once proud nation that was Israel returned from the Babylonian exile (538 BC), it found itself totally destitute, defenceless and powerless, crying in a desert of abandonment and rejection. Born in exile and carrying only the memories they had heard from their long-dead ancestors, with no city, no temple, nor political or religious structure to rely on and to identify itself with, that motley *remnant* had only Yahweh as its security and its power for reconstruction. These are the *anawim*, and the biblical *anawim* are not necessarily persons without possessions or the destitute without food or shelter. The biblical poor is every person who is called to confront life and its multifaceted vagaries without human securities, guarantees, or even dignity or acceptance, but relying entirely and exclusively on God.

The poor, suffering or hungry of the Gospel, as much as the unemployed of our tenement houses today or the people unseen behind well-manicured mansions are every woman or man for whom God remains the ultimate security. Poor are those who acknowledge that their whole life is totally dependent on others, whether for a piece of stale bread, for a word of recognition, or a gesture of dignity. Hungry is the person who lives by the precariousness of each day, grateful for the opportunity to satisfy their hunger for life with those crumbs that God sets into the lap of one's daily life (Luke 16:19-30). Poor is the person who has neither hope nor vision for tomorrow, beyond the generosity and acceptance by someone else today. Poor and hungry is the person who is aware of their need of God, the person for whom everything and everybody is a gift accepted with gratitude and compassion. Poor, suffering and hungry is the person who accepts life as it comes, with outstretched and open hands, hands that may remain empty, but also hands ready to give and share, because those hands know the real meaning of need and rely entirely on God alone.

Gospel poverty is not a contemptuous rejection of the goods of the earth, nor should we canonise hunger and human suffering as blessings to be sought after. However, when we are prepared to free ourselves from that obsessive possessiveness, then we set God free to work his ways with us. Then our life becomes a proclamation of the human possibility for total and free availability to make the good gifts of God available to everybody. Then we are truly blessed in spite of poverty, hunger, suffering and misunderstanding, because God is at work there.

It is this biblical and radical understanding of Jesus' words that we need to recover and to own, both personally and communally, if we are to understand the call of the Beatitudes of the kingdom, a call to total and radical insecurity, dependant and trusting only on God, and God alone. Moreover, with this kingdom of God on our side, we know it well: we can only be winners, whatever life puts before us.

Acceptance: the energy of healing

If we are prepared to accept Jesus' subversive but eminently practical injunctions as signposts on our journey of discipleship, then our lives will be turned upside down in a manner that we will never imagine, and in a way that only God could possibly bring about. If we accept God in our life, then we will experience healing where there is brokenness (Luke 7:36-49), joy taking over from suffering and despair (Luke 7:1-10), and life supplanting all forms of death (Luke 7:11-17).

As we look at the biblical texts, we need to let ourselves be challenged by the radical nature of the demands in the here-and-now, where we are, and as we are. Very early in the narrative and well before Jesus was to start his emblematic journey to Jerusalem (Luke 9:51) where the fulfilment of his life and mission would only come about through suffering and death, Luke introduces two significant moments that set the tone to the whole journey of discipleship. First, we encounter Jesus struggling vehemently in the desert of temptation, loneliness and depravation as he wrestles to come to terms with the uncertainty and unknown challenges that the Father has set out for him (Luke 4:1-13). Secondly, rejected by his own townsfolk of Nazareth (Luke 4:16-30), Jesus proclaims the Beatitudes, the Magna Carta of the kingdom (Luke 6:20-26), precisely by reversing the accepted expectation of the human heart.

Once again, these texts seem to defy accepted logic. At the very beginning of his ministerial journey, grappling with the unknown, Jesus said *'no'* to any exclusive compulsion with material goods, to obsession with self-importance and personal ambitions, and he rejected unequivocally control and power (Luke 4:1-13). By claiming to follow Jesus on the journey to fulfilment in Jerusalem, we are challenged to confront ourselves with the same questions and to seek our own life-giving response. For us, that challenge means to question our tendency to take the easy way out for our exclusive satisfaction or comfort, to focus entirely on our own personal needs and ambitions, to seek power and control at all costs.

Penance and self-denial have nothing to do with self-satisfying masochism, nor are they just nice traditions warming the heart. Rather, they are the expressions of that inevitable and painful change brought on by letting go of whatever holds us back from being who we are and what we are meant to be.

Abraham Joshua Heschel puts it well.

> Needs are looked upon today as if they were holy, as if they contained the quintessence of eternity. Needs are our gods, and we toil and spare no effort to gratify them. Suppression of desire is considered a sacrilege that must inevitably avenge itself in the form of some mental disorder... We feel jailed in the confinement of personal needs. The more

we indulge in satisfactions, the deeper is our feeling of oppressiveness... We must be able to say *no* to ourselves in the name of a higher *yes*.[18]

In our daily dealings, how do we respond to the compulsion to use, to have and to grasp for the sake of our own personal satisfaction, even if that means changing stones into bread, if need be? Within the web of relationship entangling our day, how do we relate to each other at home, at work, at school or just down the street? By demanding attention, centre-stage, or pecking order? Are control and self-seeking the energy and the absolutes of our life, or are we motivated by love, compassion, and understanding? This is the blessedness in destitution propounded by Jesus, confronted by him in the desert of temptation, and sanctioned in the Lucan Beatitudes.

However, we need to be wary of distorting the words of Jesus into literal fundamentalism by focusing on ourselves and on our own personal efforts towards attaining the kingdom. Paradoxically, such fundamentalist stance ultimately will destroy the very meaning of the kingdom. The radical demands of Jesus have nothing to do with literal fundamentalism. Faith and discipleship are not blind and passive acceptance of some abstract truths expressed in culturally conditioned manner of speech. Faith and discipleship must be incarnated in time and place, and challenge cultural taboos and status quo. This is the call of these senseless demands by Jesus.

---

18 Abraham Joshua Heschel, *Man Is Not Alone*, New York: Farrar, Straus and Giroux, 1955, 186,189.

Having proclaimed the blessings and the woes, Luke's narrative takes a sudden and unexpected turn, and Jesus' mission engages a new beat. His words become parables in action on behalf of the destitute, the suffering and the rejected, all the time changing people's lives and challenging his disciples to do likewise. Throughout the Gospels, Jesus is the man at work (John 4:34), constantly bringing out life from non-life, and calling forth a lived faith response from his followers. The presence of God which he proclaimed, and enjoined on his disciples as the platform of the kingdom, is now brought to bear in the lives of real peoples in the reality of each day as a personal response on the part of the disciple, not in terms of control or performance, but in terms of a personal decision to trust unconditionally this Jesus who announced himself as being sent to heal the broken and to set downtrodden free (Luke 4:18-19).

Faith is not a set of intellectual or academic propositions, and for all the challenging and subversive injunctions, Jesus did not propose a code of moral laws, or ritual precepts binding people into some abstract ideology outside of themselves and in spite of themselves (Matthew 5:17). Laws, ritual practice, and moral precepts are the natural manifestations and the human response consequent to accepting the kingdom in our daily realities. The kingdom is about fullness of life (John 10:10), but the disciple must be prepared to accept this gift of fullness of life in spite of all evidence to the contrary, and abandon themself with trusting faith in Jesus. The result of accepting God in the reality of our lives is just as radical and all transforming as Jesus' subversive demands, and Luke reminds us constantly that faith must become action energised by trust, or our claim to faith remains an ideology at worst, or a self-serving devotional practice at best.

On that plain (Luke) and on that mountain (Matthew), Jesus proclaimed a radical and paradoxical message that challenged people out of apathy and into a new awareness, and demanded a personal decision for God each day – where we are, and as we are. Moving from word into action and centering on the effect of accepting God in our life in trust and faith, Luke' narrative reiterates the same sense of subversion but from an entirely different perspective. In chapter seven, we encounter two events that are unique to the third evangelist, and both speak of the reversal and life-giving transformation that come about when one accepts the living and active presence of the kingdom as a reality in one's life, here and now.

First, Jesus heals the slave of the pagan centurion (Luke 7:1-10), and then brings back to life the dead son of the widow of Nain (4:11-17). In both cases, we have a clear proclamation of the gratuitous intervention of God to bring out life and healing wherever and whenever there is death and despair. Both events are proclamation of God's kingdom in daily life, even if – as in the story of Nain – we are even unaware of this presence, or lack the courage to turn to our God for healing. The very presence of God through Jesus is a healing presence, and all God seems to be concerned with is this sense of acceptance and trust in his presence, regardless of our condition or expectations. Destitute but open and trusting, God heals us by simply being there, as exemplified by that very human gesture of Jesus laying his hands on the bier and entering the pain of the situation by touching a dead body, at the risk of personal defilement and cultural condemnation.

Belonging to the kingdom bids us to be people of simple and uncomplicated faith, who, in their ordinary human situation, have the courage and wisdom to discover, accept, and trust unconditionally the living and healing presence of our God journeying with us each step of the way towards the personal and communal Jerusalem-fulfilment of our lives.

Trusting faith

The second event, representing one of the most challenging calls to faith as trust and abandonment to God has a Roman centurion as its main character, a pagan for any orthodox Jew, and an officer of a foreign occupier, an outcast from the Law of Moses and an enemy of the state (Luke 7:1-10). There is, however, a deep sense of humanity and compassion in this man, because he shows unusual respect and unheard-of concern for his slaves. He is also a man who respects and upholds the cultural and religious differences of an occupied country like Palestine, to the point that the inhabitants of Capernaum become his referees supporting his request to Jesus. This man acknowledges his condition of need and trust in Jesus as the only one on whom he can depend in his brokenness and destitution. These details are much more than some initial information for the reader. By highlighting the very opposite of what the contemporaries of Jesus upheld as fundamental parameters for faith, Luke opens up a non-sectarian vision both of Jesus' mission and of the nature of discipleship. Without explicit mention, Luke clearly qualifies this man as a person of faith, a faith that is not determined by culture, creed, social status or power structure, and even less by belonging to a race or a sect.

While demanding a very personal assent, faith has a necessary universal dimension, and the centurion exhibits both dimensions. Without having anything in common with the Jewish tradition, and upholding legal and legitimate authority and control over the people, he respects their faith, he accepts the presence of God through Jesus, he acknowledges his need and his unworthiness, and in his full humanity turns to him in trust. He is a man of faith not because he performs regular rituals or because he belongs to an exclusive clan, but because he lives out his relationship with Jesus with honesty and sincerity. He accept the life-giving presence of God in his life, even if he knows that he is considered a gentile and an outcast, and he trusts Jesus, in spite of who he is by birth and culture, by social status and role.

There is an interesting mix of self-awareness and trust in this man. He knows his position as a Gentile, he respects the cultural ethos of Judaism, and feels that he has no right to trouble Jesus; and because of this self-awareness, all the communication between the centurion and Jesus is done through Jewish intermediaries. First, he sends someone with the request, and then someone else with a message so full of faith that not even Jesus could resist its appeal or deny the original request.

> *Lord, do not trouble yourself, for I am not worthy to have you come under my roof; therefore I did not presume to come to you. But only speak the word, and let my servant be healed* (Luke 7:7).

These words have long entered our Eucharistic liturgy as an introduction to the Communion Rite, taking on very specific penitential connotations. However, in their original context, much more than a request for forgiveness, the centurion expresses a deep personal faith in Jesus as the only one who can bring healing to his slave. For the centurion, Jesus is not a magician or a wonder worker that needs to be physically present in order to perform some exorcism or utter magic words in order for his slave to be healed. As we often see in Mark's Gospel, this sense of a God a wonder-worker was very strong among many of those who sought healing from Jesus. For the pagan centurion, instead, the very presence of Jesus in the world is both a sign and an instrument of healing and salvation. With unconditional trust, this man expresses clearly the nature of God's living presence, and its effects in the human story and in his personal life. For him, this presence is a gift of a God who shares his creative and life-giving powers with every human being who is prepared to trust God unconditionally.

Somehow, Jesus seems unable to resist such a demonstration of faith, and not only praises the faith of a pagan, but he links specifically the miracle of healing with the faith of a Gentile, and as a consequence of the man's faith in him.

> *When Jesus heard this he was amazed at him, and turning to the crowd that followed him, he said, 'I tell you, not even in Israel have I found such faith'. When those who had been sent returned to the house, they found the slave in good health* (Luke 7:9-10).

As in most healing stories, in that final comment once again Jesus throws the inevitable challenge to his disciples who witnessed the miracle, and to us who have been confronted for a lifetime by this narrative. His words clearly question both our understanding of God and of his living and active presence in our lives, as well as the living out of our claim to faith. While we need "to know" the faith, it is relatively easy to give an intellectual assent to a set of theological propositions, perhaps expressed in highly technical and academic language that remains mostly unintelligible. In contra-position to trusting faith, we justify this attitude by the highly misunderstood term "mystery". The centurion was not appealing to any such technical proposition. He simply accepted the presence of God in his life and believed in Jesus as the source of life and healing. For him God was not the hidden one, or the judge and jury of human behaviour. God was the One here, present in his life, the one he could trust in his need without the need of quasi-magical rituals or physical presence.

Sometimes we resort to a moral code or to a set of precise rituals as the principles of faith, but these certainly do not come into play in the story of the believing centurion. While these elements are expressions of our faith, Jesus subverted the expected expressions of behaviour, pushing beyond the concept of performance and into the realm of relationship. The centurion never sought external expressions such as Jesus physically going to his home, waving his hands, and pronouncing strange words over a distressed body. On the contrary, this centurion sought a personal relationship of trust and utter dependency on Jesus as the instrument of healing.

That is why Jesus praises a pagan official of an occupying power before those very people who considered themselves God's exclusive possession and champions of orthodoxy, holding up this Gentile as a champion of true faith for Israel and for us. *'I tell you, not even in Israel have I found such faith'* (Luke 7:9). We all turn to God in our need, but often we lose sight of the God whose desire is to establish a close relationship with us in our daily experience, and so we relegate him up there or out there, outside our lives and our experience. For the pagan centurion, God is a reality in his own life and in the world around him, not conditioned by cultural, religious, racial, or sectarian categories. God is the one who alone gives life and the centurion simply trusts and abandons himself to this God, regardless of personal merits or worthiness. And that must be our God too.

Letting go and letting God

Of course, the classic event illustrating the kingdom call to human abandonment and total security on God is offered to us in the encounter of Jesus with the rich young man. This young man is sincere in his request to become one of Jesus' disciples (Luke 18:18-23). Mark's version of the same text specifically exemplifies the relationship of Jesus towards the young man as belovedness, by adding the comment *"Jesus, looking at him, loved him"* (Mark 10:21). All the right presuppositions are there; he is personally moved to follow Jesus, he is searching for the full realisation of his life, and he has kept the commandments. There is only one problem, and often we readily identify with the young man, as we too strive to become disciples in the kingdom. The young man unquestionably claims centre stage as the architect of his own life and looks upon the kingdom as his personal achievement. The man who has everything presumes that he can buy eternal life too, through his own means and on his own terms. *"All these I have kept all these since I was a boy; . . . what must I do to inherit eternal life?"* (Luke 18:18), he insists. Accustomed to have everything, he seeks more than the security of possessions inherited or achieved through his personal doing. He is seeking total control of his life. *"What must I do?"* In the end, as we know, it is precisely this I-centeredness that will be the stumbling block to the full realisation of life in discipleship. Jesus' reply is unequivocally and radically other-centeredness:

> *You still lack one thing. Sell everything you have and give to the poor, and you will have treasure in heaven. Then come, follow me* (Luke 18:22).

No, the well-intentioned rich young man cannot accept this absolute invitation to let go of everything and to turn upside down his whole life expectation by placing God as centre stage. Consequently, the encounter ends with a sad comment by Jesus, and a deep sense of pity and almost of hopeless despair for all (Luke 18:23-24).

> *When he heard this, he became very sad, because he was very wealthy. Jesus looked at him and said, 'How hard it is for the rich to enter the kingdom of God!* (Luke 18:23-24).

Jesus does not deny discipleship to the young man. With an unspoken but clearly spelt out reference to the first beatitude, he simply points out that self-realisation in the kingdom demands that he let go (Mark 10:17-22; Matthew 5:1-12; Luke 6:20-25). Let go of your personal securities and of your ready-made answers, let go of your plans and dreams and means of achieving them, let go of your strengths and your weaknesses, let go of your doubts and your certainties, let go of your yesterdays and of your tomorrows. Most of all, let go of that possessive I-approach to life, which the young man, who had everything, exemplified. It is precisely this obsession with material securities that Jesus condemns, not because they are securities or that they are bad in themselves, but because they are artificial and we are obsessed with them.

The final comment is almost pathetic. "*He became grieving*" (Mark 10:22). In the end, the young man lost everything, and most of all he lost his own self. His dream, his holy desire, and indeed his whole life work come to nothing simply because, by making his own self the centre and the focus of it all, he set his heart and his sights on the wrong priorities in life.

> *Whoever wants to save their life will lose it, but whoever loses their life for my sake will save it* (Luke 9:24)... *And he said to all, 'If anyone would come after me, let them deny themself and take up their cross daily and follow me. For whoever would save their life will lose it, but whoever loses their life for my sake will save it. For what does it profit a person if they gain the whole world and loses or forfeits themself'?* (Luke 9:23-25).

Surely, the call is as costly as its sounds, because changing patterns of behaviour, letting go of attitudes and practices that have been life-giving and held sacrosanct for a long time, prioritising our needs and constantly re-focusing on relationships with others – these are demands that cut deeply into our psyche and our value system. They leave us uncertain and confused, highlighting our nakedness, dependency, and fragility. We have to embrace death in its multi-faceted dimensions every day in order to make room for God. We have no choice if we want to be fulfilled disciples embracing the presence of God's kingdom in our life and in our world.

Trust: the key to hope

It is so easy to fall into the same trap of the rich young man, particularly when our dreams and plans overlook the twofold foundational assumption of the kingdom; namely, that our life is in God's hands, and that our hands are empowered by God's energy to establish the kingdom through us. When we have the courage to trust in God and rely on God alone for our security and the fulfilment of our dreams now and in the future, then we can journey on through excitement and struggle without fear, anxiety or compulsion, in spite of and even through setbacks and personal trials. Then we can truly rejoice and hope because there is nothing standing in the way of God guiding our journey, whatever that human journey may demand of us, or wherever it may take us.

When we discover ourselves totally destitute with nowhere to lay our head, no home to call your own, or no private self-advancement to attend to, then we will be ready to journey in discipleship free and unencumbered, and to seek and to achieve full realisation of life (Luke 9:57-62) in the kingdom and for the kingdom. Referring to John of the Cross' classic cry of "*todo*" and "*nada*", Thomas Merton proposes that discipleship in the kingdom is nothing else but the total (*all - todo*) emptying of oneself (*nothing - nada*) until one becomes wholly available to God, who cuts and moulds and shapes on his own absolute terms. The call is not about "what must I do" but about letting go and embracing nothingness (*nada*), because our destiny is to possess and to be possessed by the One who is Wholeness (*Todo*)[19] and fullness of life itself.

Only by losing all control, and trusting exclusively on God, we can achieve fullness of life, even if at times such a call will

---

19 Thomas Merton, *Wisdom of the Desert*, New York: New Directions, 1960.

appear too much to bear. Jesus' total letting go of his life on the cross in trustful abandonment to the Father was the instant that sparked off the ultimate fullness of life in the Resurrection, and his first greeting to his distraught and helpless disciples was to gift them with peace. We too will truly discover inner peace, so long as that is all we want, leaving the rest of our life-journey to the companionship of God. The disciple of the kingdom is forever the Easter person who faces death knowing that not even death could keep God away from us or nullify our hope in abandonment. Dead and buried, Jesus rose to be forever and to be with those who trusted in him. That is the foundation of our hope and our trust, fruits of letting go into God's hands.

Unlike the rich man, trust means to have the courage to acknowledge God's giftedness to us and be thankful. We need the wisdom to set the rightful priorities and live by them, knowing that God is always at work as the primary initiator and energiser. We need the honesty to admit that in the end there is but one security in our life story, God. There will come a time when our achievements, successes, and even good works will mean nothing and become non-existent. The time will surely come, through misfortune or death, when we will have nothing left to rely on except God. God will then be the only insurance policy available to us for the future and for eternity, a future and eternity that have a lasting visible expression in the kingdom here and now, in our own life, and in our relationships.

Once we have given over our complete self in trust to God, then our life may exhibit symptoms more akin to paralysis than vitality, childlike dependency instead of explosive maturity, total insecurity where we would like to see well-laid master plans. That will be the time of grace-filled call to trust in a God seeking to take over in our life, and through our absolute destitution to reach out to a world in desperate need of security, affirmation and trust. Then we will have incarnated the Beatitudes. When our paralysis becomes a compassionate walking together with the lame and the lonely in ourselves and in others, when our nakedness and radical insecurity becomes availability to God's transforming power, then the hungry will be fed, the blind will see and the prisoners set free (Luke 4:18). Then our destitution will bear rich fruitfulness, and we will have become truly ready to follow Jesus on the journey of discipleship in the kingdom, in this world and in eternity, beyond time and space.

The Cross

The Banner of the Kingdom
Luke 24:13-26

Now on that same day two of them were going to a village called Emmaus, about seven miles from Jerusalem, and talking with each other about all these things that had happened. While they were talking and discussing, Jesus himself came near and went with them, but their eyes were kept from recognising him. And he said to them, 'What are you discussing with each other while you walk along?' They stood still, looking sad. Then one of them, whose name was Cleopas, answered him, 'Are you the only stranger in Jerusalem who does not know the things that have taken place there in these days?' He asked them, 'What things?' They replied, 'The things about Jesus of Nazareth, who was a prophet mighty in deed and word before God and all the people, and how our chief priests and leaders handed him over to be condemned to death and crucified him. But we had hoped that he was the one to redeem Israel. Yes, and besides all this, it is now the third day since these things took place. Moreover, some women of our group astounded us. They were at the tomb early this morning, and when they did not find his body there, they came back and told us that they had indeed seen a vision of angels who said that he was alive. Some of those who were with us went to the tomb and found it just as the women had said; but they did not see him.' Then he said to them, 'Oh, how foolish you are, and how slow of heart to believe all that the prophets have declared! Was it not necessary that the Messiah should suffer these things and then enter into his glory?'

Struggle along the way

The disciples trudge along, shattered, angry, trying to forget. That is precisely why they return to the small village of Emmaus: to forget it all, to go back to what they know, and pretend that this tragedy never happened! A multifaceted tragedy indeed. The violent death of one man had shattered the lives of so many others as well! Like those many others, these disciples had placed all their hopes and dreams on this Jesus of Nazareth who promised so much, who had convinced them – in their own understanding at least – that the promised Messiah had finally come. He was the one who would deliver the People of God from the domination of the Roman gentiles and re-establish the glorious and eternal reign of David. But now he was dead, executed as a subversive criminal, abandoned even by his own followers. The destruction was now total. Not only was Jesus of Nazareth now a lifeless body lying in a tomb, but also that same Jesus had abandoned them to fear, disillusionment, mistrust, anger, and deep, very deep personal pain, born out of danger for their own lives. Why all this? Why had they been drawn into this tragedy not of their own making? Why had they been cheated of all their hope and future? Why?

Wrapped in their own self-pity and anger, they do not even notice the stranger who falls in step with them. He must be a real stranger if he is unaware of what has happened in Jerusalem that sparked off this deep and overwhelming pain they are now experiencing. Out of a need to enlighten the ignorant stranger, but most of all to let others know of the injustice they have been subjected to and which has caused the pain they carry, they tell him. *"We had hoped... But now!...."* (Luke 24:21). Of course, they are the victims, it is clear, and all they seek is compassion and pity!

The stranger, however, seems quite unmoved by their obvious tale of woe, and certainly he shows little feeling of pity for their plight. After listening with interest and intent to their story of self-justification, his response to them is bewildering. Someone they have never met and from whom they only seek sympathy and support, actually call them *"foolish"* and *"slow of heart to believe all that the prophets have declared"*. Then the most shattering comment of all: *"Was it not necessary that the Messiah should suffer and die and then enter his glory?"* (Luke 24:25-26).

Those words must have sounded like a hot blade thrust into their self-indulgent hearts. Pain and suffering cannot be necessary, least of all when one is asked to bear it in one's flesh because of the deeds of someone else. Those words only cut even more deeply into their pain, made more intense by the realisation of having been thrown headlong into a situation not of their own making, and totally out of their control. Pain and death are not solutions, not humanly speaking, anyway, and when one is in the midst of pain and death he/she will struggle with every fibre of energy to avoid pain and death, because life is too precious to be wasted by pain and pain is too unnatural to live with. Tragically, as we know, we humans often prefer death to suffering, and escape suffering by seeking death.

Our experience of suffering

The media is not good news! Constantly, obsessively we are bombarded on all sides and in every moment of our existence by everything that is most negative, abhorrent, destructive, and depressing in our world, in our story, in ourselves. Disasters and suffering inevitably leave us bewildered and disturbed, because in most cases, there is no logical human rationale for such events, nor for the immensely tragic consequences they bear. As we watch from the comfort of our living room, we may even become desensitised and callously resigned to it all. Suffering may seem inevitable in the end, but hardly necessary to our wholeness as human beings! Hopefully, like for the disciples of Emmaus, questions will arise, hidden, unspoken, but persistent and unresolved nevertheless. Why?... Why these things?... Why these people?... Why me? Not only natural events or catastrophic disasters leave us bewildered, but our personal, immediate, and inner worlds may collapse for a whole plethora of reasons – marriage breakdown, job loss, onset of disability, or serious life threatening illness, estrangement between parents and children, sudden realisation of the rapid passing of years into weakening old age. In all these situations, we may become so overwhelmed by adversity that we feel as if our life has lost all its meaning and purpose. Yes, we too wish we could turn away from it all, and seek shelter in the small but reassuring world of our own personal securities.

At the same time, like the disciples on the road to Emmaus retreating into their own secure world, we too may need to hear and heed those words, *"was it not necessary?"* precisely in order to challenge those attempts at denying and at escaping the pain that the two disciples in the story clearly illustrate.

If we are to accept the insights of developmental psychology, there are only two possible outcomes to such bewilderment: either an irrational and death-dealing bitterness, or a call to faith. As Erik Erikson puts it, we can either slide into despair or we can choose to embrace hope.[20] When one's earthly hopes are shattered, when our life collapses and loses its meaning, when we feel flattened and heavily bowed down, when everything seems totally hopeless, we can either fall into bitterness and despair, or enter more deeply into oneself and one's story and see the cross as the ultimate and eternal sign pointing inevitably to salvation and freedom.

That is the banner of the kingdom – the cross – and this is precisely what the stranger along the road to Emmaus points to, inviting those two followers to look at the inevitability of suffering not from the point of view of some cruel and inescapable fate, but from the perspective of a call to inevitable hope and liberation.

Suffering is not "Good News"

Embracing the cross as a call to inevitable hope and liberation carries its own dangers of fundamentalism, and it can be yet another form of escape and denial, unless we are prepared to look at it from the perspective of the Stranger walking alongside us on our own Emmaus journey. Over time, Christianity has stood

---

20 Saul McLeod, "Erik Erikson", http://www.simplypsychology.org/Erik-Erikson.html (accessed 30/12/2015).

accused of making an apology of the cross, often canonising it by pretending that suffering is good, or by escaping from its stark daily reality into an unreal spirituality of an otherworldly or an after-life reward, directly proportional to the degree or amount of suffering one has to endure throughout one's earthly experience. Paraphrasing Gerard W. Hughes, the Christian's journey is not a kind of sufferathon, where the person who suffers most will certainly win the Olympic gold. If suffering were good and life-giving, "the most effective service of God would consist in our imposing the maximum suffering on ourselves and on others".[21]

On the contrary, as the one sent by the Father to bring life in its fullness to every man, woman or child (John 10:10), Jesus did not choose the cross nor did he want it because it was good. It is true that in the gospel narratives, for Jesus the cross is the one necessary path to discipleship (Matthew 10:38; 16:24; Luke 9:23), the inevitable condition of his filial relationship, and of submissive obedience to Abba. However, Jesus did not choose suffering as a good to be sought after for its own sake, and even less to be imposed on others. In the garden, he prayed to the Father pleading for deliverance. *"Father, if it is possible, let this cup pass me by"* (Matthew 26:39; Luke 22:42), and on Golgotha, Jesus reached the threshold of despair to the point of doubting the Father's presence and love, and screamed his pain, *"My God, my God why have you forsaken me?"*(Matthew 27:46).

Though the cross is part of the human journey, it remains the archetypal and ultimate symbol of suffering and death, and suffering and death for their own sake are evil, and the fruits of evil, as the very beginning of the Judaeo-Christian story reminds us

---

21 Gerard W. Hughes, *Oh God, Why? A Journey through Lent for Bruised Pilgrims*, Oxford: The Bible Reading Fellowship, 1993, 138.

(Genesis 2). Nevertheless, unwanted and less-than-human though the cross may have been for Jesus and for the whole of humanity for all time, Jesus accepted it as part of that human and divine journey that would lead to fulfilment and salvation. The cross will be salvific only to the extent that it is an expression and an instrument of that radical Yes to the Father, a radicalness that Jesus lived and witnessed throughout his earthly life. God's will for us is life, and not destruction and death, as Jesus' first self-disclosure in the synagogue of Nazareth proclaimed and all his subsequent actions revealed

> *The spirit of the Lord has been given to me, for he has anointed me. He has sent me to bring good news to the poor, to proclaim liberty to captives and to the blind new sight, to set the downtrodden free* (Luke 4:18).

The kingdom Jesus proclaimed is not about suffering and death but for life in spite of death and suffering. To a widow grieving for the death of her only son, Jesus gives him back bursting with life (Luke 7:11-17). Lepers cry out in despair and anger at a world that rejects them and labels them unclean, only to be restored to health and dignity (Luke 17:11-19). At the risk of defilement and condemnation, Jesus holds the hand of a young girl lying in death, restoring her to fullness of life and joy (Mark 5:41). A woman afflicted by a physical ailment and by an even more painful moral stigma, is allowed to touch him, and healing and affirmation are the result (Mark 5:25-34). Jesus was not about suffering and pain for the sake of pharisaic ritual purity or moral judgment. On the contrary, human fragility and pain are the catalysts that ignite compassion in him. Jesus physically touches pain, suffering and death, and by touching and embracing that human fragility, Jesus not only condemns and heals the darkness of pain, fears and self-condemnation, but he also declares the moral imperative to remove pain, fear, suffering and death that in many ways obscure and denigrate the preciousness of each person. Gerard Hughes claims that the passive and indiscriminate acceptance of suffering as a presumed instrument towards a deeper relationship with Christ is blasphemous and a denial of Christ himself.

> Suffering, in itself, is an evil and to be avoided. While it is true that some people are ennobled by suffering, the majority are diminished or destroyed by it... Suffering does not save: its effect is normally to destroy... (and) to accept it passively and encourage others to do the same 'for the love of Christ' is to collude with evil, not to resist it.[22]

Have we ever considered the anomaly of such expressions as "the cross lies at the heart of Christian life", particularly when we verbalise such platitudes right in the midst of heroic self-giving, or as we minister for the relief of pain and suffering, fear and guilt, degradation and condemnation, despair and death? If we hold on to some distorted belief by which suffering is a sign of God's favour, and that God can only be appeased by human struggle and pain, then why deceive ourselves blind and betray all those engaged in activities of human promotion and redemption, be it in terms of justice, well being, health, or just plain companionship or compassion?

---

22 Gerard W. Hughes, *God of Surprises*, London: DLT, 1998, 138.

To claim any inherent goodness and value in pain and suffering as willed by God makes a mockery of the God whom we address as Father. To claim that God wills suffering and death for us, makes God into an angry, cruel, and sadistic puppet, who after throwing us into "this valley of tears", smugly leaves us floundering, hopeless and helpless, just to see if we can make it to the shore. This is definitely not the Abba revealed by Jesus. Such a bloodthirsty God may well make millions on a Hollywood portrayal of 'The Passion of the Christ', but, as Gerard W. Hughes puts it, "this can leave us very grateful to Jesus, but less keen on his heavenly Father".[23]

The cross: the place we share with God

Claims such as "Unless we enter into the Passion and death of Christ, we cannot share in the Resurrection" are true, but we need to grasp fully its salvific meaning, which has nothing to do with masochistic tendencies or self-inflicted stoicism.

Jesus did not embrace the cross and invite us to take up ours for its own sake, or because it was good to suffer. In the context of his first self-proclamation in the synagogue of Nazareth, Jesus gives us the key to his life and the mission entrusted to him by the Father. He has been sent *"to bring good news to the poor, to proclaim liberty to captives and to the blind new sight, to set the downtrodden free"* (Luke 4:18). In that self-proclamation, Jesus actually sets out a program of redemption from all that is evil and unjust and death-dealing in our world. However, such a task of redemption on behalf of others often demands a level of self-giving, and of courage that is painful, self-sacrificing and even death-dealing.

---

23 Gerard W. Hughes, *Oh God, Why?*, 138

The cross then becomes not only the banner of the kingdom, and the instrument of realisation of the kingdom; it becomes the place where we encounter God in Christ. Indeed, there is an even deeper level of human and spiritual consciousness where suffering, pain and death become necessary means towards discovering the real God in us and walking with us, as the disciples of Emmaus eventually discovered. Jesus invited those two disciples to look on their own suffering as the key to hope. At the same time, he is warning us that if there were no suffering, if all our longings were merely in the here-and-now, there would be no need of hope.

This is the message of Good Friday, where we see a Jesus subjected to and struggling with the most painful experience imaginable, to the point of screaming out in anguish his ultimate despair *"My God, my God, why have you forsaken me?"* (Psalm 22). Yes, Jesus reached the ultimate level of physical, emotional and spiritual agony to the point of touching and living through human despair. This means that now we can truly claim that, having taken upon himself the totality of human suffering, God, through Jesus Christ, now knows my suffering to its ultimate destructive power in death.

Having been there in the flesh, God now knows what I go through, when physical pain wrecks my body, when loneliness and abandonment crush me to death, when my future looms so hopeless that I even doubt that there may be a future at all, when I am the victim of injustice or I am called to forgive the hurt received. In Jesus, God knows rejection and insult, physical and mental abuse, betrayal and falsehood. God knows death to the point that my death becomes the only human way to enter into God's reality, just as death was the ultimate way of God entering the totality of our human reality. In the words of Thomas Keating,

> God is not just an onlooker of human history and of our individual melodrama, applauding our efforts and lamenting our failures from a safe distance. He *joins* us in our sufferings. In the crucifixion of Jesus, the impossible happens. God dies.[24]

Consequently, because God knows it all, and knows it with a knowing of the heart as well of the mind and body, now I am no longer alone in my struggles, in my sufferings, in my death. In this context, the event of the journey to Emmaus is both a self-revelation of the Risen Lord and a parable in action. Along the road, Jesus not only claims that it was necessary that the Messiah should suffer and die, but he makes himself their compassionate travelling companion. By falling in step with two people who trudge their way in darkness and pain seeking for an escape more than for an explanation, God not only dies an abominable death, but our God is also the one who walks, mostly unknown, along the road of our pain, loneliness and misunderstandings.

The necessity that Jesus speaks of to the disciples of Emmaus, is the necessity of letting God into our pain, and abandoning our false images as much as our false expectations and securities into God's hands. When we have the courage and strength to do that, then truly pain becomes redemptive and truly life-giving, because it becomes the instrument of God working his way in our life and journeying alongside us on our way. With nothing to hold on to of our own making, then only God can make us into what God has

---

[24] Thomas Keating, *Manifesting God*, New York, NY: Lantern Books, 2005, 59.

always wanted us to be. It is as if God invited us into himself through our vulnerability and dependency, even to the point of our most hellish experience. Ronald Rolheiser invites us to reflect on that creedal statement stating that Jesus "*died, rose and descended into hell*".[25] Every time we proclaim those words at liturgy we commit ourselves to accepting that whatever our personal hells, paranoias, fears, physical and emotional torments, or sense of alienation and abandonment, in Jesus, God has plumbed their darkest depths. And because of that descent into all that is evil while remaining trustful to the Father, life blossomed anew, like a flower out of the cruellest winter.

Incarnation reached its ultimate fulfilment on the Cross of Calvary, not as a blood sacrifice, but as total immersion of the divine into the human story. Then truly, the most human facets of our existence became caught up into that divine presence that did not shun the earthy and the broken, but made earthiness and brokenness constituent elements of the divine reality incarnated in the human story. God truly became human through suffering, so that human suffering might become instrument and stimulus towards our divine destiny of oneness with our God. Only in this sense can suffering be redemptive. Only in this perspective can we speak of abundant fruitfulness through suffering and death.

In the hands of the Master Craftsman

In this perspective, suffering and pain are ironical and contradictory elements throughout the gospel narratives. On the one hand, Jesus is unashamedly committed to healing and relieving pain of all

---

25 Ronald Rolheiser, *Forgotten Among the Lilies. Learning to Love beyond Our Fears*, New York, NY: Doubleday, 2005, 158-159.

types and at all costs. On the other, he is equally obsessed with instructing his slow-learning and unbelieving disciples that he must suffer and die (Matthew 16:20-22; 20:17-19; Mark 8:31-32; 9:12; 10:32-34. Luke 9:21-23; 17:25; 24:25-27). Indeed, Jesus makes no secret of the fact that death itself is the *sine qua non* of all forms of discipleship (Matthew 10:37-39; 16:24-25; 24:9-10. Mark 8:33-35. Luke 9:23-25; 14:26-27).

Reflecting on the fact that "*we are consigned to our death every day, for the sake of Jesus*", Paul writes to the Christians of Corinth,

> *We are only the earthenware jars that hold this treasure, to make it clear that such an overwhelming power comes from God and not from us. We are in difficulties on all sides, but never cornered; we see no answer to our problems, but never despair; we have been persecuted, but never deserted; knocked down but never killed; always wherever we may be, we carry with us in our body the death of Jesus, so that the life of Jesus, too, may always be seen in our body... So death is at work in us, but life in you* (2 Corinthians 4:7-12).

By bringing into relief Jeremiah's image of the clay and the potter, Paul points to our destiny to fulfilment through death, because that is the way Jesus fulfilled his mission in obedience and abandonment to the Father. With the prophet, let us go down to the potter's house and observe the Master Craftsman at work; and then let us enlarge and personalise the image a little.

> *The word that came to Jeremiah from the Lord: 'Come, go down to the potter's house, and there I will let you hear my word". So I went down to the potter's house, and there he was working at his wheel. The vessel he was making of clay was spoiled in the potter's hand, and he reworked it into another vessel, as seemed good to him. Then the word of the Lord came to me: Can I not do with you, O house of Israel, just as this potter has done? says the Lord. Just like the clay in the potter's hand, so are you in my hand, O house of Israel* (Jeremiah 18:1-5).

Clay – amorphous mass, ordinary, cheap and common. Yet there is nothing cheap and common for the potter who discovers beauty and potential and preciousness within that amorphous commonality. Our high-tech assembly-line productivity has lost the sense of relationship that the artisan feels and lives with the object and materials of their work. It is not thus for Jeremiah's potter. He sees beauty within, and he feels the moral imperative to release such beauty. However, that release is so painful, slow, unrelenting pain, uncontrollable by the clay itself. Cutting, tearing, shaping, beating, spinning, and spinning over and over again. Yes, as clay, I am out of control and I have no telling what my destiny is, or what the craftsman wants to make of me. Occasionally, things seem to slow down; but I barely catch my breath when the look on the craftsman's face tells me that I am not quite the masterpiece that he has in his mind. It is then that I find myself crunched again into a lump of shapeless mud, only for the process to start again. More tearing, more water, more shaping and spinning and squeezing. Finally, the fire – slow burning fire! It is all so painful! I do not know why or how long. I only know that eventually the Master Craftsman, in his own good time, releases me from the fire and holds me in his hands with the smile of satisfaction, the joy, and beauty of the final masterpiece from his hands, held in his hands. After his struggles to achieve his dream and the most harrowing experiences on my part, I am in his hands, a unique, unrepeatable masterpiece in the potter's hands! I may be small, fragile, and paper-thin, but a unique masterpiece nevertheless. Indeed, the preciousness lies precisely in that smallness and fragility, a fragility that may break and shatter at any moment, but, paradoxically, strengthened by every attempt to knit the pieces together.

I am that amorphous clay and the paper-thin masterpiece worked by the hands of the Master Potter, who struggles with me in order to achieve his dream. This is the kind of language by which we need to re-express our human-divine identity in the kingdom and our relationship with the God who journeys with us, sharing our struggles and pain, until both of us achieve the primal dream of God. This is the kind of truthfulness that we have to re-appropriate and own, if we are to structure our life, and our own very self in terms of what each of us is meant to be in this human-divine relationship called the kingdom. In the Christian perspective, fragility is preciousness, brokenness is potential, death is openness to life, and Easter Sunday is always subsequent to Good Friday, because God has been through all the dualities and contradiction of human life that we can possibly experience in our story.

This is neither stoic fatalism nor a canonisation of suffering. That would be blasphemous in the Christian understanding of reality. The problem is accepting the painful process of breaking up of our husks of suffering, fear, and self-centredness, within the darkness that we experience in ourselves and all around us. God shared that darkness in order to bring us all into the explosion of life and light of Easter morning.

Conclusion

At the Last Supper, as Jesus gave explosive expression to his feelings for his disciples, he reminded them of the vine, the image that captures both richness and ambiguity intertwined as the story of discipleship.

> God wants to prune me. A pruned vine does not look beautiful, but during harvest time it produces much fruit. The greatest challenge is to continue to recognise God's pruning hand in my life. Then I can avoid resentment and depression and become even more grateful that I am called upon to bear even more fruit than I thought I could.[26]

Like the disciples, we may occasionally feel confused, bewildered and afraid. We may not like to own what the message reveals to us or about us, and the temptation to escape, rationalise, and blame may appear too strong to resist. Like the fragile vine of our own self, we will often feel stripped, pruned, cut, and left bare. Yes, we may feel that the news is too good to be true and we do not quite measure up to our own expectations. We may hear the call to let go of our fears and anxieties, and walk through brokenness and suffering in trust. We may be touched at the very core of our

---

26 Henri. J. Nouwen, "The Farewell Discourse", in Michael O'Loughlin (ed.), *Henri Nouwen – Jesus: A Gospel*, Maryknoll NY: Orbis Books, 2001, 91-92

being with a mixture of joy and pain, hope and sadness, energy and fragility. We may feel bound and locked by our brokenness. Yet our brokenness and suffering are the place of our encounter with God who shared it in Jesus, and shares it with us every day.

When emptiness seems the only content of our broken life, when memories of past and uncertainty of future fill us with fear, condemnation and isolation, when our clayishness is too much to bear, let us have the courage and the wisdom to remember that it was necessary for the earthenware jar to be shaped, and moulded, and torn, and reshaped again, and fired many times over, with the Master Craftsman totally immersed in that amorphous mess. In those clayish experiences, let us pray for the courage to acknowledge the one who journeys with us, and recognise the pain of deep love born out of the stripping and tearing that heralds the passing from winter into spring. *"I am the true vine, you are the branches, and my Father is the vinedresser"* (John 15:1.5).

In the words of Jurgen Moltman,

> Our faith begins at the point where atheists suppose that it must be at an end. Our faith begins with the bleakness and power which is the night of the cross, abandonment, temptation and doubt about everything that exists! Our faith must be born where it is abandoned by all tangible reality; it must be born of nothingness and it must taste this nothingness and be given it to taste in a way that no philosophy of nihilism can imagine.[27]

---

[27] Jurgen Moltman, "The Crucified God", in Ronald Rohlheiser, *Forgotten Among the Lilies*, 155.

Resurrection

The Impossible is Real
Mark 16:1-8

When the Sabbath was over, Mary Magdalene, and Mary the mother of James, and Salome bought spices, so that they might go and anoint him. And very early on the first day of the week, when the sun had risen, they went to the tomb. They had been saying to one another, 'Who will roll away the stone for us from the entrance to the tomb?' When they looked up, they saw that the stone, which was very large, had already been rolled back. As they entered the tomb, they saw a young man, dressed in a white robe, sitting on the right side; and they were alarmed. But he said to them, 'Do not be alarmed; you are looking for Jesus of Nazareth, who was crucified. He has been raised; he is not here. Look, there is the place they laid him. But go, tell his disciples and Peter that he is going ahead of you to Galilee; there you will see him, just as he told you.' So they went out and fled from the tomb, for terror and amazement had seized them; and they said nothing to anyone, for they were afraid (Mark 16:1-8).

The human heart is prisoner of a life-long paradox. Enslaved by an insatiable yearning for love, peace and joy, but most of all for life in its fullness and forever, such deep and intense longing shatters against the inevitability and finality of death, which not only puts an end to our hearts' yearnings, but obliterates the very possibility of life itself. From a purely human perspective, death is horrid, non-negotiable, and all destructive. Unless, of course, we are prepared to believe in an empty tomb that only a few hours before held a dead and mangled body, an emptiness screaming the humanly unthinkable that the one who lay there before is alive, beyond and in spite of death.

That is the challenge of Easter: to believe that the ultimate and impossible longing of the human heart is no longer a mirage, but a reality. Life explodes in and through death. The stories that the liturgy puts before us at Holy Week and Easter speak of horror and death, but at the same time, they proclaim the impossible. Life has blossomed in its fullness in spite of the horror of death.

Sabbath Day in the Upper Room

Let us imagine the atmosphere in that Upper Room on that evening after Passover, the great annual festival commemorating an apparent human impossibility exploded into reality for those who lived through it many centuries before. Passover celebrated the central event of Israel as a nation and as "the people God had chosen". It celebrated freedom from slavery by a powerless and anonymous band of slaves against the might of Egypt. It was a yearly celebration and a memory projecting the heart into a yearning for a future full of hope for all generations to come.

However, on this occasion, their longing hearts harboured

only disappointment, sadness, fear, and resentment. Jesus' disciples were not in the mood for celebration that night. Indeed, you could cut the air with a knife; air full of emptiness, of anger, of fear, of disillusionment, and of mistrust. To the end, they had failed to understand who Jesus really was, what his mission was about, and their motives for following him were often more dubious than praiseworthy. Nevertheless, those disciples had staked their lives for Jesus who promised so much for their personal future and their misguided expectations of political liberation and freedom from their oppressive political, social, and religious culture. In trust, they had gambled both present and future, whether it was two leaky fishing boats or a profitable tax collector's table, leaving behind all their personal securities and families in order to follow the preacher from Nazareth, who promised so much and spoke joy and peace to the outcasts. They had gambled it all because they believed in him.

For whatever reason, and not necessarily the most praiseworthy, that band of ignorant and simple people had left behind the security of their home and trade to follow this young preacher from Galilee who seemed to promise so much. *'We had hoped that he was the one to redeem Israel'* (Luke 24:21), two of them complained on the way of home and escaping from it all. Of course, it is easy and attractive to follow and to trust the Lord when he speaks to us words of affirmation and healing (Luke 15); when, in our own imagination, his message sounds like a radical call to arms against the hated Romans (Luke 12:49-53); when he works spectacular deeds like feeding five thousand people on two fish and five barley loaves (Luke 9:10-17). It is easy to claim discipleship when we let our imagination run wild and we create our own style of discipleship, twisting and misplacing the words of the Lord to suit our own expectations (Matthew 20:20-23; Luke 22:24-30). It is all so easy, then.

Now all those self-styled expectations have vanished; all those dreams of first and second place in the kingdom have turned into a nightmare of deception and fear. All that following the Lord now seems completely futile and cruel. Now the young man from Galilee who worked wonders and spoke of such promise was dead, the most ignominious death of a rebellious slave, and their own world had crumbled into despair and deceit. Now all they had to hold on to was the memory of a dead teacher, of a wonder worker executed like a fraudulent criminal. Yes, they felt cheated, let down, and utterly hopeless. Their longing hearts could now harbour only disappointment, sadness, fear and resentment. Their dreams and plans shattered, all that was left now was to go back to what they knew before – fishing, farming, and tax collecting, trying to put out of their minds that whole tragic chapter, in the hope that time, if ever, would heal the wounds of their misguided adventure.

An empty tomb

In this scenario, the light of hope is trapped by darkness, and the energy of life has been swallowed up by the all-embracing gloom of death. It is dark outside that Upper Room, the place of promise and intimate friendship just a few hours before; a darkness that seemed to exude from the all-embracing blackness gripping the hearts and souls of those who had witnessed the unbelievable tragedy of our Good Friday.

Just before daylight has the strength to break out, the only sign of life is shadows, as three black-clad figures shuffle hurriedly and stealthily through the narrow lanes leading out of the village.

In the darkness, they are looking for the darkness of a tomb. Only a mother grieving the cruel and untimely execution of her son can comprehend the pain of loss and death. It is all pervading and overwhelming! One more visit to "the place they laid him" (Mark16:6), for one more tear, one more memory, one more embrace of that cold unmovable stone that seals away forever life and any loving embrace.

Suddenly, the outer darkness turns into inner despair. Unexpectedly, the tomb is open and empty. The ultimate sword piercing the heart of a mother! Tombs are meant to hold dead bodies, delivering a strange message of marriage between finality and eternal presence at the same time. An empty tomb is a sad and cruel reminder of absolute nothingness, without presence and without memories. The cruel game of tragedy and pain has now reached its ultimate climax in an empty tomb, freezing the human psyche into absolute fear and horror. Even the last fickle reminders of life now have been obliterated . . .

. . . Unless, of course the unthinkable, the unbelievable, and the impossible happen, by which the empty tomb becomes the ultimate sign of life through death and beyond death! This is the message of a "young man, dressed in a white robe" who, in Mark's account stands at the place of death; but a message that in its apparent absurdity does nothing to allay the fears of those who persist on looking for a dead body in an empty tomb.

> *Do not be alarmed; you are looking for Jesus of Nazareth, who was crucified. He has been raised; he is not here (Mark 16:6).*

He has been raised! What does that to mean in the midst of

darkness, loss and despair? Suddenly, the overwhelming message of the frightened women takes on a sense of illusory incredulity. In the midst of overwhelming gloom, death, and heart-wrenching memories, the rest of the disciples are confronted with the cosmic unthinkable and impossible. Jesus stands there, in their midst, once again reassuring and affirming them, eating with them, inviting them to touch him, and speaking words of peace. An unreal mixture of bewilderment and hopelessness suddenly explodes into a sense of wonder and joy that defies human words, and projects those who lived through it into a completely new level of reality and self-understanding. By the empty tomb and in that Upper Room, the disciples experience a radical event that defies human rationality but proclaims that the impossible has become real. Jesus is not dead, but alive. No logical process or explanations hold any value here, because Resurrection delves into the deepest level of the human heart, awakening precisely that ultimate and eternal longing for life in its fullness and forever.

In that Upper Room, the disciples discover that the impossible is now not just a possibility but a reality for them, before their very eyes and in their hands. If we but accept it, that becomes also our experience. When the one we love walks the streets and greets us again after being dead and buried for three days, then everything is possible, and there are no longer limits to our yearning, hoping and dreaming. In that upper room, they experience in the flesh that not even death could keep Jesus away from them. The Lord has truly risen, as he said he would!

In that Upper Room, where the freedom and hope of the first Passover had died with the memory of the crucified one, now they experience the ultimate freedom from the slavery of fear and death, and supreme hope reassures the yearning heart that whatever the journey ahead, life and not death is the final destiny. In the face of such impossibility, the ultimate certainty for the disciples was a sudden awareness that only a direct intervention of God in human history could have brought about a transformation of such magnitude as to bring life out of the very depths of the tomb, and push the limits of our yearning beyond the barriers of death. Only God could have done this, and this God is standing right here in their midst, beyond all human possibilities or power of understanding.

Transformation, not information

In a bizarre parody of Easter, someone suggested that Jesus did well most things, but failed miserably on the most important one. Had he chosen to walk this earth in our times, full of ubiquitous technological wizardly, a minute bug inside the tomb would have revealed to the whole world in real time what happened in that place of death, and confronted us instantly with undisputable evidence for our faith and belief. Apart from the strange presuppositions underlying such a suggestion, the best one can say is that probably our electronic wizardly would have returned nothing but the silent emptiness of the darkness of death.

It is an acknowledged fact that historically and chronologically, the various Resurrection narratives make little sense, and it is a futile exercise to pretend to set out some logical and coordinated sequence of events in time and place. As an experience of Jesus, dead and risen again, the disciples and the narrators are totally at a loss in their attempt to portray something wholly other, without any measurable resonance, and totally counter to normal human experience. Hence, when it comes to details of place, time, situations and protagonists, the telling is confusing and in some case contradictory.

When we look at the various Easter narratives, we find a total lack of sequence and logical rationality. In total confusion, and without any literary connection to each other, the four evangelists range across a whole gamut of details, times and places, painting the diverse reactions of those who lived through the event. Time seems to be suspended and geographical references are boundless. Jesus seems to appear simultaneously in different places, while sometimes one person, or sometimes a multiplicity of characters seem to be the recipients of the same appearance, according to different narratives. Taken as a whole, the Easter stories make no sense; and rightly so, because the Gospels are not about information but about transformation. Information seeks the why's and how's of some vacuous and mysterious resuscitation of a body, where living energy is held in suspense to be revitalised by human intervention. Jesus' Resurrection, on the other hand, is a total and radical transformation, challenging and supplanting all that is non-life, and exploding into fullness of life where absolute and total death reigned supreme.

Easter is about life, tapping into life experience and demanding a personal life response from each person within the diversity of situations and in their understanding of life and the world. Resurrection is an experience transcending human categories of measurement and analysis, yet powerful enough to energise a radical and eternal transformation, investing totally the lives of those first disciples as much as the lives of all those who claimed discipleship. Resurrection belongs to the realm of faith, or it has no meaning. The one thing we know for sure about the Resurrection of Jesus is that we are not dealing with some miraculous unexplainable resuscitation of a dead body, but with a powerful encounter with our God and with our own self.

In this multiplicity of responses, a common thread runs through all the Resurrection stories, linking the diversity of personal experiences into the proclamation of the Easter Alleluia as the individual and collective event of salvation. In every narrative, there comes a moment where a shift takes place and that is the saving moment of the whole event. This is the shift from unbelief to recognition of Jesus, from concern with self to concern with Jesus as the revelation of God's love, and from obsession with death to rejoicing in life. When the first witnesses cease to search for a dead body, and their obsession with death and grief turns into recognition of Jesus as the living and undying presence of God in their personal and collective life, then Resurrection becomes real and saving for those who lived through the events.

One particular Resurrection narrative is a classic example of this duality of vision and shift of perspective, bringing together and at the same time contra-posing two opposite perceptions of the same event by the disciples (John 20:3-10). Following the bewildering message of the women who find the empty tomb, frightened and confused, Peter and John rush to the burial place. John, much younger, outruns his companion; but, in deference to the older man, he stops and allows Peter to enter the tomb first. Here the Gospel writer makes a very significant observation. Peter looks into the tomb first and he sees the burial cloths but no sign of the body of Jesus. John, in turn, looks into the tomb, and we are told that *'he saw and believed'* (John 20:8). Both men look at the same event under the same circumstances, but their perception and understanding runs in opposite directions. Peter is searching for a dead body, just as the women were in the darkness of very early morning, or as Mary of Magdala was doing when she asked the gardener to tell her where they had hidden the body of Jesus (John 20:11-18). On the other hand, looking at the same setting, John *believed*, seeing through the gloom of death and emptiness the sign of the living Lord. The true disciple is the one searching for Jesus as the revelation of the living and life-giving God, and in that search, their eyes are opened and they experience Resurrection.

The same shift of perspective occurs in the narrative of the two disciples on their way to Emmaus. In a vain attempt at forgetting completely the tragic events that have entrapped them and the crushing darkness within, they escape from Jerusalem. Trudging along, their thoughts dark and their hearts utterly closed within themselves, they become completely unaware of reality, except for their own predicaments and their longing for self-pity (Luke 24:13-35). Trapped within their own selves, they do not notice the stranger who comes up and falls in step with them. All that matters, really, are their personal problems, their own sense of having been let down and betrayed, and this stranger must know that they are the victims of injustice and deceit.

The real tragedy, however, is that with this self-centred focus on the negativity, they missed the point of it all; namely, the living presence of God journeying with them. Focusing exclusively on themselves rather than the Unknown Stranger who walks with them, they are at pains to wallow in self-pity and they tell him their sad and mournful story. By contrast, the stranger invites them to move away from their navel-gazing, self-pity by tapping into the depth of their heart and engaging their personal and collective memory of God with his people. Only after being addressed as *"foolish and slow of heart"*, and the stranger finally sharing the intimacy of hospitality and table fellowship, their eyes are then open and there is the sudden explosion of recognition. Yes, *"the Lord, has risen indeed"* they call out (Luke 24:34). Emmaus is not just an escape or a pretence. Emmaus is a challenge to us and to believers of all times to let go of our expectations, and to make choices based not only on immediate perceptions, or on how we view things and events, but to look at the world with the eyes of God and energised by God's presence in spite of any evidence to the contrary.

Faith is seeing and believing, but, to achieve faith, the disciples must be prepared to move on from seeing what one wants to see, into allowing oneself to see in spite of what one actually sees. Easter calls for a reversal of action and of perspectives. There lies the key. It is all a matter of perspective, a looking at the world and its history from a very different place, from the perspective of life or from the perspective of death. Then we will discover life anew, a life teeming with goodness and the power and presence of God, in spite of all appearances or personal expectations. Then we will be able to celebrate Resurrection.

Fullness of life may demand that we stand peering inside an empty tomb, like Mary and the other disciples, often so overwhelmed as to focus entirely our search for a dead body, with little understanding, nothing to show for our efforts, and nothing to hold onto. Like for Mary and the Emmaus disciples, we must stop focusing on the signs of death and accept that God, in Jesus, is standing there beside us, alive, calling us by our name, urging us to embrace the apparently human impossibility as the place where God is waiting to abolish our death and give us life.

Easter is here and now

For God, there is only present, and the Christian Story is never information about a past challenging human rationality or relegated to dusty history books. The word of God is *always about us, here, now*. The experience of the disciples is not just an event of two thousand years ago, and our celebration is not merely a yearly ritual, no matter how heart-warming or emotionally charged it may be. It is not a matter of retelling that Jesus is alive and once again with his disciples, a palliative message we proclaim to ourselves to quieten the burning yearnings and restlessness of our hearts. For us believers, the Word of God is always addressed to us and is about us, and the proclamation that "*He has been raised; he is not here*" in spite of death is, at the same time, both our commitment and our story to be lived today and for all time, where we are and as we are. Easter is a living and lived experience as real and as personal as sharing a meal of fish together, or encountering a stranger on the road, or strolling along the beach, as some of the Easter narratives tell us.

Our Easter rejoicing is not just a memory of Jesus who conquered death in Palestine two thousand years ago, but a proclamation to the whole world that that conquest marks out our own destiny for all time. Having immersed himself totally into humanity to the very depths of ultimate death and despair, then our humanity becomes the place where God is and wants to be, even in death. If not even death kept Jesus trapped in its clutches, the same is true for us in our full humanity, and nothing, absolutely nothing can separate us from the love and life of God made visible in Jesus Christ, as St Paul reminds us (Romans 8;39).

However, so long as our God remains a dead body in an empty tomb, and we are not prepared to accept the reality that he is alive beyond the death and pain that often invade daily life as well as our flesh and blood, then all our festivities are empty make-beliefs, leaving us, like the disciples, in a place of darkness and fear. Although each one of us has our challenges and our sorrows in life, and may at times feel trapped in helplessness, or we despair of present and futures, there is an inner awareness in us that can lead us to believe that love is stronger than hate and life is stronger than death.

We are the ones called to confront seeming impossibilities of long ago and far away, and respond to it with our lives here and now. That is the crux of the Christian story incarnated in the Resurrection of Jesus. Like the disciples seeking some sense in the darkness of daily life, we are the actors in and respondents to the Easter experience, embracing the paradox of a rich source of hope and soothing peace and of deep love when and where everything in us and around us points to darkness and hopelessness. Mary despairs; Peter is struck silent, not knowing what to make of those abandoned burial cloths; John sees the same thing as the fisherman of Capernaum, but John sees through the appearances and believes. That is our Easter story too: seeing and accepting life through and in spite of death within and all around us.

Like for the first disciples, life for each of us can so easily turn into a scenario of loss of immeasurable consequence, of emptiness, and of hopelessness without rhyme or reason, testing faith to its very limits. Underlying all the Resurrection narratives is the assertion that, because of Easter, fear turns into courage, grief into joy, absence into presence, loss into hope, darkness into light, and distance becomes intimacy. As the original pre-Easter story tells us, life can easily turn into a scenario of loss of immeasurable consequence, of emptiness, and of hopelessness without rhyme or reason, testing faith to its very limits. Consequently, to celebrate Easter means to live on the edge of impossibility and to call it the highway to complete reality and fulfilment. No matter what our individual and collective stories may be, Easter must become an injection of courage empowering us to make our daily deaths turning points of encounter with our God, places where God is at work in spite of all appearances to the contrary, or what our disillusioned hearts may try to tell us.

Our life will have harsh moments; our world will confront us with incomprehensible tragedies; our souls and bodies will grapple with darkness and scream with pain; our hearts will yearn for freedom and intimacy. But because the wounded Jesus left behind an empty tomb and walked back into the lives of those who were totally broken and desperate, then we can hope against all hope. Death and suffering are not the end of the story, and we can rejoice in the midst of sadness, and the darkness of our struggles will inevitably have a life-giving and love-enriched conclusion.

From now on, the only way for us to look at death and see life beyond death is to gaze into an empty tomb, yearning not for a dead body, but embracing life in its fullness through that absent dead body. Faith in the Resurrection is seeing through death, hearing through the silence deep in our hearts, rejoicing when the world weighs heavily on our shoulders. Faith in the Resurrection is acknowledging God's presence when loneliness seems to enshroud us on all sides, and embracing and being embraced by our God precisely when physical, spiritual, emotional, and psychological death is all around us and dominates every dimension of our lives.

Having experienced Resurrection, now the disciple is called to let go of everything that is death-dealing: fear, anxiety, hopelessness and guilt. On the contrary, joy, hope, trust, and peace are the hallmarks of this season of transformation and new beginnings. Are we such people of transformation, of new beginnings, of renewed energy and of fresh awareness? Alternatively, are we just celebrating another empty ritual reminding us only of the passing of time and the inexorable cycle of seasons? Are we perhaps gazing at an event of the past with no significance and even less bearing on our daily lives? Easter is not a time or a ritual. Easter is a commitment to accept God and to reveal God's presence whatever our human story may put before us.

As a harbinger of peace, joy and hope, Easter must become a stimulus that kindles the burning yearnings of our hearts for life and love, through the energy of our living and loving God – the God whom not even death could keep away from us.

A verb of transformation

Privacy is not of God or of faith, and Easter's call to transformation and new beginnings, of energy and of renewed sense of presence, carries a double dimension. Easter is not a passive attitude but an active verb. Immersed in the joy and peace that comes from the realisation that not even death can keep God away from us, then the world must know the truth in us and through us. Adopting an unexpected grammatical twist to the word "Easter", Gerard Manly Hopkins speaks of Easter not as noun relating to an event of the past, but as an active verb implying a life-long, ongoing process of life beyond death, in the reality of each individual's life journey. Confronting a tragedy and loss of life one Easter Sunday morning, including among its shipwrecked victims four Franciscan Nuns on their way from England to the Americas, the poet reminds us that Easter is a verb of cosmic transformation into a totally new reality of hope, peace, and faith-filled joy, in spite of all conflicting manifestations.

> "Let him easter in us, be a dayspring to the dimness of us, be a crimson cresseted east".[28]

For all its power of transformation, the resurrection of Jesus is wrapped in silence, and we do not encounter any spectacular Old Testament theophany. Yet, as if by an irresistible compulsion and urgency to spread the news, the disciples, fired by excitement and wonder, proclaimed the message to each other through an impromptu communication network of word of mouth. The women frightened and bewildered, tell the disciples (Matthew 28:8), Luke 24:10), and Mary, after her incomprehensible meeting in the garden, does likewise (John 20:18). Similarly, having recognised the Risen Lord at the breaking of bread, the Emmaus disciples immediately *"returned to Jerusalem"* to make the unlikely proclamation, only to be told that their news was already second hand (Luke 24:33-35). Just as the original disciples could not hold to themselves the experience of their encounter with the Risen Lord, but had to scream it to the world, so our belief in the Resurrection must become a verb committing us unconditionally to become ambassadors of the Good News in our world, or our

---

28 Gerard Manley Hopkins *The Wreck of the Deutschland*

faith is a futile looking into a hollow, dark, and empty tomb.

In a world where death has become a tragic, multi-dimensional daily reality of war, racism, terrorism, street violence, exploitation, abuse, abandonment and destitution, words like hope, peace and affirmation may sound hollow and almost offensive to victims. Yet, Easter screams to the world that in this very world hope, peace, and goodwill are possible in spite of everything else. Jesus' first greeting to his distraught and broken disciples was, '*Peace be with you!*' (Luke24:36), together with the message that he has gone ahead of them into Galilee where they will see him (Mark 16:7, Matthew 28:10).

In Scripture, Galilee is "*the Galilee of the nations*", a potpourri of cultures and traditions. Because of this, Galilee is also the place of simplicity and ordinariness, where everyday life unfolds with all its unchallenged commonality and sometimes its tragic realism of struggle and suffering. That is the Galilee of our lives, and where we are called to live and accept the Easter proclamation and, in turn, become witnesses and proclaimers of the living and active presence of God beyond death.

Having been touched and called to review and renew our perceptions, our attitudes and our behaviour, transformation can only be authentic when these elements exude naturally from the realm of self to become energy for new perceptions, fresh attitudes, and stimulating behaviour for others. Grammatical verbs speak of activity and action, and we must be the instruments of Easter revelation because the Word of God makes us both recipients and actors in the Story, and commits us to be ambassadors of the presence of God and bearers of joy and peace in the real world of every day.

Every time evil and hurt are conquered by forgiveness and love, every time a simple gesture of friendship raises a smile in a brother or sister, every time we open our hands and reach out to that person in need of companionship and compassion, Easter becomes an active verb. Every time we have the courage to face life without losing heart and nurture a single moment of peace and serenity in someone else, death is supplanted by life. In all these times, Easter becomes real, we re-live it in ourselves, and we bring it about in our world.

Conclusion

All our life stories – both individual and collective – are dotted with incidents that reveal the active presence of God in our life. Often, however, such experiences remain forgotten, tucked away in the recesses of our memory, overgrown with concerns with our own agenda or with the pain that they may engender. At the same time, when looked at from a different perspective or revived in hindsight, for the person of faith these are glimpses of God walking by our side and revealing his presence in spite of brokenness or even death. Friendship, healing, courage, hope, love, compassion, forgiveness – these are only a few of the glimpses of God with us in spite of any negative and painful experience that dot our life journey.

Bringing these glimpses to consciousness must spur us on to future hope in spite of the pain of loss and darkness of tomb within us and all around us. We need to change perspective and look at our story from the point of view of life and not of death, because death has been conquered and subdued by life in Jesus' Paschal Mystery of death and resurrection. Having revealed himself as the

Living One in spite of death on all sides, Jesus calls his doubtful disciples and this confused and fragmented world into the ultimate awareness of life screaming to the universe and for all time that not even death could keep Jesus away from his disciples. Therefore, we can face our future into eternity with courage and hope and have no fear of brokenness and personal darkness because not even death can ever keep God away from us. That is our destiny and an infallible source of peace and joy, come what may, because for God the impossible is real.

Forgiven

A Kingdom of Healing and Forgiveness
Luke 15:1-32

Then Jesus said, 'There was a man who had two sons. The younger of them said to his father, "Father, give me the share of the property that will belong to me." So he divided his property between them. A few days later the younger son gathered all he had and travelled to a distant country, and there he squandered his property in dissolute living. When he had spent everything, a severe famine took place throughout that country, and he began to be in need. So he went and hired himself out to one of the citizens of that country, who sent him to his fields to feed the pigs. He would gladly have filled himself with the pods that the pigs were eating; and no one gave him anything. But when he came to himself he said, "How many of my father's hired hands have bread enough and to spare, but here I am dying of hunger! I will get up and go to my father, and I will say to him, 'Father, I have sinned against heaven and before you; I am no longer worthy to be called your son; treat me like one of your hired hands.'" So he set off and went to his father. But while he was still far off, his father saw him *and was filled with compassion; he ran and put his arms around him and kissed him. Then the son said to him, "Father, I have sinned against heaven and before you; I am no longer worthy to be called your son." But the father said to his slaves, "Quickly, bring out a robe – the best one – and put it on him; put a ring on his finger and sandals on his feet. And get the fatted calf and kill it, and let us eat and celebrate; for this son of mine was dead and is alive again; he was lost and is found!" And they began to celebrate.*

'Now his elder son was in the field; and when he came and approached the house, he heard music and dancing. He called one of the slaves and asked what was going on. He replied, "Your brother has come, and your father has killed the fatted calf, because he has got him back safe and sound." Then he became angry and refused to go in. His father came out and began to plead with him. But he answered his father, "Listen! For all these years I have been working like a slave for you, and I have never disobeyed your command; yet you have never given me even a young goat so that I might celebrate with my friends. But when this son of yours came back, who has devoured your property with prostitutes, you killed the fatted calf for him!" Then the father said to him, "Son, you are always with me, and all that is mine is yours. But we had to celebrate and rejoice, because this brother of yours was dead

and has come to life; he was lost and has been found" (Luke 15:11-32).

It could be an everyday occurrence in any of our inner city suburbs, so commonplace it no longer rates a mention in the morning papers. Unfortunately, blinded by the plague of street-kids, we are no longer able to see the human drama that entangles the plague. In the first place, that street-kid is the fruit of the life and love of two people from whom, tragically, he has severed all connections, thus creating mutual disavowal and rejection. For whatever reason, the fracture of relationships has become a chasm that at times may never be crossed or bridged. Losing sight of that parent/child relationship will create its own social milieu, and a personal world of shame, guilt, condemnation, judgment, anger, social separation and self-pity which may appear unredeemable for those caught up in its spiral.

Yet, regardless of the apparent psychological disintegration, I propose that the chasm is only a sociological and cultural malaise that does not deny the natural order of things and the destiny of each person. In this apparent disintegration, there remains one certainty, unaltered and unchanging. In spite of all attempts at renouncing, denouncing, or denying on either side of the chasm, somewhere there is a man and a woman who are father and mother, who having given life and love, have lost all sense of relationship with a son or daughter. That is the undeniable reality of human nature. For eternity, whether the protagonists are alive or dead, that child will always be the son/daughter of that man and that woman, the fruit of their life and love, and nothing will ever negate or obliterate the relationship of life given and received that they share. I may not want to admit it, but I cannot deny that my life is inextricably linked with other people, and my relationship with my mother and father is life-giving and eternal, regardless of the vagaries of time and place, or social conditions.

Relationship is both the key to the issue and the remedy to its solution. No social band-aid or psychological palliative will ever heal the rift, if we fail to re-establish the proper children/parent relationship. Only by acknowledging and re-establishing broken relationships will people who are apart come together again, and heal the rift that separates them.

Luke's well known story of the son who leaves home and then returns, as Jesus told it long ago, is precisely a story of relationships. It not only mirrors the plight of youth homelessness today, but it makes a clear statement about personal identity in relation to the nature of God, and about the relationship between God and us, as well as among ourselves. In both cases, it is only in terms of relationship that we can understand our God and heal the brokenness and homelessness that resides deep within our own psyche and our communal story. It is all a matter of relationships.

Who is your character?

The story revolves around three protagonists: a father and his two sons, each character representing a very distinct and specific personality, each of them incarnating typical attitudes by which we often relate to God and to one another. The story, like all the gospel parables, addresses fundamental issues of identity, raising the question of who God is for us and about the way we respond to God, challenging us about making value choices, incarnating attitudes, and living out our faith commitment as individuals and as a community.

The personal stories of the two sons begin from diametrically opposite stances; they run in totally opposite directions, and eventually lead to two equally opposite and unexpected conclusions. In a way, the two sons personify the full range of values, life attitudes, and reactions of the human heart, a heart that is so restless, confused, and reckless when it comes to confronting itself with God.

The two personal stories never intercept until the final critical climax, and even then indirectly and at a distance from each other. At the same time, the two stories are not irrevocably disjointed. In the middle of the story – beginning with the younger son and ending with the elder of the two – stands the father as the unchanging, non-judgmental, and fixed centre point that links together individual and collective dramas. As if to give substance and meaning to two brotherly but distant bookends, in the middle stands the father, whose undivided and all-embracing love becomes the point of conjunction and of stability between two apparently irreconcilable attitudes. Much more than the drama between a foolhardy and thoughtless young man who eventually discovers and admits to his misdemeanours on the one hand, and on the other, a self-righteous brother who will not accept either mistakes or reconciliation, this is the story of a father whose unchanging love reconciles opposites.

In the face of unfaithfulness and injustice, the father refuses to pass judgment, but rejoices at being recognised as father even by his ungrateful son, while, at the same time pleading with his older one to look beyond the sinfulness of a wayward brother and to accept him and embrace him precisely as a brother. The father of the story is only interested in re-establishing relationships, a three-way, life-giving relationship between father and two brothers. He is not interested in judgment, sinfulness, unfaithfulness, waywardness, lip service, anger, broken promises or brotherly injustice.

That is the fundamental revelation about the identity of our kingdom-God. All our Father-God is seeking is to be recognised as father and, like the two sons of the story, for us to recognise one another as brothers and sisters. As we know, the Word of God is not just about chronology, history, or social mores. The parables of Jesus are addressed to us and about us here and now, and so the question must be asked: as I claim belonging to the kingdom, where do I stand? Am I open and trusting in God's love for me, or do I identify more readily, and maybe more comfortably, with the rebellious son who leaves home to seek a justification by self-styled securities and pleasure? On the other hand, am I rather more like the older son, whose relationship with the father is based entirely on fearsome respect, self-righteousness, and the acquisition of personal merits?

Leaving home – self-interest and rebellion redeemed

The scene opens with the younger son holding centre stage. Young, idealistic, and reckless, he is so trapped in himself and in his own self-interest that he is totally unaware of the pain and injustice engendered by his bold demand for his share of the family property. He has neither any feeling for the love and devotion of his father, nor any sense of respect or justice towards his family. Nor does he display any personal concern or responsibility as to how he will dispose of the gifts lavished upon him by a doting father. He simply leaves home and wastes his money. From a psychological perspective, this younger son typifies the young child for whom the world is their personal possession, and the only rationale for life-values is self-interest, pleasure seeking, security and personal satisfaction. While this is the natural world-view of a young child, when this kind of self-centeredness and possessive control lingers on as the life-value into adult life then we have domination, violence and dysfunctional personalities.

However, confronted with a crisis, he becomes aware of the consequences of his recklessness, and his thoughts go back to his household where he belongs, and to his father. No matter how much he has strayed or betrayed his life-giver, that fundamental thrust back to his roots comes to the fore. He remembers who he really is, and all he wants to do is to go back to where he came from. Self-acceptance is the first step towards reconciliation, letting go of fear, guilt and self-condemnation and reactivating our awareness of where we belong. As Richard Rohr says:

> We have for too long confused holiness with innocence, whereas holiness is actually mistakes overcome and transformed, not necessarily mistakes avoided,[29]

This is the beginning of reconciliation: accepting one's mistakes and responding to that fundamental human drive that urges us to return to where we really belong, to recognise that fundamentally we are children of the kingdom.

However, this self-acknowledgment is only the first step towards re-establishing the relationship. The young man has not yet thought of his father's love; and the journey back home towards full reconciliation has only begun. Full re-integration in

---

29 Richard Rohr, *A Spring Within Us*, SPCK, 2018, 232.

the kingdom demands a life-long ongoing process of growth into self-awareness and decision-making, towards full acceptance of that one fundamental truth of the journey of faith that says, "God accepts me and loves me as I am, and not as I would like to be, or how I think I should be". Confronted with his personal destitution, the first reaction is one of self-pity and shame. He acknowledges his condition, but his first concern is still locked within himself. He has not yet come to the full realisation and acceptance of the love of the father. In a way, he is looking for a solution to his immediate problem, a sort of survival kit, a way out of his miserable situation, or a ritual purification for his wrongdoings.

Consequently, his first reaction is to focus on himself, admit to his wrongdoings, and enumerate his mistakes, in the hope of being re-instated, if not into the family circle, at least as one of the paid servants. His understanding of the father is certainly not in terms of love, but of justice, where wrongdoings have to be paid for, and belonging to the household is a matter of hierarchy, and of merit or demerit points. It makes sense, then, to attempt some sort of bargaining that may help us to keep our head out of the mire. In this perspective, we do not have reconciliation and healing, but only a ritual purification that will set me right for a while, but it will never re-establish the father-son relationship that was there in the first place. Belonging to the kingdom is not a matter of bargaining, ritual purity or self-justification, but of accepting a God who has nothing to do with bargaining or personal merits, but embraces me as I am with unconditional love.

When reconciliation is reduced to a ritual of purification, then we do not really seek to re-establish our relationship with our God, but we settle and/or bargain for some immediate solution, a palliative for a troubled conscience. In that case, we reduce God to a stern and angry judge from whom we can only hope for a lenient sentence, but never quite a full re-instatement into the family home. When reconciliation is reduced only to a ritual practice, then we operate out of self-pity and of fear of punishment, but never out of love of God and from our God. When reconciliation is reduced only to a ritual practice, then we control the process, never allowing God to reveal his true face as a father full of tenderness and mercy, who rejoices beyond all human expectations, and invites everybody to rejoice with him when he sees the son come back again after rejecting the family and abandoning the home.

It all revolves around that word *father*. More than in the admission of his foolishness, the solution lies in the recognition and admission of fatherhood and in that recognition the young man finds the energy to retrace his steps home and accept his relationship with that man who never forgot him, nor gave up hope of him ever coming back. Beyond his self-pity and his fears, there is a father waiting for him, and he recognises him by that very name. "*I will go to my father and say: Father*" (Luke 15:18). There lies conversion. The shift from a justice-image to a life-giver image of his father becomes the decisive spark that will urge him to turn his steps towards home, in trust. Only the acceptance of our God as the Father revealed by Jesus will heal us of our sins and guilt. Only trust in this Father – as against any personal effort at self-purification – can bring about true conversion and fullness of life in our brokenness and infidelity. Only the acknowledgment and personal appropriation of a Father-God who waits for our return can bring about total healing and joy.

Waiting at home - love

Luke 15 is unquestionably not primarily about a son who betrays the love of his father, or about another son who refuses to forgive that original betrayal. The real core of the story lies in the patient waiting of the father for the son's return. Past infidelity, ungratefulness, abandonment of home, rejection of family, wastefulness of resources, loose living – none of these seem to come into consideration, as far as the father is concerned. He does not even contemplate the possibility that his waiting and hoping will all be in vain. He just waits, without ever giving up hope that the son will return home – a waiting founded exclusively on the one rationale that, humanly speaking, seems utterly irrational and even unjust. He is the father and that young man is his son. That is all that matters.

Such behaviour on the father's part must have come as a shocking revelation to Jesus' hearers, creating precisely the kind of dissonance that runs through all the parables. Not only did it run counter to their accepted code of behaviour between father and son, as well as to their whole social and religious construct strictly governed by retributive justice, but such behaviour undermined radically their idea of God on which such a construct rested.

For the Pharisees, the sinner was a person devoid of all dignity, and, consequently, the sinner could only consider himself or herself nothing more than a social and moral outcast, abandoned by God and condemned by humanity (John 8:1-11). Through the telling of the parable, Jesus wants to redress precisely this distorted perception in order to restore the sinner's self-image on the one hand, and challenge the condemnatory attitude of the leaders on the other. Jesus' intent is to lead his hearers to a new understanding of God and, consequently, to a totally new self-image on the part of the sinner, as well as to a new perception of sin and brokenness. No matter how hardened a sinner a person may be in the eyes of human justice, Jesus invites his hearers to a self-image based on a personal, living, and intimate relationship of God with every human being. Jesus challenges the images of self and of God by presenting a God who loves freely and who accepts to be loved in return only in a relationship of freedom and respect of personal dignity. The God of Jesus of Nazareth is a God who remains forever present and waiting, even in the absence of love or in the rejection on the part of the sinner, to offer this sinner the possibility of a radical change and conversion. A God whose offer of forgiveness is absolute, unconditional and universal.

Through this story of homecoming, Jesus is trying to convey a new perception of God and of self, a kingdom perception based on mutual and personal relationship between God and humanity. However, God's word is addressed to us and is about us today, right here and now, and one hopes that, as we seek reconciliation and forgiveness, such disclosure is just as shocking and disconcerting for us here today as it was for his contemporaries. While acknowledging personal sinfulness and brokenness, we need to move away from a pathological concern with ourselves that engenders guilt, shame, self-condemnation and the fear of punishment. On the contrary, we are invited to re-imagine, first of all, and then to appropriate our God as the One who is caught up in the same drama of sin and brokenness that we are, however never as a judge, but only as a Father, full of tenderness and mercy, gratuitously and unconditionally lavishing love on the sinner-son.

The wayward son is quite satisfied with becoming a hired servant. He has not yet understood fully the deep relationship of love that binds him to his father, and so he begins his well-rehearsed bargaining plea, *"I am no longer worthy..."* (Luke 15:21). Once again, the sinner will attempt to control the process of reconciliation on their terms, by putting forward conditions, even though couched in words and attitudes of shame and guilt. Yes indeed, the Good News probably is too good to be true. Accepting that we are loved and loveable in our brokenness is a harsh demand because it deprives us of all control, and we just have to accept love as a gift.

No effort of mine will move God to change his mind about me or his opinion of me. No amount of breast-beating will make me more or less worthy of God's love. No list of sins admitted to over and over again, with obsessive accuracy of details, will reinstate me into the household. The only controlling element in my seeking forgiveness is God's unconditional love for me, and I have absolutely no control over that element. I have no choice but to accept that, regardless of how sinful I may be, or I may think I am, I am wrapped in God's love like in a rich new cloak, and gifted by him as with a precious ring that a lover has unexpectedly placed on my finger to show their love for me.

The father is certainly not interested in the son's well-rehearsed speech or his proclamation of a long list of misdemeanours. No one needed reminding about those, least of all his own father. His past behaviour was all too obvious to everyone, but that was now past and it had no relevance in the present. Healing, reconciliation, and re-instatement into the family come when the son finally decides to place his trust in his father's love, believing that this father would accept him back, in spite of his unfaithfulness and sin. On that one surety, and on that alone, he retraces his steps and goes home to his father. Are we prepared to trust that we are loved and embraced in our brokenness and sinfulness, or are we more at ease with many words that will focus only on our misdemeanours, thinking that God is a slow learner that needs to be reminded, repetitively, of all the wrongs we have done?

I am always fascinated by a small detail common to all the stories of healing and forgiveness in the Gospels. Nowhere in these events do we ever encounter an enumeration of ailments or a long list of sins. The sick will call out for healing from Jesus, but their ailments are painfully obvious to all. It is precisely in that call of trust that healing ultimately takes place. So often Jesus will comment on their faith and trust. *"Your faith has saved you"* (Luke 7:50; 17:19; 18:42). As for the forgiveness stories, not one of those people who are publicly assured of forgiveness will say a word about their sins. These may be painfully obvious sometimes, as in the case of the woman caught in adultery (John 8:1-8), or the Samaritan woman in the house of Simon the Pharisee (Luke 7:36-50). As for the likes of Zaccheus, not only were his misdemeanours a matter of public knowledge, but indeed he wallowed in his selfish arrogance, and seeking forgiveness was the last thing on his mind that morning when he was caught up a tree (Luke 19:1-10).

In the end, trust, and only trust, is the key. The Father certainly trusted his son in the almost irrational belief that one day that son would come back. And his trustful hope is rewarded. He is not interested in long catalogues of sins, and he will simply not give the son a chance to make his little sorry-speech, or to wallow in self-pity. He is simply ecstatic for that son *'who was dead and has come back to life'* (Luke 15:24) and all he wants is to give full vent to his explosive joy and to celebrate life. Nothing else matters.

Staying at home – self-righteousness

By its very nature, celebration implies others, community, friends and family. Not surprisingly, then, we call on these others to join us in our rejoicing, because there cannot be celebration any other way. On the contrary, few things are more hurtful to the human heart than a deliberate rejection of an invitation to a family gathering because one does not want "to meet that person, after all they have said or done!" That is precisely the situation that the father – who loves his children unconditionally, no matter what these children may have done – has to face. The older son simply refuses to join in the celebration because he cannot accept either the return of his wayward brother or the gratuitous love of his father. Unfortunately, there can be no celebration without the forgiving presence of that older and, in many ways, faithful son. The tragedy of the whole situation is that that son is perfectly correct in his many claims to faithfulness towards his own father and his family. He has done all he had to do, and done it very diligently, if not lovingly, as we are led to surmise by his reaction.

But precisely there lies the tragic side of his life-story. He has always operated towards his father on a model of subservient obedience and human justice, and now he cannot accept that his father not only operates out of love, but also that he is actually calling him to operate out of that same love for his brother. In his "correct" behaviour, the faithful son has turned self-righteous, precisely because his behaviour was stimulated not by relationship but by law, not by being-with the father but out of fear of making mistakes, not by acceptance of other people's mistakes but by obsessive legal purity. Consequently, on his side of the ledger, the only conceivable and possible course of action is total and absolute rejection of wrongdoing and condemnation of the sinner.

Unfortunately, in the end, that side of the ledger places him alongside his brother, not because he has to admit to anything wrong in his past life, but because he clings to his own personal rights now. Like his brother, but unbeknown to himself, the older son is in desperate need of conversion, beginning with a conversion of his understanding of fatherhood and of God. In his obsession for correct behaviour, he must move away from the slavery of a relationship based on duty and into the freedom of a relationship based on love. That is how things operate in the kingdom – Jesus seems to say – then and now.

Conversion is not a mere psychological process on the part of the sinner who returns to God. Conversion is a radical transformation of the image of God that both sinner and righteous person alike must undergo in their own lives. The root of sin does not lie so much in wrongdoing, but in the erroneous and self-centred understanding of father and fatherhood that both sons carry with them. The younger one, in order to rid himself of this erroneous and oppressive image, takes refuge in the strategy of pleasure by rejecting the father and leaving home. The older one, instead, in order to win favours from the same father, and to keep him good and on side, seeks the strategy of duty expressed through a servile religiosity and moralistic purity. Both sons, however, miss the fundamental point that Jesus came to reveal –namely, that our God is a Father of gratuitous mercy and unconditional kindness, bonded to us by a deep and unconditional love-relationship. The celebration of homecoming and the joy of being re-embraced by the Father can only come about to the extent that we let go both of guilt born of sin and of presumption born of self-righteousness.

To the end, the father is obsessed with re-establishing proper relationships with both children and between them, not because of what the children have done or not done, but simply and solely because they are his children. While the wayward son sought a relationship based on self-assertion and the older one insisted on duty and self-righteousness, the Father operates exclusively on the father-son-brother relationship

In the dialogue with the father who is inviting him to come into the house and join in the celebration for the return of his brother, the older son gives full vent to his displeasure and emotions. He never acknowledges his sibling as *brother* or *my brother*, calling him a very distant and derogatory *"this son of yours,,, who has devoured your property with prostitutes"* (Luke 15:30). The older son focuses entirely on what his brother has done, without ever accepting the fundamental reality that he is his brother. There is more that judgment in these words; there is total rejection and condemnation both of his brother and of his own father. This rejection is the fruit of his refusal to acknowledge the relationship of *brother* and *son* and stressing, instead, the wrongdoing that *that* brother/son has committed. By contrast, the father retorts with the language of father-son-brother relationship, on which healing and forgiveness rest.

> *We had to celebrate and rejoice, because* **your brother** *was dead and has come back to life, he was lost and has been found* (Luke 15:32).

Both sons need healing through accepting the call to relationship born of love, or the joy for the return of one will only provoke the distancing and rejection of another. As we see in the parable, healing through acceptance and love is both personal and communal.

Children of a prodigal Father-God

This page of the Gospel demands that we convert from an attitude of servile religion to one of celebration in freedom centred on a self-consciousness of being children of God. God loves us not because we are good or do good deeds, but only because God is Father, and all he can see in us is children, fruits of his life and love. There is no need of self-justification, nor is there any place for condemnation of self and most of all of others.

Of course, this is where the parable of the prodigal son becomes most challenging in real terms. Accepting that we are freely loved, now we have no option but to return this love freely and unconditionally to each other, because we all share equally the undivided love of the Father. We can claim that God is an integral part of our life, and rejoice in being forgiven, only to the extent that we are prepared to go beyond the brokenness of others, remove all labels, suspend all judgment, and accept others as the brothers and sisters that they are. Yes, these may well be the very people who have hurt us and hurt us deeply; those who by their way of life do not conform to our expectations; those whose weaknesses and shortcomings have a public face, and perhaps fill us with embarrassment and shame; those who are likely to continue hurting us. That is precisely the point of the story.

The father trusted that his son would come back, and his trust was rewarded. However, now he has no guarantee that, once forgiven, the son/brother will not sin again, nor can we place conditions in reaching out to each other in forgiveness. Have you ever noticed how this parable, like all the Gospel narratives of forgiveness and healing, is open-ended, leaving us with a feeling of unfinished business for us to complete? At the end of the whole saga, there is no conclusion, and we are left wondering if the older son did actually accept the invitation to join in the festivities and to embrace his brother, or whether the younger son, in another moment of folly, did not actually leave home once again in search of other adventures?

I really believe that these are not just idle questions. The Father has trusted that his son will come back after all, but there is no guarantee that, once forgiven, the son/brother will not sin again. That is precisely the point of the story. The call to forgiveness of those around us must be unconditional and universal, or our own forgiveness is void. Regardless of past events or future possibilities, these are the brothers and sisters whom we are called not only to encounter, but also to re-embrace and to rejoice with.

The love that heals us becomes true and authentic for each of us individually and all of us collectively, only when it becomes brotherly love towards all, when it awakens a personal responsibility and commitment for the good of all, and when it engenders trust and courage in the face of all human brokenness, particularly the brokenness of those who share our life in the myriad of ways that we experience every day. If we are truly convinced that God loves us unconditionally, forgives us gratuitously, and gives back to each of us our human dignity as son/daughter, together with a renewed sense of trust and hope, then we must open ourselves absolutely to human frailties and brokenness.

That is the absolute demand of healing in the kingdom. We must make the first move towards meeting and embracing with trust those who are overburdened with sin, guilt and shame for their mistakes, those who have lost all meaning and self-awareness of brokenness, those who have lost the very sense and taste for life. Either our response to the call to forgive each other is unconditional and universal – without expectations or pre-conceptions on our part – or we will never be forgiven ourselves. I remember an old priest who, trapped by dementia in his later years, among a number of fascinating peculiarities, had developed his own version of the Lord's Prayer, introducing an interesting variation that worked wonders during liturgical celebrations, especially when one did not know what was coming. After the words, *"Forgive us our sins as we forgive those who sin against us"*, he would throw his arms up in the air, and in an extremely theatrical gesture and a booming voice he would call out, "Please, Lord, don't take me seriously!" If nothing else, one has to admire the honesty of the man who took seriously what he was saying.

In the kingdom perspective as proclaimed by Jesus, the social dimension of reconciliation and forgiveness is unequivocal and non-negotiable. As we pray for forgiveness and healing, we leave ourselves no choice but to open ourselves to those realities where human dignity is at lowest ebb. Are we prepared to take seriously the words we pray each day, several times a day *"Forgive us our sins, as we forgive those who sin against us?"* Are we aware of the commitment we take on each time we utter those words by which we proclaim our readiness to forgive each other with the same measure with which God forgives us, knowing full well that God's measure is measure-less, universal and unconditional?

In the Lord's Prayer that we utter every day, have we ever allowed ourselves to be challenged by that small preposition '*as*'? In all honesty, we need to begin with a variation to the words we utter, that the Lord of healing may touch our hearts and lead us to forgive others as God forgives us, so that in our dealings with each other we reflect the kingdom as the action and presence of God in our world. That is precisely what Jesus did, particularly in the way he welcomed sinners, in his trust towards those who had gone astray, and in his ultimate forgiving act on the Cross.

We will never be true disciples in the kingdom, nor will we ever reflect an authentic image of God and Church in our lives, unless we learn to imitate the forgetfulness of God. Like the father of Luke 15, God can only see a new creation in each of us, saint or sinner we may be, unencumbered by any handicap or baggage that the past or human frailty may have laid on us. This is the living witness of Jesus in word and deed, right to the final instant of his earthly life. This is the challenge thrown at us by the prodigal Father in Jesus' story. This is the commitment we take on each time we dare to paraphrase "Teach us to forgive others, as you forgive us", because the loving, forgiving and prodigal Father-God of the kingdom can only be experienced and witnessed through a three way dynamic of unconditional and loving forgiveness: God-self-each other.

Eucharist

Breaking Bread in the Kingdom
Matthew 26:26-30; John 6:53-57

While they were eating, Jesus took a loaf of bread, and after blessing it he broke it, gave it to the disciples, and said, "Take, eat; this is my body." Then he took a cup, and after giving thanks he gave it to them, saying, "Drink from it, all of you; for this is my blood of the covenant, which is poured out for many for the forgiveness of sins. I tell you, I will never again drink of this fruit of the vine until that day when I drink it new with you in my Father's kingdom....

Very truly, I tell you, unless you eat the flesh of the Son of Man and drink his blood, you have no life in you. Those who eat my flesh and drink my blood have eternal life, and I will raise them up on the last day; for my flesh is true food and my blood is true drink. Those who eat my flesh and drink my blood abide in me, and I in them. Just as the living Father sent me, and I live because of the Father, so whoever eats me will live because of me.

Revealed at table

It may sound like a trivia question, but have you ever noticed how often the Gospel narrative seems to link significant events of recognition or of revelation by Jesus within the context of a meal? I propose that this link between a meal and seeing or encountering Jesus carries a very specific significance when it comes to the resurrection stories, where Jesus reveals himself to the disciples as who he really is beyond any personal agenda and expectations, the Risen Lord, the God-with-us beyond death and suffering.

In the Upper Room, Jesus said his earthly good-byes during that intensely emotional experience of the Last Supper, an experience exuding a powerful sense of intimacy and revelation: intimacy between Jesus and his disciples, and revelation of who the disciples are for God and who God wants to be for the disciples. Having said good-bye through the symbolic instrumentality of bread and wine, just a few hours later, the resurrected Jesus seems to pick up the same theme again from where he had left, and a significant number of the resurrection narratives are told again through the same symbolic vehicle of food and drink (Luke 24:28-31, 41-44; John 21:1-15).

I believe that the ultimate expression of this rapport between the recognition of Jesus and table fellowship takes place not so much at the Last Supper, as Christian Tradition has probably handed down to us, but as the conclusion of the Emmaus story (Luke 24:13-35). To the end, the slow learning disciples fail to recognise Jesus, even if he walks alongside them, all this time opening the Word to them. As they reach home and evening is setting, the Stranger is making as if to journey on his way, but they invite him to stay with them. Jesus readily accedes to the invitation, and, accepts to share their hospitality and their table fellowship. In that cultural context, the guest is sacred and, as the sacred custom demanded, his presence is honoured by asking him to break bread at the table gathering. Breaking bread! That is the clue, the moment of ultimate revelation that the Lord whom they sought, and presumed dead and buried, was truly with them.

> *Then their eyes were opened and they recognised him (Luke 24:31).*

The breaking of bread then becomes the very paradigm of revelation and of recognition of who Jesus really is, and having recognised the Lord at their table, the disciples *ran* back to Jerusalem to proclaim and to rejoice in the knowledge that the Lord is not dead but alive. He is not buried, but he is actively present. He is not distant, but he is right there in the midst of their doubting, grieving and unbelieving.

Jesus is the one who shares our table fellowship to energise us into a new vision, into a new vitality, and into a new hope. Is that what our *breaking of bread* along our personal life journey really is: recognition, new energy and commitment to hope? Or perhaps are we satisfied with an empty and repetitious ritual where the only recognition that we acknowledge is the satisfaction of our personal needs and agenda, and our protestation of unworthiness? Addressing the theme of Eucharist within the context of discipleship, Pascual Chavez writes,

> (Believers) live eucharistically, not so much because they often celebrate the Eucharist, but

because they live Eucharist and spend their life for others.[30]

Thus, the breaking of the bread is both the ultimate moment of recognition of Jesus in the life of the disciples, and the primary source of energy that must propel the disciple to reveal to others this same presence in the world. Nourished, the disciple must become a nourisher.

Some friends of mine tell the story of their grandfather who, having survived the rigours and the starvation of the Second World War, like thousands of others, had migrated from Europe to this country, to start a new life and try to forget the horrors of the past. As he got older, however, and began to show signs of dementia, he developed some very distinctly personal behavioural quirks. One such mannerism had to do with memory and food. The destitution of food during his experiences as a war prisoner became crystallised in his fading mind, becoming the rationale of his message and of his actions. As the story is told, occasionally he would get up in the middle of the night, and startle the whole household by knocking at bedroom doors and calling out at the top of his voice, "Eat! Eat!" As people got up to quieten him down, to their surprise, just outside each bedroom door, every member of the household would find bread rolls laid out ready for eating.

The painful memories of starvation and misery of his youth had become an obsession; but so also his concern for those who lived with him. He did not want to re-live those bad memories ever again, nor did he want any of his family to suffer deprivation any more. Thus, his way of showing concern was to provide for them

---

30 Pascual Chavez, "Making the Eucharist in Order to Make Oneself Eucharist" in *ACTS*, http://www.sdb.org/ENG/Documenti/2007/2_24_66_1_23_.htm

real food, and encourage them to eat. Somehow the memory of the past became a stimulus for present action, not only by inviting the members of his household to eat, but also by providing the food that would heal his own memories and sustain those who heard his story.

On reflection, it all sounds so familiar. Memory, recognition, food and drink shared, bread broken and wine drunk in fellowship – this is Eucharist.

Food: the fundamental need

Food plays a fundamental role in our lives, both individually and as a community. Not only does it nourish and sustain our daily life, providing energy for growth and work, but most of all, food shapes our life style and our social interactions. Indeed, food has the power to create and/or destroy completely social groups and cultures. Every day we are exposed to the shocking revelation of destruction and havoc wrought by lack of food in Africa and Asia, as well as most of the two-thirds of the world. Our own suburban sprawls are not immune to this tragedy, a tragedy so vast and so deep that we cannot comprehend. We feel so helpless in confronting it. Indeed, in spite of or even because of media saturation, we have been lulled into an almost inert sense of hopeless complacency.

Economic poverty and destitution are not virtues, and the lack of food is a tragedy that screams indictment and condemnation to the universal human conscience. Life deprived of food becomes cheap and meaningless. A hungry person will leave home and country, as the plight of millions of refugees the world over demonstrates so graphically and so tragically to us these days. If need be, a hungry person will kill a fellow human being in order to obtain the basic necessity of life, food. Historians and sociologists tell us that both the search for and the super-abundance of food are primarily responsible for the thousands of wars and social upheavals that have shaped and written the history of humankind over the last forty centuries.

Have you ever stopped to think of what happens to food? The very moment we ingest food, a whole biological/physical process is set in motion, which will transform that food or drink into something wholly different and powerfully life-giving. Whatever our likes and dislikes, the food we eat quickly becomes flesh and blood and bone – energy for growth, for work, for enjoyment, and for healing. The food we eat becomes what we are, not only physically, but emotionally and spiritually as well. Indeed, our life style, our mutual relationships, our pattern of work and growth are shaped and conditioned to their deepest level by what we eat and by our eating habits.

These experiential considerations are important, as they open up vital insights into the mystery of the Eucharist for each of us individually, and for all of us as a community of believing disciples. The evangelist Matthew tells us that

> *While they were eating, Jesus took a loaf of bread, and after blessing it he broke it, gave it to the disciples, and said, "Take, eat; this is my body." Then he took a cup, and after giving thanks he gave it to them, saying, "Drink from it, all of you; for this is my blood of the covenant, which is poured out for many for the forgiveness of sins. I tell you, I will never again drink of this fruit of the vine until that day when I drink it new with*

> *you in my Father's kingdom* (Matthew 26:26-30).[31]

'Take and eat . . . This is my body!'

Only a God madly in love with human beings could have set up such a dramatic scenario as to make himself food, to create that total even physical and personal intimacy with every human being who is prepared to enter into it.

When we think about it, the words of Jesus are quite shocking and almost crude; and nowhere more so than in John's Eucharistic discourse (John 6:22-66). The fourth evangelist makes only a passing mention of a meal during Jesus' Last Supper with his disciples, and even then, only in the context of the washing of the feet during the Passover meal,

> *He got up from the table, took off his outer robe, and tied a towel around himself. Then he poured water into a basin and began to wash the disciples' feet and to wipe them with the towel that was tied around him* (John 13:4-6).

The parable in action of the washing of the feet also carries a strong Eucharistic weight, but in a very different context. The author of the Fourth Gospel, instead, develops a very powerful Eucharistic teaching in chapter six of his Gospel, within the context of another very significant meal: the multiplication of the loaves and fishes, where Jesus feeds thousands out of five barley loaves and two fish (John 6:1-14). Once again and very significantly, the

---

31 See also Mark 14:22-26; Luke 22:14-20; 1 Corinthians 11:23-25

evangelist places a crucial event in the ongoing narrative of the self-revelation of Jesus within a context of food and drink. The multiplication of the loaves and fishes must have held a unique significance for the early Christian tradition, judging by the fact that this food-centred miracle occurs six times throughout the four Gospel narratives, with Matthew (14:13-21 and 15:32-39) and Mark (6:30-44 and 8:1-8) retelling the story twice, alongside Luke (9:10-17) and John (6:1-65).

What is more significant, however, is that in John's version, immediately after the spectacular miracle, Jesus introduces an 'I-discourse', thus accentuating the self-revelatory nature of the story, by confronting his hearers with such shocking realism that many of his followers could not accept the "intolerable language", and turned their backs to him (John 6:66). They did not recognise him because this was certainly not the Jesus-Messiah they were expecting or looking for.

> *Jesus said to them, "Very truly, I tell you, unless you eat the flesh of the Son of Man and drink his blood, you have no life in you. Those who eat my flesh and drink my blood have eternal life, and I will raise them up on the last day; for my flesh is true food and my blood is true drink. Those who eat my flesh and drink my blood abide in me, and I in them. Just as the living Father sent me, and I live because of the Father, so whoever eats me will live because of me* (John 6:53-57).

Jesus pulls no punches, nor does he mince words. With that absolute authority and total integrity that marked all his life and ministry, he tells us to *eat* his *flesh* and *drink* his *blood*. If we feel uneasy and a little shocked at the realism of these words, we should not be dismayed. We simply join the majority of his listeners who, after an abundant feed in a desert place at no expense at all, could not accept the reality of God's intimate presence in their life that Jesus was trying to reveal to them. They turned their backs on him, and "no longer went about with him" (John 6:66-71), because they could not accept a God so intimately immersed in our flesh and blood as to become our flesh and blood through the symbol of food and drink. There is a tremendous sadness and a deep loneliness in those final words of Jesus to his disciples at the end of the story: "*So Jesus asked the twelve, 'Do you also wish to go away?'*"(John 6:67). The same poignant but challenging question is addressed to us when, perhaps, "breaking bread together" has become a mere ritual, and we fail to see the living and active presence of God yearning to nourish us and walk with us at all times.

The God the Jews had come to know over the centuries was El Shaddai, the "God on high", the "Protector" of Israel against its enemies, the 'Law Giver' and the 'Just Judge' (Psalms 11:4; 75:7; 82:3; 91:1-2, 14-15; 93:4; 96:10; 113:5; Isaiah 31:5; 33:22; Hebrews 1:3). The people of Israel prayed to him in their need and paid strict ritual homage, to ensure his favours and continued protection. In many ways, some of us will readily identify with this kind of faith and with this image of God. The problem is that when that happens, we fail to see that the God Jesus came to reveal is the totally "Other" God, the *Abba*, who longs for intimacy with his children, to the extreme of complete identification with my life and your life. Such longing for intimacy has no more powerful expression that through the sign of food and drink.

What Jesus is saying is that in the Eucharist meal God becomes part of our very self, our flesh and blood, our bone and tissues, part of our struggles, joys, sorrows and hopes. God's total self-giving becomes the energy by which we live, grow and die. Yes, God is my energy, no matter what I am, or what I may think I am. No matter what may ever happen to me, God becomes my strength and my hope, because, by sharing at the Eucharistic meal, I assume him into my life and very body, into my emotions, my achievements, and even into my mistakes. Ours is no longer a God of fear or the 'Distant One' of those shocked first followers of Jesus. Ours is a God who shares our experience fully and deeply to the point of becoming flesh of our flesh, and bone of our bone, as well as energy for our becoming.

> When we consume the consecrated bread and wine... we are engulfed in an infinite embrace ... creating ripples that radiate to every level of our being, body, soul and spirit, and flooding with the inexhaustible energy of divine light, life and love.[32]

Total self-giving for total identification!

> *Take, eat; this is my body... Drink from it, all of you, for this is my blood of the covenant* (Matthew 26:26-28).

The critical question is "what kind of recognition do we carry to our Eucharistic celebrations, or accompanies our daily life after the Eucharistic encounter?" Truly, my body is his body, his life,

---

[32] Thomas Keating, *Manifesting God*, New York NY: Lantern Books, 2005, 34-36.

and his total self. St Paul calls it "incorporation", oneness of intent and experience (Romans 6:10-11), and St Augustine, instructing his newly baptised, captures this same realism when he proclaims, "Let us rejoice and give thanks that we have become not only Christians, but Christ". Henri Nouwen put it beautifully:

> God not only became flesh for us years ago in a country far away. God becomes food and drink for us now at this moment of Eucharistic celebration, right where we are together around the table. God does not hold back; God gives all.[33]

No wonder the early Church called its ritual meal *Eucharistia*, a word meaning precisely *Thanksgiving*. We have reasons to give thanks indeed, and to rejoice and to hope!

'Do this in memory of me'

The fact that the four accounts of the Lord's Supper in Matthew (26:26-30), Mark (14:22-25), Luke (22:14-23), and Paul (1 Corinthians 11:23-27) differ more or less markedly in expression and details reflects the different traditions out of which they grew. While this may be interesting biblical scholarship, the one linking factor among them all is the injunction of the Lord to "*do this in memory*" of him. This has far more serious and personal implications than mere theological speculation. Each community saw the injunction *to do* as addressed to them, in their real and

---

33 Henri Nouwen, ed. Michael O'Loughlin, *Jesus – A Gospel*, New York, Orbis Books, 2001, 87-88.

very specific cultural and religious situation, in their actual needs and struggles, in their rejoicing and hoping, in every individual and communal attempt at coming to terms with the Lord who was no longer physically present with them, after promising them that he would not leave them alone (John 14:18).

Matthew actually adds the words *"all of you"* – *"Drink all of you from this"* (Matthew 26:27). In Eucharist, God becomes who we are, where we are, as we are. No barriers, no holding back, no distinctions of worthiness or unworthiness, first or last, saints or sinners; all are made one in the energy born of the presence of God in their lives and in their community. The doing in memory of the Lord's Death and Resurrection, all together, implies a community dimension as the vital and foundational element of Eucharist, such that we cannot afford to overlook it without destroying the very nature of the mystery.

We all have had the experience of eating together, an experience which is often linked with some very special and personal event. A family gathering, a successful business or academic achievement, a visit from a relation or an intimate friend after a long absence – like the story of the prodigal son illustrates (Luke 15:11-32) – an anniversary, a wedding or a birthday, and even after the sadness of a good-bye, or a funeral. These are but a few occasions when we feel the need to be together, occasions when we invite our friends and relations to share a meal or, someone would say, "to chuck a party", or just "to have a drink".

What matters least of all on these occasions are precisely the food and drink as elements in themselves. It is the feeling of celebration, sharing, and intimacy, of togetherness and affirmation, of joy, compassion and hope that really bring us together. What gathers and binds a group of individuals into a celebrating community is a need to *be with* others in mutual presence, and allowing others to be with us. The food and drink shared and consumed on such occasions by *all* of us *together*, certainly have an important role to play as the instruments and symbols that give meaning to our gathering, both signifying and creating that common-union of ideals and intent that brought us together in the first place. However, just as we cannot envisage a celebration without the symbols of food and drink, so we cannot pretend to invite someone to share our meal, unless the basic attitudes of togetherness, friendship and mutual acceptance are already there.

Eating bread and drinking wine together does not automatically create community, as we see all too well in our age of fast foods and grabbing from the fridge. At the same time, we need the symbols of eating and drinking to express the oneness that binds us together around the table. Neither the symbols of bread and wine in themselves, nor the mechanical, quasi-magical, and monotonous repetition of what the Lord said or did, will ever constitute or create Eucharist. Rather, Eucharist is the sharing here and now of those attitudes of mind and heart symbolised by the breaking of bread and pouring of wine, all together, in memory of the Lord. It was precisely in a peak moment of powerful togetherness, of deep intimacy, of good-byes, and of bewilderment, of memory and dreams, of death and of life, that the Lord Jesus 'took bread... said the blessing... gave it to his disciples", and told them to do the same.

In writing about early Christian communities, Luke tells us:

> *They devoted themselves to the apostles' teaching and fellowship, to the breaking of bread and*

> the prayers... All who believed were together and had all things in common; they would sell their possessions and goods and distribute the proceeds to all, as any had need. Day by day, as they spent much time together in the temple, they broke bread at home and ate their food with glad and generous hearts... and having the goodwill of all the people (Acts 2:42, 43-47).

Clearly, the coming together to break bread and to do what the Lord did was only subsequent to and a necessary consequence of the *fellowship* (Κοινονια) and of the total and mutual sharing of their whole life. Then, and only then, Eucharist made sense to those early believers as total *Communion* with the Lord and with one another. The Eucharist can never and must never be reduced to a private "me-and-God-and-no-one-else" kind of devotion, because then we would neither celebrate memory, nor do what the Lord did on that one night of his earthly life.

> When participation in the Eucharist is understood more as a precept to be fulfilled than a Grace to be accepted; when we go to Mass for the gifts which God has waiting for us rather than for the Gift which is God himself, we are driven to the conclusion that even though the external forms seem Christian, the reality is far from being so.[34]

---

34 Juan E Vecchi (2000), "'This Is My Body Which Is Given For You'", *ACTS of the General Council of the Salesian Society of St John Bosco, 81*(April-June 2000), 18.

The early Church never thought or spoke of Eucharist except in terms of *oneness* and *community*, because *that* is what the Lord intended it to be. On the contrary, Paul had some strong words of condemnation for the Corinthians who had lost sight of the deep significance of what they were doing, to the point of total disregard of each other's needs.

> *For when the time comes to eat, each of you goes ahead with your own supper, and one goes hungry and another becomes drunk*
> (1 Corinthians 11:17-21, 26-34).

I wonder what the Apostle and those early Christians would say if they were to witness some of our Eucharistic celebrations today.

Eucharist: to become bread and to do Eucharist

From this perspective, the Eucharist becomes both a *challenge* to think and to live in a certain way, and a *commitment* to build up the Body of Christ together with our brothers and sisters. "*Do this in memory of me*" has truly been called "a dangerous memory", because, when taken at face value, those words are far more than an exhortation to repeat a ritual. Jesus is not asking us simply to repeat a ritualistic performance, but to do what he did, and what he was about to do for his disciples and for the whole world.[35]

In John's account of the Last Supper, we do not find any direct reference to Eucharist or its institution, but what is unique to the

---

35 John Baptist Metz, in Theresa F. Koernke, "Eucharist, Spirit, Dangerous Memory", Downloads/217-Article%20Text-1032-1-10-20130409%20(1).pdf (accessed 3/12/2018).

Fourth Gospel is the long goodbye conversation of Jesus with his disciples over five chapters (John chapters 13-17), preceded by the action of Jesus washing his disciples' feet (John 13:1-13). That gesture substitutes the narrative of institution, spelt out in Paul and the Synoptics. More importantly, that parable in action expresses the total self-giving of God to us, through what Jesus will do the next day. However, it is important to note that at the end of the gesture of absolute self-giving, Jesus enjoins on his disciples,

I have set you an example, that you also should do what I have done to you (John 13:15).

Thus, both the narrative of the institution in the Synoptics and the washing of the feet in John, express exactly *the same sentiments* of Jesus towards his disciples, and *the same message* to his disciples towards each. The total self-giving of Jesus, in view of what was to happen within a few hours culminating in his total abandonment to death, is exactly what the disciples have *to do* to each other in memory of him. "*Do to each other what I have done to you*" (John 13:15).

Celebrating Eucharist then means to take seriously Jesus' powerful and unequivocal injunction to incarnate in real terms the attitudes that fired Jesus, as he broke bread with his disciples on that last evening of his earthly life. We have *to do* Eucharist and *be* Eucharist. We have to wash one another' feet, and break bread for each other. On the dynamic memory of Jesus' self-giving today and every day, we must become bread for each other, and people will only recognise Jesus as the self-giving God in every facet of real life through our own personal self-giving to each other.

Interestingly enough, the old man in our original story was remembering the struggles, celebrating his present blessings and healing his memories through a ritual that made him do something for others. He, who had experienced famine and suffering, felt the need to *do something* for others, so that the memory became a healing gesture for himself, and a commitment to make abundance available and nourishing to his household.

To break bread together means availability to each other without distinctions or personal judgments. It means to go out to those we live with in spontaneous and joyful self-giving, even at the expense of one's own likes and dislikes, or personal plans. It means readiness to bear one another's burdens, even when we feel that our crosses and burdens are more than we can carry. It means fostering harmony through sensitivity to another's needs and mutual encouragement. It means taking up one's responsibility for the welfare and happiness of every member of the community, regardless of status, tasks, or personalities. It means readiness to forget and forgive when we are hurt, and hurt deeply, as well as readiness *to accept forgiveness* from brother or sister; and accepting forgiveness is far more difficult that to offer forgiveness to another person. It means fostering each other's God-enriched gifts and talents of human qualities by affirming, encouraging and rejoicing.

Precisely because of all this, the Eucharist can never be reduced to a personal devotion or a routine chore. I am led to the Eucharist because of my encounter with God, who sends me to meet my brothers and sisters and to be in fellowship with them.

The practical implications, of course, may be staggering! What about when I refuse to meet my brother and/or sister? It is no use, then, to protest faithful observance of the law on the rhythm of an alarm clock, or shielding behind correct political stance. It is hypocritical to entrench oneself behind private devotions, pretending that my many personal prayers at thanksgiving time will become the magic wand that will settle differences, if I am not prepared to take the first step towards a settlement and reconciliation (Matthew 5:23-24). It is idolatrous to think that God will turn war into peace and hatred into love as if by magic, and change both mind and attitude of that brother or sister who is different from me, if I remain entrenched in my own views, and my personal agenda. The Eucharist builds the community; we have heard it so many times. But the very celebration of Eucharist presupposes human conditions of people in the real concrete milieu of each moment who are prepared to accept into their own lives that very unity of intent and relationship that the Eucharist signifies.

Because we share at the table of the Lord, we must let ourselves be challenged. Failing to accept the challenge is to make a mockery of the Eucharist. Already Augustine had warned us, "The faithful know the Body of Christ, only if they do not neglect to become the Body of Christ".[36]

All this makes heavy demands of time and energy. It frustrates and tires us out; it hurts and leaves us shattered. That is why the Fathers of the Church spoke of becoming bread; bread for the hungry, bread that is broken, cut, torn, chewed up, and transformed. All this hurts, and it hurts very deeply and intensely! Joyce Rupp puts it beautifully.

---

36 St. Augustine, On the Gospel of John: 3:3.

> To follow Jesus in discipleship means that sometimes I will be rejected and misunderstood; I may not see results in my ministry and I will need to give when nothing seems to be returned. "To follow" is to serve when the body and the spirit are weary and to never know what lies ahead... Sometimes we feel like there is a part of us that's been *eaten out* and *chewed on*... We will expects some emptying to go on in our lives, some eating up to take place. But it will not destroy us... We can be sustained and strengthened by our love of God and our faith in his ever-abiding presence.[37]

Our contribution to this Eucharistic *common-union* may appear small, probably insignificant to world wisdom, but it absolutely essential nevertheless. John links his most powerful teaching on Eucharist to the miracle of the multiplication of the loaves and fishes, where the almost insignificant contribution of a small boy who was prepared to share the poverty of his means, five loaves and two fish, became the instrument by which thousands of people were fed. Equally significant, however, is the comment that, in the end, those very disciples who were protesting destitution and inability to avoid being implicated in a gesture of human promotion, are the ones to whom Jesus entrusts the task of distributing the divine-imbibed abundance to the hungry and tired in a desert place (Matthew 14:15, Mark 6:3044; Luke 9:10-17; John 6:1-14). There is a clear link between sharing Eucharist and

---

[37] Joyce Rupp, *Fresh Bread and Other Gifts of Spiritual Nourishment*, Notre Dame, IN: Ave Maria Press, 1987, 118-119

becoming Eucharist by making ourselves available to God, who then works his way through our destitution.

Commenting precisely on this specific Gospel event, Basil Pennington writes:

> What happens in our lives is not measured by our talents, nor even by our dreams, but by our willingness to say yes to the Lord each day and use our gifts as he inspires and directs… How many loaves do you have? Really, the number is not important. He can do as much with one as with seven. We all have the gift of life, the power to love, to be there with him for others. Given that, there is nothing we cannot do with him, in him, through him.[38]

That is the only way that the energy of God, promised by Jesus at the Last Supper, set free by the Spirit at Pentecost, and imbibed by each of us individually and all of us together at Eucharist, is set free to energise the world, and proclaim to all without distinction that God is madly in love with each and every one of us, uniquely and personally, and that our destiny is to be one with him in κοινονια with the whole world.

---

38 M. Basil Pennington, *Who Do You Say I Am? Meditations on Jesus' Questions in the Gospels*, (Hyde Park, NY: New City Press, 2005, 87-88.

"Opus Operandi"

The "Doing" in the Kingdom
Luke 10:25-37

Just then a lawyer stood up to test Jesus. 'Teacher,' he said, 'what must I do to inherit eternal life?' He said to him, 'What is written in the law? What do you read there?' He answered, 'You shall love the Lord your God with all your heart, and with all your soul, and with all your strength, and with all your mind; and your neighbour as yourself.' And he said to him, 'You have given the right answer; do this, and you will live.' But wanting to justify himself, he asked Jesus, 'And who is my neighbour?' Jesus replied, 'A man was going down from Jerusalem to Jericho, and fell into the hands of robbers, who stripped him, beat him, and went away, leaving him half dead. Now by chance a priest was going down that road; and when he saw him, he passed by on the other side. So likewise a Levite, when he came to the place and saw him, passed by on the other side. But a Samaritan while travelling came near him; and when he saw him, he was moved with pity. He went to him and bandaged his wounds, having poured oil and wine on them. Then he put him on his own animal, brought him to an inn, and

> took care of him. The next day he took out two denarii, gave them to the innkeeper, and said, "Take care of him; and when I come back, I will repay you whatever more you spend." Which of these three, do you think, was a neighbour to the man who fell into the hands of the robbers?' He said, 'The one who showed him mercy.' Jesus said to him, 'Go and do likewise (Luke 10:25-37).

Answers beyond questions

A striking feature of the gospels' parables is the way Jesus often seems to take the bait from those who challenge him, only to become very soon subversive in his turn, by throwing the challenge back to his questioners, thus leaving both hearers and readers facing unexpected questions about themselves, their relationship with God, and with one another. The parable of the Good Samaritan (Luke 10:25-37) is a classic example of this technique (see also Matthew 22:34-40 and Mark 12:28-34). Jesus' reply on a point of law put to him by one of the leaders projects one far beyond a simplistic yes-or-no type of answer that the enquirer was seeking in order to justify his personal religious and moral stance.

The parable of the Good Samaritan is undoubtedly one of the best-known and best-loved Gospel stories, and the sense of contrast between Jesus and his self-righteous opponents could not be more striking, engaging both the fundamental understanding of God revealed by Jesus as well as the moral imperative that faith in this God enjoins on the believer. A recurring and common problem for Jesus' contemporaries – as much as for us and for the believers of all time – is that endemic attempt at separating faith and life, whereby faith is reduced to a comfortable legal performance towards God, with little relevance or commitment to the daily situations one has to live through. This is the one-dimensional attitude of the human-divine relationship underlying the lawyer's query. On the one hand, such understanding reduces God to the role of a pre-programmed dispenser of mercy and love for personal demands that gratify one's self-righteous ego, and on the other, it justifies moral judgment and distance from fellow human beings, especially those who do not meet our expectations.

Taking the cue from a real event that probably occurred along the notorious road through the mountainous barrenness between Jericho and Jerusalem, Jesus reverses the expected roles as well as the motivations of the various characters, making the response to the lawyer's inquiry unquestionably clear and shockingly challenging. Most of all, Jesus' response dismantles categorically any semblance of distance, selection, or distinction that the lawyer clearly entertained almost as a moral precept. By breaking down the walls of prejudice, Jesus opens up our vision to encompass and to embrace every person on the road of life, regardless of race, creed, culture or social pecking order.

The story begins with the lawyer approaching Jesus for all the wrong reasons, except self-justification, and ends with a Samaritan – a reject of society – who had nothing to justify himself for, playing the role of instrument of God's presence and mercy expected of leaders and of all "those who know best".

'Teacher, what must I do to inherit eternal life?' (Luke 10:25). Innocent and reasonable as the question may seem, by remarking that the lawyer wanted to justify himself, the evangelist Luke is quick to point out that, in reality, it is strongly mischievous and

subversive, particularly on the lips of a lawyer. The man steeped in the knowledge of the Law, and therefore an authority in matters political, social, and especially religious, needed no reminder of *the golden rule* linking love of God and of neighbour as a single commandment. That was a primordial tenet handed down from the ancient writings (Deuteronomy 6:5 and Leviticus 19:18), and he would have learnt those words by rote long before, since his infant days on his mother's knees and teaching them to so many others.

> *You shall love the Lord your God with all your heart, and with all your soul, and with all your strength, and with all your mind; and your neighbour as yourself* (Luke 10:27).

Good question – wrong motivation

Yes, the lawyer knew the golden rule, but what really motivated the request of the learned man was not so much a need for a deeper personal relationship with God through the dictates of the ancient covenant, as much as a double mischievous intent. By tapping cleverly into Jesus' message about the kingdom, and asking him what one must or must not do *to inherit eternal life*, the lawyer first challenges Jesus' teaching in relations to the Law, and secondly seeks a key for self-justification of his own stance on faith and life.

As it occurs frequently throughout the Gospel narrative, the contrast between Jesus and those whom John call "the Jews" revolves around some facet or norm of law and, like in this case, the challenge is usually couched under a direct reference to the ancient dictates of the Torah. In this way, Jesus would almost inevitably fall into some contradiction, whether with the Law, or with his teaching about a God of mercy and love that sounded so utterly revolutionary to the champions of orthodoxy of his time. In the story of the woman condemned to death for adultery (John 8:1-11), we are told explicitly that

> *They said this to test him, so that they may have some charge to bring against him*' (John 8:6).

Likewise, in Matthew, over the issue as to whether it was lawful to pay taxes to the Roman emperor, we are told that

> *Jesus aware of their malice, said, 'Why are you putting me to the test, you hypocrites'?* (Matthew 22:18).

In the case in point, Luke prefaces the story of the Good Samaritan, precisely with the warning that '*just then a lawyer stood up to test Jesus*' (Luke 10:25), and a few lines later the evangelist insists,

> *But wanting to justify himself, he asked Jesus, 'And who is my neighbour?* (Luke 10:29).

The lawyer is clearly intent on trapping Jesus by his own words.

> The lawyer demonstrates that he knows very well what to do to receive eternal life. He asks the question to force Jesus to compromise himself. If he gives the standard response that everyone already knows, he is brining nothing

new to the Mosaic Law and does not deserve his fame. If he responds in another way, he can be accused of being a heretic.[39]

The second intent of the lawyer was to set boundaries for his own religious and moral behaviour, so that he could justify his own stance in relation both to God and to other people, a stance based on personal preferences and convenience. He knew perfectly well what the Law intended for the treatment of his neighbour, but by pleading ignorance he would feel justified in his intent to categorise people by restrictive labels of distinction, selection and rejection according to what suited him.

"Who is my neighbour?"

In answer, by telling the story of an unfortunate stranger who is attacked and thrashed by thugs, Jesus casts the question back to the lawyer, defying him to give his personal response from within his own life experience, as the place of encounter with God's gift of eternal life through outreach outside of himself, in love and compassion to all.

For a start, we are not told anything about the *"man who was going from Jerusalem to Jericho and fell into the hands of robbers"*. The person could be anyone, an enemy, or a stranger, maybe a non-Jew, and having been assaulted, he may be injured, there may be blood, or he may even be dead. All these possibilities militate in favour of distance, non-involvement, and judgment, and against approaching the man on grounds of physical, moral, and religious purity, or defilement. The fact that both a priest and a Levite are

---

39   Raniero Cantalamessa, *The Gaze of Mercy. A Commentary on Divine and Human Mercy*, The Word Among Us Press, 2015, 159.

two of the four protagonists of the story brings to the fore a strong moral and religious dimension to the whole situation. One needs always be careful to uphold ritual purity, lest one draws divine punishment on oneself. Of course, in all this, the unexpressed intention being, "I come first on all counts and too bad if someone else has to suffer abandonment and disregard, or pay for my religious convictions".

On this score, both priest and Levite were perfectly justified in their behaviour. Indeed their action was sanctioned by the Law, which demanded absolute ritual purity for those who exercised a religious office (Numbers 19:11-13; Leviticus 21:1-4). The priest and the Levite are faced with the dilemma of choosing between observing the Law, or reaching out in compassion and mercy to a stranger in the most unfavourable circumstances. They chose the security of the legal observance, and the stranger was abandoned to die alone. The lawyer would have most certainly approved of their *"passing by on the other side"*, in order to avoid personal contamination and impurity, whether such purity/impurity dilemma was real or imagined. But Jesus openly points in the opposite direction, contesting precisely the priority of one's needs, yes even religious needs and legal observance, overreaching out in compassion to a broken and battered unknown individual, the very refugee of our neighbourhood streets, perhaps.

Having challenged his hearers by indirectly calling into question the right behaviour of "those who know", Jesus does not hesitate to denounce their self-righteousness. Typically, he pushes well beyond their self-determined bounds of decency, acceptability, political correctness, or righteous understanding and convictions. Having remarked poignantly on the behaviour of the priest and

Levite as those who, having come to the place, *"saw him and passed by on the other side"*, Jesus shocked his audience by introducing into the story the one unwanted and the unexpected character, the one person that, in their consideration, was the one most questionable to notice the victim and even more to offer help and compassion.

> *But a Samaritan while travelling came near him; and when he saw him, he was moved with pity. He went to him and bandaged his wounds, having poured oil and wine on them. Then he put him on his own animal, brought him to an inn, and took care of him. The next day he took out two denarii, gave them to the innkeeper, and said, "Take care of him; and when I come back, I will repay you whatever more you spend* (Luke 10:33-35).

The introduction of the Samaritan was not only a shocking turning point in the story for any self-respecting Jew of Jesus' time, but it must have sounded as a personal and shameful indictment of the lawyer and of all the leaders of his time. By upholding the behaviour of a despised gentile, rejected by society as an infidel, with no social standing and even less moral righteousness, Jesus completely subverts both understanding and praxis. For Jesus, God's mercy destabilises all human categories, breaks through all cultural or religious distinctions, and can express itself through the most abject and undeserved human endeavours.

No self-respecting Jew would even dare to approach a Samaritan, let alone expect an act of selfless pity from such a person. The cultural, religious and social divide between Jews and

Samaritans was deep-seated, embracing every level of private and public life, and the barriers between them carried strong moral implications. The sliver of land wedged between fertile Galilee to the north and the seat of political and social power of Judea to the south was a land disdained equally by the simple but faithful Galileans and the learned and powerful leaders of Jerusalem. Over its twisted and sometime tragic history, Samaria had become a cultural and religious potpourri, mixing local pagan customs and cultic mores with the foundational Mosaic tenets, to the point of abandoning the sacred and ancient traditions of Yahweh's people. For any law-abiding Jew, infidelity to the covenant and an unscrupulous mix of semi-pagan religious beliefs and practices, had long detached Samaria from Jerusalem; and its inhabitants were looked upon with suspicion by any law-abiding Jew of Jesus' time.

The term Samaritan had become synonymous with betrayal, depravity and unredeemed sinfulness, and there was no greater insult than being addressed as a Samaritan. The very land of Samaria became a land of defilement and contamination, and anyone journeying north-south through Palestine in Jesus' time would carefully avoid setting foot on the very soil of Samaria, to avoid becoming morally tainted. There were only two safe routes possible to this traveller: either journey through the barren desert beyond the Jordan and then cross the river again once into the Judean hinterland, or seek the same destination by sea, aboard some leaky fishing boat arching into the Mediterranean to the west. Yes, the *dangers of a desert* land (Trans-Jordan region), and the *loneliness and uncertainty* of a long sea voyage was far more preferable to any contact with the *unfaithfulness* of Samaria. In a subtle way, through his response to the lawyer and by bringing into play a Samaritan as the unlikely hero, Jesus says that the self-righteous person is worse than a Samaritan.

Against this background of cultural and religious barriers and taboos, Jesus proclaims the unfaithful enemy as the champion of those who seek eternal life, as well as the instrument of God's mercy. In this context, the whole story is a blatant challenge, not only to his contemporaries, but also for us the readers. God's mercy defies personal merits or cultural categories, as Ambrose of Milan reminds us: "Mercy, not kinship makes someone a neighbour".[40] However, to be real and life-giving, this gift of mercy needs a direct human intervention of self-less giving without distinction or prejudice. It is only through this human intervention on behalf of each other that we will discover and experience God's loving mercy towards us. In the Beatitudes, his Magna Charta of the kingdom, Jesus openly declared that to experience the joy of God's mercy at a personal level we have to be instrument of mercy to the world. *"Blessed are the merciful, for they will receive mercy"* (Matthew 5:7).

The need to acknowledge every one as neighbour irrespective of culture, status, beliefs or personality, is an unquestionable and inevitable consequence of our claim to faith. We can do no greater violence to God's Word and to our claim to faith than to avoid reaching out in compassion to the needy and broken who walk with us along the road. The Samaritan, on the other hand, unencumbered by self-imposed bounds of religiosity or prejudice, did not hesitate to become the compassionate stranger for the broken stranger. He had no need to ask, "Who is my neighbour?" or "How far can I go to help this person?" because he had no fear of

---

40 Pontifical Council for the Promotion of the New Evangelisation, "Exposition of the Gospel of Luke, 7, 84", in *The Parables of Mercy*, Huntingdon IN: Our Sunday Visitor Publishing Division, 2015, 27

defilement, contagion or uncleanliness, and even less did he need to make distinctions or choices, or put up walls of separation of ritual or cultural purity. Because he knew rejection in his own life, he could identify with the rejected, and the broken, and so he felt compelled to share compassion without seeking self-justification through excuses, distinctions or idle questions.

Visceral compassion

We are told that, on seeing the man who had fallen into the hands of robbers, the Samaritan was *"moved with compassion"* and immediately set out to care for him. We find a similar expression and an equivalent reaction from Jesus himself, when he encountered the widow of Nain grieving for her dead son being carried to his burial (Luke 7:11-17).

> *When the Lord saw her, he had compassion for her and said to her.' Do not weep'. Then he came forward and touched the bier, and the bearers stood still. And he said, 'Young man, I say to you, rise!' The dead man sat up, and began to speak, and Jesus gave him to is mother* (Luke 7:13-15).

Note the striking and shocking similarity between the Samaritan of the parable and Jesus facing defilement by touching the bier and restoring life to a dead body and joy to a distraught widow and mother. In both cases, compassion becomes the most authentic expression both of God's mercy towards us, and of the moral imperative urging us towards reaching out to each other. Compassion is the concrete expression of mercy and it is the operative word in both divine and human outreach movements.

However, often the term carries connotations of passive helplessness and of feeling "sorry" or "pity" for someone in need. Etymologically, however, compassion expresses a dynamic and active movement derived from two Latin words, *cum* (with) and *passum* (step or walk), conveying a sense of *falling in step with* someone, and journeying together with a person in need. Thus, compassion is that appropriation of another person's needs and a decision to become *actively involved* with this person and confront together whatever the situation may be.

Unencumbered by fears, prejudice or taboos, the Samaritan feels the suffering of this man and is almost instinctively driven to appropriate the suffering in a deeply personal manner. Even more realistically, in the original Greek text of this parable, the term compassion derives from a word that refers to internal organs or from the mother's womb. Literally, compassion implies a "visceral movement", as Pope Francis describes it, a powerful energy welling up from the inside one's very self, that moves one into becoming mercy personified towards the victim.[41] Veronica Lawson speaks of mercy as "womb-compassion" giving and protecting life at its most foundational stage and welling up from the inner core of our being where the heart beats.[42]

Pope Francis comments beautifully:

> The Greek verb that indicates this compassion... derives from the word that indicates internal organs or the mother's womb. It is similar to the love of a father and mother, who are

---

41 Ibid, 26-27
42 Veronica Lawson, *The Blessing of Mercy*, Morning Star Publishing, 2015, 32-35

> profoundly moved by their own child; it is a visceral love. God loves us in this way, with compassion and mercy. Jesus does not look at reality from the outside, without letting himself be moved, as if he were taking a picture. He lets himself be involved. This kind of compassion is needed today to conquer the globalisation of indifference. This kind of regard is needed when we find ourselves in front of a poor person, an outcast, or a sinner. This is the compassion that nourishes the awareness that we, too, are sinners.[43]

Having by now recognised the complete reversal of his parameters, the lawyer could not but admit that the stranger was the true neighbour, because that despised Samaritan alone had reached out to put someone's needs ahead of his own, without personal considerations. The neighbour, whoever he may have been, came first, while for the lawyer moral and religious self-righteousness was the primary concern. In that cultural context, for an observant Jew, the Samaritan was the most unlikely person to lend a hand and take responsibility. Yet, because he stepped through prejudice and personal agenda, the man on the road was healed and given back his life.

As Pope Francis proclaims incessantly, God's mercy towards us is unconditional and visceral, because God cannot but love us out of his own nature, and God cannot but express this love for humanity precisely in a visceral manner. That is also the nature of mercy exemplified by the Samaritan, and that is the demand

---

43 Pope Francis, *The Name of God is Mercy*, Bluebird Books for Life, 2016, 92

that Jesus makes of the lawyer and of all of us. We cannot but love totally out of our conviction of being loved totally by our God. Any excuse to avoid the confrontation is a denial of both God and self, and no amount of religious practice or legal observance will re-establish the relationship with our God, which we have formally rejected by refusing to become involved in this dynamism of human-divine love.

Clearly, compassion is not so much a matter of doing or of contributing to a cause, but of *being with the other*, especially the other in need. It is not simply a matter of benevolence, or of being nice to each other, of feeling pity or good will from the comfort of our armchair, or even of engaging in some warm-hearted form of humanitarian altruism. It is no longer sufficient to ask who our neighbour is, or why one should love one's neighbour as oneself (John 13:34). We need *to become neighbour* to one another with the compassion with which God loves us, and reach out to each other in a living, dynamic and visceral manner, without conditions, fears, or personal agenda. We can never justify ourselves or hide our moral responsibility behind personal needs, inadequacies or brokenness. Awareness of belonging to a wounded humanity and belief in a compassionate God of love demand that we own both the brokenness of the Samaritan, and the wretchedness that we encounter abandoned along the road, or that surrounds us on all sides. Jesus did that, even at the price of his own life.

This incredible page of Luke's Gospel is all about overcoming distinctions and putting oneself out in whatever way one is capable of, in order to reach out to someone else, whoever or wherever this someone else may be. Like the victim on the road to Jericho, we all need support and welcome, and, like the Samaritan, we are all called to make our time, energy and talents available to each other. To believe in a God of visceral love impels us to have the wisdom and courage to be Samaritans, unafraid, and free of prejudice, motivated only by compassion and love for the broken and the abandoned, not in old Jericho, or on the screens of our high resolution television sets, but in our community and family, on our streets, in our neighbourhood and immediate environment, today, and for the rest of our life journey.

> We cannot claim to be truly disciples of Jesus unless we are totally engaged in honouring his presence in each one, and in building and nurturing this community to be a living witness of that presence.[44]

Conclusion

Objects of God's visceral love must generate concrete and down to earth love and compassion towards everyone else without distinction, or God's love is dissipated and the world will never know peace, justice and hope, but only divisiveness and self-destruction. To proclaim that God is love and that Mercy is the name of God is our inalienable commitment and moral duty to be instruments of the same divine-sanctioned compassionate love and mercy where we are. We have no choice but to incarnate visceral compassion in this world of ours, which often appears to have lost all sense of the other(s), and where there is no room for the powerless, trapped by prejudice and injustice, or ignored in unyielding social, political or religious structures. Faith impels

---

44 T.J. Brady, http://cathnews.com/cathnews/30435... (accessed 11/10/2017

us to be Samaritans for those abandoned into chronic loneliness, because they have passed the use-by-date of economic usefulness, for those who are silenced by the bullishness of the powerful, or discriminated against by economic policies.

Energised by God's visceral love and mercy, we leave ourselves no option but step into the shoes of those who flee war, famine and inhuman situations, and land helpless and hopeless on our doorstep, or are pushed back into the high seas because we just do not want them. Unless we are prepared to pour the oil of compassion and of healing presence on these and a myriad similar conditions, and to pay out of our own person for the redemption of these situations that hem us in from all sides, then we betray any claim to belonging to the kingdom and to faith in a God of mercy, who loves us with the love of a father and mother, and enjoins of us to do likewise universally and unconditionally to each other.

Community

Foot Washing in the Kingdom
John 13:1-20

Now before the festival of the Passover, Jesus knew that his hour had come to depart from this world and go to the Father. Having loved his own who were in the world, he loved them to the end. The devil had already put it into the heart of Judas son of Simon Iscariot to betray him. And during supper Jesus, knowing that the Father had given all things into his hands, and that he had come from God and was going to God, got up from the table, took off his outer robe, and tied a towel around himself. Then he poured water into a basin and began to wash the disciples' feet and to wipe them with the towel that was tied around him. He came to Simon Peter, who said to him, 'Lord, are you going to wash my feet?' Jesus answered, 'You do not know now what I am doing, but later you will understand.' Peter said to him, 'You will never wash my feet.' Jesus answered, 'Unless I wash you, you have no share with me.' Simon Peter said to him, 'Lord, not my feet only but also my hands and my head!' Jesus said to him, 'One who has bathed does not need to wash, except

> *for the feet, but is entirely clean. And you are clean, though not all of you.' For he knew who was to betray him; for this reason he said, 'Not all of you are clean. 'After he had washed their feet, had put on his robe, and had returned to the table, he said to them, 'Do you know what I have done to you?'* (John 13:1-20).

One of the striking features of Jesus' parables is the strong sense of "otherness" and of *community* that runs through the various narratives. Although the kingdom-parables of Jesus have a very personal appeal, challenging our relationship with God, this relationship can only be expressed and achieved through relationship with each other. The parables of the kingdom always contain a plurality of characters, interrelated and often in contrast with each other, thus highlighting a strong sense both of diversity and of community underlying the nature of the kingdom and its realisation in the here and now. Jesus' story telling invariably challenges his hearers to look beyond themselves, at their own lives in relation to those around them: their families, their neighbours, their strangers, and even their antagonists and opponents.

Therefore, we hear of landowners reaching out to unfaithful and ungrateful tenants to whom they have entrusted their property. As tenants, their very identity depends on the generosity of their landowner and, in the end, their refusal to accept the offer of relatedness ends in self-destruction (Matthew 21:28-46; Mark 12:1-11; Luke 20:9-27). In a similar vein, Mark has Jesus repeatedly telling us not to hide the light under a bushel (Mark 4:21-25), but to keep our lamps burning (Luke 8:16-18. 11:33-36), so that others, seeing the light, may believe and find their way into the kingdom through the flickering flame emanating from our lives.

> *You are the light of the world. A town built on a hill cannot be hidden. Neither do people light a lamp and put it under a bowl. Instead they put it on its stand, and it gives light to everyone in the house. In the same way, let your light shine before others, that they may see your good deeds and glorify your Father in heaven* (Matthew 5:14-16).

Likewise, in the classic parable of "the Good Samaritan" (Luke 10:25-37), the learned doctor of the law was only concerned with justifying his own stance of separateness and self-righteous distinction as a faithful and observant believer. In response, Jesus tells the story of the man who fell among robbers, thrusting his enquirer, and us as well, out of self-centredness and into an other-centred perspective. With a clever change of perspective, Jesus shifts the focus from self to *self-with-others*, and asks a scholar of the Law to do the same as the despicable and unfaithful Samaritan had done to an unknown stranger.

Jesus is very personal. He does not say "those who follow me", but addresses his audience and us with the very personal pronoun *you*. Clearly, the very commitment to faith in Jesus thrusts us inescapably into a community dimension as the place of our personal encounter with God and of the fulfilment of the kingdom in our world. Privacy is definitely not of the kingdom. On the contrary, the disciple is never a spectator but a primary actor, and the living and active presence of God will only become a reality through the disciple's conversion from a mentality focused on self to a committed action of self-with-others. Without a direct and affirming reference to others, there cannot be any personal relationship with God, as the parable of the Pharisee and the tax collector praying in the temple clearly points out (Luke 18:9-14).

The community of the kingdom

Through the parables, by accentuating plurality and an active relationship with each other, Jesus' teaching and mission carries an unmistakable community intent. Indeed, throughout the Gospel narrative, he is clearly the community builder, calling people *to follow him*[45], instructing his would be followers on the meaning and implications of the decision *to stay with him*[46], and in the end, at the Last Supper, praying to the Father *that they may be one*. The Fourth Evangelist dedicates a quarter of his Gospel narrative (chapters 13-17) to Jesus' long conversation in the Upper Room the night before he died, a conversation revealing *love* as the energy bonding himself to the Father and the disciples to one another, and ending with a prayer to the Father, *"that they may be completely one"* (John 17:14). Community building is thus the crux of Jesus' last will and testament left to his disciples, those very ones who were now entrusted with the mission of spreading the kingdom.

Jesus is not removing us out of our reality, nor is discipleship possible in isolation from our daily experience, because both our

---

[45] See Matthew 4:19-25; 9:9; Mark 1:17-20; 2:14; 10:21; Luke 5:10-28; 9:59; 18:22; John 1:39-43
[46] See Matthew 4:23-25; chapters 5 - 7; 8:1-4.18-22; 9:14-17.27-31; 10:1-42; 12:15; 13:1-58; 14:13-21; 15:1-39; 16:5-12.24-28; 18:1-39; 19:2.23-30; 20:20-34; 21:1-11. Mark 2:15.18-28; 3:7.13-30.31-34; 4:1-33; 5:24; 6:6a-13; 7:1-23; 8:14-21.34-38; 9:33-37.42-50; 10:1-16.35-52. Luke 5:33-39; 6:1-5.17-49; 8:9-21; 9:1-6.23-27.46-62; 10:1-12.17-20; 11:1-13; 12:1-59; 13:1-9.11-30.57-62; 14:7-14.25-34; 16:1-31; 17:1-10.17-37; 18:1-30; 19:1-27;John 6:2.

relationship with God in faith and our mission to the kingdom are not extra or out-of-this-world experiences. Faith can only find expression in the relationship with one another and within the confines of where one is at any one time. That is why, at the end of the long Johannine discourse of the Last Supper Jesus prayed to the Father:

> *I am not asking you to take them out of the world... May they be one, as we are one, I in them and you in me, that they may become completely one, so that the world may know that you have sent me and have loved them even as you have loved me* (John 17:14, 21-23).

Kingdom and community are inseparable and complementary in the Gospel narratives, and one cannot exist without the other. Indeed, for the Fourth Gospel, if we accept the kingdom as the living and active presence of God in our daily experience, clearly there is no way of responding to God in discipleship except in togetherness and oneness. Community stands at the very heart of faith and mission in the kingdom.

However, following the Paschal events of Jesus' death and resurrection and his return to the Father, the early Christian communities were soon faced with a particularly testing problem. It was clear that during his earthly life Jesus had gathered around himself a community. Now that he had left them and entrusted them with his own mission of spreading the kingdom, what happened to that community, and what was in reality this kingdom he had proclaimed and revealed? Indeed, what was the meaning of community when Jesus of Nazareth was no longer the one to lead the way and meld them together in unity, or the one they could look up to? How could the believers express that final injunction "to be one" through their diversity of backgrounds, their different understandings and perceptions, their varied cultural and social categories, and their personal experiences? How could they live that unique personal relationship with God that discipleship implied, and, at the same time, express it within the community's shared belief in Jesus?

These are not academic questions locked in some historical time capsule of long ago. The challenge of the early communities is the never-ending ongoing challenge for each individual and for the Church community for all times. Like the early community, we need to question ourselves constantly as to the relevance of this Jesus' presence in absence now in our Church and Christian communities, and on the meaning of this kingdom in the here and now, at all levels of our experience.

Sandra Schneiders invites us back into the Upper Room and points to the experience of the Last Supper as the paradigm of the new kind of community, a paradigm that is both revelatory and empowering at the same time. It reveals the active presence of Jesus once he was no longer physically with us, and it empowered the community to incarnate the new mode of being in the kingdom. As a paradigm, the community of the Last Supper transcends time and space, and thus it becomes a model for understanding our own community. It is there that we need to look, if we are to understand and live out our call to community. In particular, we need to take seriously two metaphors that are central to the event of the Last Supper and intimately connected as a double parable, one expressed in narrative form and the other in personal and communal action.[47] First, Jesus opens the Last Supper with the highly symbolic gesture of washing his disciples' feet (John 13:1-20), and then he proceeds to explain the parable in action through frequent and powerful references to the imagery of the vine and the branches (John 15:12-16).

The two expressions are intimately connected. The personal life-relationship between God and each of us individually imaged through the vine and branches can only be incarnated and become a credible witness through the relationship of service to each other expressed in the washing of the feet. This powerful dynamism of God's love for us individually becomes the only and unequivocal yardstick of the love the disciples must have for one another within the community. Just as Jesus became the living witness of the active and loving presence of God in our history, so the disciples are to witness the same active and loving presence through each other in community. There is no escaping the two imperatives of *abiding* in God's love as branches enlivened by the vine, and *loving* one another as the expression of this universal energy making us *one*, as Jesus enjoined on us and prayed for us. Unlike Matthew (5:54) and Luke (6:27.35), John makes no mention of loving one's enemies, because we either accept and love one another, or we do not, and to refuse to love means to abdicate totally any claim to discipleship.

In the kingdom, we will witness to Jesus and become credible signs and effective instruments of God's loving presence only by living fully and in a deeply human and real way the life of love we claim to share. If the life we live is the life of love for one another, then people will know and take notice (John 14:31; 17:20-24), and the energy becomes contagious.

---

47 Sandra M. Schneiders, "The Foot Washing (John 13:1-20): An Experiment in Hermeneutics", *Catholic Biblical Quarterly 41/1* (January 1981).

'Now I am no longer in the world, but they are in the world... Holy Father, protect them in your name... so that they may be one, so that the world may believe that you have sent me (John 17:11, 21).

At a more personal level, when we try to structure a discipleship in terms of a personal spirituality divorced from the social dimension and relatedness to others in terms of justice, service and open acceptance, our efforts are naive, futile, and ultimately self-destructive (John 15:4-6).

A parable in action

Kingdom faith demands totality of mutual love expressed through service, equality, and real friendship, precisely the kind of service, equality, and deep friendship, which Jesus expressed through the symbolic action of washing his disciples' feet.

Although the Fourth Gospel gives large space to the Last Supper discourse, the author makes no mention of the *'institution of the Eucharist'*, having already dealt with the Eucharistic teaching at length and in depth in terms of the bread of life in chapter six (John 6:25-69). Instead, John's Gospel substitutes the institution with the parable in action of "the Washing of the Feet" (John 13:1-20). However, though narratively diverse and quite distinct, both events carry the same strong Eucharistic undertone. In the symbolic gesture of washing his disciples' feet, Jesus explained what he was going to do next day. Just as the broken body and the blood spilled on the cross will always be the ultimate manifestations of Jesus' total and unconditional self-giving love for his disciples and in trustful abandonment to the Father, the Johannine community has always identified the washing of the feet as the expression of the same self-giving, carrying the same injunction of unity and love that must exist among all those who belong to the kingdom. Rather than being an abject sign of self-abasement (*kenosis*), by washing the feet of the disciples Jesus proclaims that the giving of one's life for one's friends (John 15:13), sisters and brothers, is the ultimate sign of love and the final glorification of the Father (John 17:5, 22, 24).

While we must be wary of deceiving ourselves into some masochistic or emotional sentimentality by which we canonise suffering, spilling of blood, and death for their own sake, these are the necessary consequences of availability and service to each other, because any form of self-giving will always entail pain and some form of death to self. The cross will always remain destructive and obscene to humanity, but discipleship demands that we be totally and unconditionally available to others at whatever cost to self. It is only through this unconditional availability and pouring out of self that full life will sprout from the vine, and community will be redeemed from the level of a utopian idea at best, or of cohabitation at worst.

The very language adopted by the tradition carries a striking and radical similarity between the Synoptics' narrative of the institution and John's washing of the feet. In Luke, after inviting his disciples to share broken bread and spilled wine, he enjoins on them to "*do this in remembrance of me*" (Luke 22:19). Strikingly, at the end of John's washing of the feet, Jesus says to his disciples, "*For I have set you an example, that you also should do as I have done to you* (John 13:15). That *doing* that Jesus refers to has nothing do to with some repetitious memorial ritual, but everything about *doing to each other what he is about to do for his disciples:* giving himself totally and unconditionally to the Father on their behalf.

Thus, Jesus' gesture is a powerful catechesis in action. It reveals both that faith/love attitude which must inform the kingdom, as well as the mode of realising interpersonal relationships within community. By vesting as a servant and taking on the role of the slave towards the landlord (John 13:4-5) and of a disciple towards the master, Jesus reverses the accepted roles of authority and turns upside down the presumed order of power. Jesus makes no secret about the fact that service is the fundamental expression of the love relationship in discipleship. *'I have set you an example, that you also should do as I have done to you'* (John 13:15). Clearly, in his social and religious milieu, Jesus is not about political correctness, and in the Christian community either everything is on a level of deep friendship, or it is nothing at all, because any form of pecking order makes community impossible.[48] Service can only be understood and exercised from a position of equality and within a relationship of friendship and love. Jesus himself declares equality and friendship fundamental to community building and revelatory of our relationship with the Father.

> *I do not call you servants any longer, because the servant does not know what the master is doing; but I call you friends, because I have made known to you everything I have heard from my Father* (John 15:15).

---

48 Matthew 10:20-25; 16:24-28; 20:20-28; 23:11-12; Mark 8:34-9:1.35-37; Luke 9:23-27; John 12:25-26; 15:15-20.

"Us" versus "Them"

The need to acknowledge each other and everyone else as neighbour and object of mutual love, irrespective of culture, status, beliefs or personality is an unquestionable consequence and responsibility of our claim to faith. We can do no greater violence to the kingdom than to avoid reaching out to the needy and broken who walk the road with us. This call to openness and mutual friendship in relationships within the kingdom is a recurring theme running through most of the parables of Jesus, and this gesture of washing the disciples' feet is but a visual expression of what Jesus has repeatedly proclaimed in word and life (Luke 10:25-37; 18:9-14).

In the Gospels, Jesus is clearly at home with Samaritans, public sinners, Roman soldiers, children, Pharisees, and rough fishermen who deny him to his face, and double dealers who physically sold him to his enemies. Likewise, when it comes to choices, he is inevitably on the side of the rejected and the discriminated. Consequently, if we dare to claim belief in Jesus, we have to look at how we perceive and understand others, and then confront the challenge of identifying our own stance in life from the perspective of our faith claim. Any form of discrimination, distancing and separateness on grounds of us-and-them makes a lie of our claim to faith. Such a stance becomes an open denial of the active presence of a loving God in our life and in the life of those discriminated against, or from whom we distance ourselves, because they speak another language, express a different culture, worship in a church, a synagogue, a mosque, a temple, or shun and condemn worship altogether.

Ironically, the observant Pharisee of Luke 18:9-14 was perfectly correct in his claims. He had fasted and given alms well beyond the call of the law, and he had been scrupulously faithful to his religious, social and economic duties. His prayer even had a hint of thanksgiving, acknowledging the gift of faith Yahweh had granted him. Unfortunately, totally focused on himself, even his prayer becomes self-centred and self-directed, a litany of his self-credentialed virtues; and God had better remember them! As for others, he can only pity them and label them a bunch of thieves, rogues, adulterous, tax collector; and reject them; and he at pains to remind God of that too. Not that the man is very insincere, and we can assume that his words are truthful and he is an honest, deeply religious person, meticulous in his observance of law and ritual. Equally, the much-maligned tax collector most likely was the exact opposite, just as the Pharisee describes him. The trouble is that his very self-justification in terms of himself and of rejection of others leads to his unequivocal condemnation by Jesus.

On the other hand, the very name 'publican' was synonymous with unfaithfulness and dishonesty. No, he had not fasted, he had not paid his dues in goods, money, or kind, as prescribed by the Law, and probably his private life was a bit of mess. The head-bowed publican had little of himself to thank God for, and he could only beg for mercy and forgiveness. Of course, as often happens with Jesus' parables, the end of the story is surprising, paradoxical, and shocking to his hearers. Correctly truthful, the publican acknowledges his brokenness and simply trusts in God as his only security, without claiming any personal merit or distinction. The Pharisee trusts no one but himself, while the sinner trusts nobody else but God who alone in the end can justify, heal, and give life. In this case, the very one who is universally condemned and rejected because of his lifestyle, is justified.

Typically, Jesus reverses the expected order of priorities and personal expectations by condemning the self-righteous one totally closed within himself, and justifying the universally acknowledged sinner, because this sinner is not about comparing himself to anybody else, and even less judging others on whatever grounds. In the economy of God's Reign, justification and uprightness are in direct proportion to our personal stance towards each other, and in inverse proportion to our self-centredness, personal achievements and self-righteousness.

Foot washing in the community

The message is clear. The new order of the kingdom demands that we be prepared to undergo a radical conversion in the way we see each other and in the kind of relationships that govern our mutual behaviour. We need a new perspective that begins with overcoming distinctions and putting ourselves out in whatever way we are capable of doing, in order to reach out to someone else, whoever or wherever this someone else may be. Like the victim on the road to Jericho, we all need support and welcome, and like the Samaritan, we are all called to make our time, energy and talents available to each other. Belonging to the kingdom requires wisdom and courage to become involved in our community through our sharing of energy, ideas, talents, and goodwill for the life of everyone around us.

The challenge, of course, is to incarnate these attitudes and perceptions as well as behaviour in the humdrum of each day. Each individual and all of us need to ask the question each day in every diverse situation of life, and each of us must find their own response. The practical implications of this God-dream in terms of community life are radical and frightening in the extreme, giving rise to some fundamental questions about community and about Church as a whole. Whatever our personal response, it must be lived out against the foundational principle given to us by Jesus' action. Unless we can achieve friendship and equality with all those we serve and live with, we will not serve at all, but we will only dominate. In the end, it is a matter of making room for God, and allowing God to operate through us and in spite of us, trusting in God's presence and energy, even when everything seems to militate against our understanding or even common sense.

At the washing of the feet, Peter's response and the ensuing dialogue with Jesus is typical of the struggle of coming to terms with Jesus' demands against the natural tendency to control, select, compare, or set boundaries within the social context of the kingdom. In his typically fiery way, Peter objects to having his feet washed precisely because Jesus seems to be doing the wrong thing, to the wrong person, and for the wrong reason. What Peter is really rejecting is the challenge to his expectations of authority structures based on power relationships, and on an unbending attitude for "the way things are done". He demands that things be neat, and tidy and efficient, so that *he* knows where *he* stands in terms of rights and duties. Most of all, Peter is refusing a model of salvation through service and through death to self. Within a group of believers or a Christian community, service in terms of power is often bipolar: authority to subject and subject to authority, each direction taken unilaterally, can be destructively comfortable. While the exercise of authority may well boost someone's personal ego even with tragic consequences, blind acceptance of authority (sometimes falsely couched under the guise of a passive or dismissive "it is God's will") can often be a useful alibi for relinquishing all responsibility to someone else and refusing to make decisions. Such childish refusal not to become involved by hiding behind some fake unavailability or incompetence destroys community and stifles all forms of spiritual growth.

Service requires as much giving as receiving and readiness to accept service from another person is as much a sign of human maturity as it is an element of growth for the whole community. The complete sharing of the foot washing may requires that I remain open and available to others sharing their charisms as well as their pain with me. It may well be that service to the community consists in being served rather than serving others. This is not just a consequence of the passing of time and of weakening of bodily strength, but is undoubtedly the hardest demand of discipleship, because then, truly, I have no control and no power. Availability to being served is a true call to growth into deeper intimacy and total openness to love. It is a call to allow the love of the foot washing to be given to us by those around us in community.

Responsibility, affirmation, brotherly/sisterly love, forgiveness, equality, support, compassion, mutuality, empathy – these are not just nice words. They are moral imperatives and radical demands at all levels of society on which we gamble the credibility of our faith and our very lives as believers and disciples. This means that every time I dare to pray the Lord's Prayer and utter the words, '*may your kingdom come*', I do not tell God what he should do about it, but I take on the inescapable "*doing*" of the washing of the feet. In uttering those words, I place myself centre stage not as a passive spectator of a pie dropping from the sky, but as an active actor fully involved in the role of making the God's active and living presence a concrete reality of peace, justice, and down to earth love, here and now. Jesus claimed that the kingdom is here (Luke 17:21), and in the words of Francis of Assisi, we are to be the instruments of its realisation here and now, without personal expectations, without prejudice, and without distinction of any kind.

In those words, I commit myself to a kind of openness that goes far beyond liking, putting up with, encountering, or living next door with someone I do not like. I have to become friend with everyone, yes also with the brother and/or sister who has been unjust and hurtful to me and maybe to everyone else too.

Foot washing calls me to be and to become a compassionate traveller with everyone I meet on my daily journey, conscious that my journey will affect theirs, and their journey will affect my whole life. Presence to each other, so central a spirituality of preciousness and intimacy expressed by Jesus in the Upper Room, can only be real when I discover in the other my fellow co-traveller, a person endowed with undreamed-of richness and tired out by all kinds of human weakness. This is the neighbour needing foot washing from me: my time, my energy, my friendship, my recognition, and my affirmation of his/her God-empowered giftedness, as much as I need these gifts in return.

Foot washing demands availability of time and energy, when I have neither and cannot afford either.

Foot washing requires awareness and sensitivity of times and situations, and especially to people where they are at, without prejudice, violence or imposition, role stereotyping or categorising of cultures, ages or social status, but always ready to affirm and support the goodness that God has put there in each of us individually and all of us collectively.

Foot washing means personal responsibility and ready initiative to see and meet new and unexpected situations, and letting your light shine rather than hiding it under a self-styled comfortable bushel of false humility, claiming personal liminality for fear of becoming involved.

Jesus claimed that *"the kingdom of heaven has suffered violence, and the violent take it by force"* (Matthew 11:12), and we may experience violence within ourselves as we try to incarnate this divine presence of the kingdom in our world. Our whole self may resent reaching out to the lost, the hurtful, the unclean, or the physically and morally broken. However, we have no choice but to reach out to these, and incarnate attitudes of mercy and companionship in our mutual relationships, just as we have absolutely no choice but to share our commitment to discipleship. Human frailty, weakness, misunderstandings, and shortcomings will always make heavy demands on our commitment, often obscuring the vision and weakening the resolve. There, in that weakness and in those heavy personal demands, lies also the greatest challenge to authenticity and the stimulus to that fruitfulness inherent in the metaphor of the vine that Jesus repeatedly refers to alongside the washing of the feet.

In a world that proclaims that self-assertion is the norm of success, that individualism is absolute, that economic usefulness is the sole criterion for social acceptability, that material advancement is the ultimate goal in life, that labelling and stereotyping is the accepted mode of determining social relationships – in such a world, the kingdom becomes a disturbing but vital counter witness. Sharing our life of love and support with our brothers and sisters without distinctions or conditions proclaims to the whole world not only the possibility of true and authentically human love energised by God's very life and shared by every individual person, but it proclaims also our readiness to make ourselves available to bring about a world governed by justice, equality and love. The kingdom is here, and the daring and brave will bring it about. We must be those trusting, wise, and courageous ones who will have to make it happen or it will never happen at all. God relies on our weakness to bring about his kingdom of oneness in justice and peace, and we must make it happen through our openness, trust, readiness and that one universal energy called mutual love, which alone breaks down barriers, eliminates distinctions and individuality, and makes us all what Jesus prayed for: may they be one.

MISSION

The Stranger in the Kingdom
John 21:1-19

Gathered there together were Simon Peter, Thomas called the Twin, Nathanael of Cana in Galilee, the sons of Zebedee, and two others of his disciples. Simon Peter said to them, 'I am going fishing.' They said to him, 'We will go with you.' They went out and got into the boat, but that night they caught nothing.

Just after daybreak, Jesus stood on the beach; but the disciples did not know that it was Jesus. Jesus said to them, 'Children, you have no fish, have you?' They answered him, 'No.' He said to them, 'Cast the net to the right side of the boat, and you will find some.' So they cast it, and now they were not able to haul it in because there were so many fish. That disciple whom Jesus loved said to Peter, 'It is the Lord!' When Simon Peter heard that it was the Lord, he put on some clothes, for he was naked, and jumped into the lake. But the other disciples came in the boat, dragging the net full of fish, for they were not far from the land, only about a hundred yards off. When they had gone ashore, they saw a charcoal fire there, with fish on it, and bread. Jesus said to them, 'Bring some of the fish that you have just caught.' So Simon Peter went aboard and hauled the net ashore, full of large fish, a hundred and fifty-three of them; and though there were so many, the net was not torn. Jesus said to them, 'Come and have breakfast.' Now none of the disciples dared to ask him, 'Who are you?' because they knew it was the Lord. Jesus came and took the bread and gave it to them, and did the same with the fish. This was now the third time that Jesus appeared to the disciples after he was raised from the dead.

When they had finished breakfast, Jesus said to Simon Peter, 'Simon son of John, do you love me more than these?' He said to him, 'Yes, Lord; you know that I love you.' Jesus said to him, 'Feed my lambs.' A second time he said to him, 'Simon son of John, do you love me?' He said to him, 'Yes, Lord; you know that I love you.' Jesus said to him, 'Tend my sheep.' He said to him the third time, 'Simon son of John, do you love me?' Peter felt hurt because he said to him the third time, 'Do you love me?' And he said to him, 'Lord, you know everything; you know that I love you.' Jesus said to him, 'Feed my sheep. Very truly, I tell you, when you were younger, you used to fasten your own belt and to go wherever you wished. But when you grow old, you will stretch out your hands, and someone else will fasten a belt around you and take you where you do not

> wish to go.'(He said this to indicate the kind of death by which he would glorify God.) After this he said to him, 'Follow me' (John 21:1-19).

Lost and betrayed

Let us engage our imagination and picture the scene in the Upper Room, late on that fateful Friday afternoon, through the Sabbath and into the dawn of the first day of the following week. Can we imagine the scene in that room on that evening? After the tragic events of the previous forty-eight hours, or of what the Christian tradition celebrates with the apparent misnomer of Good Friday, the disciples had found refuge in the Upper Room, their hearts numb with intense emotions, their minds dazed by a choking conglomerate of memories and disillusions.

These people had gambled their life for this Jesus. Admittedly, in the end, most of them failed to understand who Jesus was or grasp his message and the purpose of his ministry. Indeed, their motives for following him were not always commendable, and even less kingdom-oriented, often allowing their own agenda to obscure and silence the message of Jesus they claimed to follow. The request of the mother of the two sons of Zebedee asking that her two sons be number one and number two in the kingdom is a classic example of such misunderstanding and misguided motivation (Matthew 20:20-23). Nevertheless, they had taken the risk. Whatever their personal expectations, they had put their trust in Jesus of Nazareth who spoke with authority and stood up for the downtrodden. His message and deeds were proof enough for them to believe that he was the Messiah, and so, in spite of their egocentric expectations, they had followed him in good faith for three years. Gambling their present and their future, they had left behind home, jobs and personal securities in order to follow him.

Now, trapped by guilt and fear, that decision to follow the young preacher from Galilee seemed so futile and so tragic in its outcome. Hiding in shadowy distance and deceit, they had witnessed it all. All but one of them had disappeared at the sight of his plea. One had actually betrayed him for blood money. Moreover, the one who had so boldly declared that he would stand by him even in the face of death (John 13:37), had actually denied him to his face (Matthew 16:21). They had seen him captured, tried, and executed, the ignominious and horrendous death of a rebellious criminal, before being buried in a borrowed grave.

In that abandonment and hasty burial, all his claims and promises were now buried with him, and so were their hopes, their plans, and their future. Would the same fate await them who had trusted and followed him? They felt cheated, let down and hopeless. All they had to hold on to now was the memory of a dead Master and of an incredibly tragic personal story. The Lord was dead, and even the grave had become the ultimate sign of total annihilation. Graves are meant to hold dead bodies; but on the evidence reported by some women who had visited the grave before daybreak on the third day, this grave, now apparently empty, seemed to taunt them in their sense of ultimate annihilation and absolute nothingness. Yes, they felt cheated, let down, and utterly hopeless. Their heart could harbour only disappointment, fear, bleakness and anger. .

In this ambience, nothing made sense for those people gripped by fear and mistrust, except the need for security and personal safety. Seeking peace of mind and refuge of body, they sought shelter behind locked doors and gathered in the Upper

Room, the place of memory and of intimacy with the Teacher. Moreover, much more than behind heavy bolts and beams, these people were unreservedly locked within themselves, in their fears, their guilt, their hopelessness, and in their anger. It was dark all around, but the inner darkness was far more intense and death-dealing than any pre-dawn absence of light could possibly be. In that same room, Jesus had said his final good-byes, and they had heard his passionate words of consolation and encouragement, though now those words sounded so hollow and almost mocking.

The scenario is one of loss of immeasurable consequence, and of emptiness. Their dreams and plans shattered, they would try to put the tragic chapter of their story completely out of their mind, and perhaps time would heal the wounds of their misguided adventure, if that would ever be possible. Engaged in a cruel game of hopeless waiting, all they could do now was to let the furore simmer down before returning each to what they knew before, their fields, their nets, and their tax collecting. That was all what was left, and that was their final decision for the time ahead: going back into a past that was no more by putting the whole cruel chapter of their present story out of their minds, in a futile hope of forgetting forever the tragic and unfortunate events that brought them to this point.

Escapes and alibi

Casually, almost to relieve the tension of his dark thoughts and crushing fears, Peter makes one of those impulsive decisions so typical of the impulsive rough old fisherman of Galilee. "I am going fishing!" he blurts out. "At the very least, I am returning into my familiar ground, where I belong, and doing what I know", he would have thought. Like the disciples of Emmaus, in an effort to quash their pain and the memory of the whole tragic venture, they leave Jerusalem, the place of promise now turned into disillusionment, suffering and death, and they choose to return to the tried and true of familiar places and fulfilling jobs. They go fishing, back into their world, and so escape the present sad reality crushing all energy and hope out of their hearts and minds.

What Peter is really doing is escaping from the tragic reality that is confronting him. In his mind, returning to the tried and true of what-I-know will enable him to forget, to pretend that it never happened, to exorcise his demons, and to put it all behind as a bad dream. Peter is searching for security by escaping into the past and in the only situation that he knows, a fishing boat on the lake. Unfortunately, in hindsight, in so doing he is refusing to confront his present situation and to face the tragic and painful decisions that the future will inevitably demand of him. In an attempt at redeeming himself, Peter takes refuge in his own personally styled securities of the past. He rejects entirely both present and future. Focused entirely on himself, wallowing in self-pity and angry at the breakdown of his own expectations, he goes back to the past and to the things he knows and likes as the only way to safeguard his own future. By embracing the tried and true of a static past as the only safeguard of his present situation and of his future life journey, he relies on fictitious alibis, and he refuses to grow through the present situation, uncomfortable and painful though it may be.

Some of the disciples join him, and we are told that they spend the night shrouded in the darkness, and in the silence and loneliness of the once familiar lake, a darkness and loneliness that are but a reflection of their state of mind and of the emptiness of their hearts. The darkness is much deeper inside them. Their hopes shattered, their fears, loneliness, and tiredness crushing, and the result is emptiness of the soul. Yes, it is all emptiness and failure, within their hearts, as much as in their boat.

Now they are returning, their fishing nets limp and empty, coming out of the darkness of the night, a silent darkness eating away inside them. They are hopeless and exhausted, crushed by disappointment and loneliness, with nothing to show for their endeavours. Not that they, the acknowledged fishermen of Capernaum and districts, are in a mood to discuss their fruitless struggles, or talk to anyone for that matter. But they are not alone. There on the shore stands a lonely figure looking out at them as they strain to bring an empty boat to shore. I must confess to a chronic fishing ignorance, but I know that the worst possible question you could ask a fisherman who has little or nothing wriggling in his fishing bucket, is precisely the question of whether "they are biting". It is better to leave the likely response to the imagination. As if to mock them in their misfortunes, the stranger on the shore asks them precisely the one question they just do not want to hear. No, they caught nothing; they have to admit it, even if that admission hurts even more than the failure itself. Even that past into which they have escaped turns into meaningless nothingness.

What's more, that stranger on the shore, unrecognised, alone at the breaking of the day, seems to mock them in their misfortune. Not only does he ask the one question they do not want to hear, he even dares to dispense senseless fishing instructions. Fancy telling a seasoned fisherman like Peter, after a fruitless and frustrating night on the lake – his lake! –how to catch fish, now that the sun is rising! The silent thoughts of those disciples spell it out so eloquently: "This fishing instruction is totally senseless!" Given what we know of the impulsiveness of Peter, we can well surmised that what followed is more of a dare to prove a point, than trusting enthusiasm at the invitation of the stranger to do something that made no sense. He throws the nets.

If this sounds like a familiar story, it is indeed the familiar story of each believer. A story, however, that makes Easter what it is meant to be: a healing and living reality for all of us here today. None of us is immune from pain and loss. When darkness strikes deep and personal, when the unexpected and the unwanted take the shape of normality, when hope has become a mirage, then God has become the Absent One. Then we want to ignore, deny, and hide into illusions. Then, we are the disciples desperately pretending to escape the painful reality before us, struggling aimlessly and fruitlessly in the dark of illness, loneliness, misunderstanding, abuse, or rejection. And all the time with no results for our efforts. Like the disciples, unless we accept and confront the negativity of the present and move through rather than away from the challenges of whichever kind, we will remain forever empty handed, unfulfilled, without future and without hope.

When brokenness, misunderstandings, and the most diverse manifestations of suffering and death grip our bodies, minds and heart, healing demands honesty and courage, beginning with the admission that we are people in need and do not have all the answers. When we are steeped in darkness, pain, and failure, healing begins with confronting the whole scenario and owning it as our reality, without present alibi, past blame, or escape into a future of fictitious fantasy. Healing begins with embracing the situation now as the only place where the Lord we have betrayed, or who seems to have disappeared from our experience, is to be found.

The plunge of blind faith

"And there stood Jesus on the shore... ", an unknown and unrecognised stranger out of the early morning shadows, alone on a silent shore, inviting professional men to do things that have neither sense nor logic.

Without conviction and against all fishing-sense, the disciples accepted the challenge of the Stranger and lowered their nets. The impossible happens. The catch of their lives! Although it had all begun in dramatic circumstances, this was an exceptional catch. Once more, humanly speaking, it just did not make sense, but the message was clear. Only the Lord could pull this one off. Seeking self-pity and wrapped in their personal anguish, they fail to remember and to recognise the Lord who called them friends (John 15:14.15), and reassured them that he would never leave them orphans (John 14:18.27). Suddenly, the Lord, whose parting had brought about this inner darkness and all-pervading emptiness, stood there on the shore, at dawn, almost unwanted, certainly unrecognised.

The impossible now is not only possible, but real. The one they had seen condemned, crucified and buried three days before, is now standing there before them, beckoning them and advising them on something that they know better than most. That is what we celebrate at Easter, and this is the foundational statement of our Christian faith and hope: accepting that the impossible is now real, and that not even death could keep God away from us. Indeed, that stranger on the shore of our life seemed to taunt us, because it appeared just not humanly possible. Unless of course they are prepared to see a presence beyond the sensory experience, and remember the recent past when the Lord had reassured them that

> "(in) a little while, and you will no longer see me, and again a little while, and you will see me" (John16:16),

and accept that for God even human impossibilities are not only possible, but real.

If there was one thing Peter knew, it was how to catch fish, and this was neither the place nor the time for such a business. Dare or trust, the redeeming feature for Peter and the disciples was that they had the courage to accept the challenge even if only to prove the stranger wrong. They followed his ill-advised invitation to throw the nets where they were adamant that there was nothing. Paradoxically, that one moment of daring faith became the turning point, not only for the surprising and unexpected catch, but a life turning point for Peter and the disciples themselves. In that one blind and senseless acceptance of the Stranger's word, they experienced Resurrection, they discovered the presence of the Living One, and they encountered the God whom not even death could keep away from them. That is Easter: the courage and wisdom of blind faith that proclaims and lives, energised by the absolute conviction that not even death can keep God away from us.

Like the disciples, we may not even recognise the Stranger-God asking us to walk paths that do not make sense. Our life plans and expectations can be subverted, and we may still wonder about God's ways, seemingly so meaningless to our human rationality. However, one thing is now sure: in the midst of our darkest night of confusion and death, everything becomes possible because God is there, looking at us, forever present to us, as we trudge and struggle without apparent success and wonder what our future may hold.

Through such experiences, are we prepared to take the plunge of faith against any fishing sense? Faith does not deny struggle and darkness, but accepts the senselessness of the unwanted and the unknown. Somehow, God is there, struggling with us, even when we fail to recognise his presence in us and all around us. Faith is taking the plunge blind, in the conviction that, if not even death could keep God away from us, then everything, absolutely everything is possible for those who put their trust in this Stranger-God.

Glimpses and memories of an unrecognised presence

Faith is trust energised by memory. How do we respond to God's unexpected revelations in our lives? If we pause and honestly consider our personal lives, we become instinctively aware that our collective and individual stories are dotted with a myriad of incidents that reveal the active presence of God in our journeys. However, an almost pathological focus on past mistakes or an obsessively self-centred approach to reality often nullify the life-giving power of such experiences. When viewed in hindsight, for the person of faith, these experiences buried in the depth of our psyche are glimpses of God strewn along the path of life. Friendship, healing, courage, hope, love, compassion, and forgiveness – these are but a few of the glimpses of God in our past life, and we need to bring them to consciousness and let them spur us on to future hope. If we are to be people who encounter the Risen Christ, and not just look for a dead body in empty tomb (like the pre-Easter Mary of Magdala), we must engage memory and thus recall what God has done for us along our personal journey.

Have you ever stood alone, wondering on the why of suffering, feeling empty about the present and hopeless about the future, or asking yourself where God is? How often in our lives, we find ourselves confronting the apparently impossible and unimaginable, the humanly senseless and hopeless, all along calling out to an absent or dead God. An impossible God often seems to be asking us to follow impossible paths. Sometimes, our sense of failure and loss is such that our best energies seem to be channelled at forgetting, ignoring, pretending or seeking consolation and future in a long-lost past of our own making.

The great catch of fish set up a whole range of reactions from the disciples. Bewilderment, unbelief, and questions rush with the unleashed energy of a tsunami into the minds of those caught in the extraordinary catch. However, only one is able *to see* through it all. "*It is the Lord!*' cries out the Beloved disciple. For John, the event sparked a glimpse of memory of what the Lord had done, and that glimpse obliterated the very concept of a dead Lord, but brought this Lord alive into the reality where they were now.

This morning encounter by the lake leaves no doubt that our God is the God of unexpected demands and surprises, calling us constantly to acknowledge the presence in absence of this God through openness of mind triggered by memory. Amid the excitement of the moment and the busyness of hauling ashore the unexpected catch, only the Beloved disciple *remembered*, and he had no hesitation in acknowledging and proclaiming the Stranger on the shore as "*The Lord*". The memory of what Jesus had done and the significance of the event left no doubt in his mind that only the Lord could bring all this about. *"It is the Lord!"* he cried out, convinced that only the Jesus he knew could have done this. This glimpse of memory was sufficient to engender a typical attack of recklessness on Peter's part. Ignoring and abandoning the astonishing haul of fish, Peter instinctively jumped into the water to reach that very Master whom he has denied to his face in the darkest moment of their life together, but now present in his life.

Unfortunately, as if driven by an endemic paranoia of guilt and victimhood, all too often when we look back, our memory becomes almost automatically gripped by the less savoury fare of our stories, focusing readily on misfortunes, setbacks and personal mistakes. Undergirding this menu of self-pity and self-justification is an unspoken notion of a God judge and jury all at once, a despot who, after throwing us into the maelstrom of human fragility and brokenness, stands aloof and distant, scrutinising our vain attempts at survival and personal salvation. This perception annihilates any possibility of a loving God-presence in our life, and we completely fail to acknowledge and appropriate the many experiences of life-giving divine presence that have energised us and brought us to this point of our story.

At the same time, as life unfolds, we all encounter experiences that seemed insurmountable, causing a great deal of pain and grief at the time; and yet, they turned out to be marker events highlighting our journey. If nothing else, we have travelled through these trying moments, and we have grown because of them, and in spite of them. We have survived in situations that originally seemed hopelessly crushing, finding an undefined but real energy to journey through individual and communal struggles and infidelities. We cannot ignore the concrete and down-to-earth love and care that people have lavished on us, sometime unbeknown to us. Most of all, we cannot obliterate that silent and deep seated awareness of the goodness that is inherent in our spiritual DNA, breathed into our human frame at the very beginning of time by the Creator, who found us very good (Genesis 1:26-27). For the person of faith, these are glimpses of God, and they can become significant stimuli towards facing new and unexpected challenges ahead and spurring us onto future hope.

All of us have lived through such significant experiences that have touched us and unexpectedly transformed us into who we are, and we must acknowledge them and bring them to consciousness as energy for life now. We cannot deny friendship given and received, courage and determination of an elderly family member, hope and joy at encountering and embracing after a long absence, the birth of a child after a less than optimistic doctor's prognosis. We cannot dismiss or forget similar experiences without denying the active and living presence of God in our story. These are the glimpses that tell us that no matter what the human drama may throw into our face, our God is forever present and totally caught in that drama to sustain, guide and reassure us. We must have the honesty and the courage to engage memory and call out with the Disciple, "*It is the Lord!*", or we will never survive the present and only deny all hope for the future.

Faith is trust energised by memory, and if we are to encounter the God Jesus came to reveal, and not just brood over our tribulations nurturing an endemic depressive self-hatred, we must engage memory and recall what God has done for us along our personal and communal journey. By remembering the past, we have reasons to rejoice in the present and to embrace the future with confidence and hope, because he is there, and he will be there forever, calling out, "Come and have breakfast with me", because from now on not even death can take us away from each other. "Nothing, absolutely nothing can come between us, except mutual and eternal love" (Romans 8:31-39).

Called into intimacy

Easter is not a day or a season recalling an event of long ago, but a verb enjoining on us to live in the awareness and acceptance of an eternal God-presence seeking us, standing by us at all times and in all circumstances, and inviting us into a personal life-giving relationship. That is the one security of Christian faith, and the source of that peace Jesus came to bring to his broken and hopeless disciples on that morning by the lake. Referring to Francis of Assisi's insight that "the one we are looking for is the one looking for us", Barbara Fiand writes:

> We are... "gazed upon" and have been from the beginning. This initial luring, this invitation to plunge into the Mystery that haunts all of us in various forms – even unrecognised ones – throughout our life... is therefore primordial.[49]

For the believing disciple, somehow God is in the struggle and darkness, struggling with us, even when we fail to recognise his presence in our own life and all around us. Even in the midst of

---

49 Barbara Fiand, *From Religion Back to Faith*, New York, NY: The Crossroad Publishing Company, 2006, 59

our darkest night of confusion and death, God is there, looking at us, present to us for good, and forever.

What John 21 is saying to us is that our life plans can be totally subverted and at times God's ways may appear quite meaningless and even subversive to human expectations. But for the person of faith, God is forever the "God of surprises" as Gerard Hughes reminds us, standing and watching us and eventually inviting us into his friendship and life, as the final scene illustrates. Having revealed himself as the Living One in the midst of the darkest night of confusion and in spite of death, in a gesture of deep familiarity and sincere welcome, Jesus calls those very ones who had let him down, denied him, and abandoned him to the most horrendous of deaths *friends*. He invites his doubtful and confused disciples into table fellowship, the ultimate sign of togetherness, acceptance, and love. *"Come and have breakfast"*, he encourages them.

One of the fundamental expressions of all religious cultures is the ritual of the meal, and, in the biblical tradition, the meal takes on a sacramental significance not only as a symbol but as an actualisation of the relationship between Yahweh and his people. For the biblical person, sharing a meal together is both the sign and the instrument of deep personal intimacy between the individual and God, and an expression of the deep friendship of the participants with each other.

Table fellowship dominates much of Jesus' life and teaching, reaching its most powerful climax in the Supper of the Upper Room. There, in the context of a sacred meal, Jesus gives free rein to his emotions for his disciples, reassuring them that in spite of whatever lies ahead, there will always be an unbreakable, three-way oneness between the disciples and Jesus, the Father, and the disciples among themselves. That was his last will and testament and his goodbye gathering that they would remember for the rest of their lives (John 13-17), and which we celebrate for all times at the Eucharistic table. Regardless of their personal and collective stories, he is the one who is forever with them, and reminds them of this divine and human oneness through table fellowship. He invites them to gather around a charcoal fire with bread and fish cooking on it – a gesture carrying a powerful Eucharistic sacramental flavour, a "sacred moment" (sacrament). *"Come and have breakfast"*.

The final destiny of the disciple is to enter into a personal relationship of love and intimacy with God, and nothing will frustrate this primordial dream of God. That is why he is there, hidden but ever-present to everyone, irrespective of who we are or what we have done. No matter what life may have in store for us, God wants to share fully every experience in a loving relationship so intimate and eternal that not even death can break or nullify. We do not seek nor create intimacy through personal faith and mission. We must simply make ourselves available to God entering into intimacy with us.

The God who lived fully and tragically our life experience to the ultimate degree of crucifixion and death is the very God who will not allow us to be swallowed up in death and darkness ever again. On the contrary, he calls us into a personal relationship of care, welcome and deep love.

Such an invitation to a personal relationship, however, holds also a serious and inevitable challenge, thrusting us unconditionally into an intensely passionate community dimension. As the disciples are invited to the banquet of bread and fish, so we too are called to his table with each other. The Eucharistic is both the expression and the vehicle of encounter with the Risen Christ, not through a ritual but through the living interaction of those who share table fellowship. Eucharist is a gift of presence and a commitment to be with, and it is only through this community interaction that we encounter the Risen Christ and both experience and express the living and loving presence of God with us. After all, Jesus summed up his last will and testament in that all embracing and life-giving energy called love.

> *As the Father has loved me, so I have loved you; abide in my love. If you keep my commandments, you will abide in my love, just as I have kept my Father's commandments and abide in his love. I have said these things to you so that my joy may be in you, and that your joy may be complete. 'This is my commandment, that you love one another as I have loved you* (John 15:9-12).

The mission

It is difficult to imagine the plethora of feelings that, tsunami-like must have stirred mind and heart for those disciples as they sat on the shore consuming that unplanned and unexplained abundance of fish and bread.

> *Now none of the disciples dare to ask him, "Who are you?" because they knew it was the Lord* (John 21:12).

In the face of what God works in our life, we cannot escape a certain lingering doubting Thomas syndrome. Maybe it is too good to be true, and an unacknowledged sense of guilt and unworthiness lingers deep and persistent in our psyche making us, rather than God, the centrepiece of our story. Consequently, Jesus, as he always does throughout the gospel narrative, takes the initiative and opens up the conversation by focusing not on their brokenness but on healing love. Three times he addresses the same question to Peter. *"Simon son of John, do you love me more than these?"* (John 21:15-16).

As if using a strange ploy of reverse psychology, by the triple question to Peter on whether he loves him, Jesus seems to elicit from the old fisherman of Capernaum a response to the love Jesus himself offers to the man who denied him repeatedly. That triple declaration of love that Jesus seems to be seeking goes far beyond an affirmative assent of "Yes, I love you", but generates an explosive energy rising from deep inside Peter's psyche and investing the totality of his being. Peter's response is fascinating. How would we feel being asked the same question three times? Do we begin to doubt, or may get upset? That is exactly what Peter does: he gets upset. Our God is a God of persistence who just will not let us go, and that can be upsetting to our understanding and our personal agenda. After answering positively to the same question twice, Peter felt hurt, and in typical Peter-fashion, he becomes rather forceful and emotional. He is hurt and angry at this persistence, while Jesus seems to be satisfied only after the third response, not an academic head answer, but a response bursting out of Peter's heart, full of emotion and energy.

> *When they had finished breakfast, Jesus said to Simon Peter, 'Simon son of John, do you love me more than these?' He said to him, 'Yes, Lord; you know that I love you.' Jesus said to him, 'Feed my lambs.' A second time he said to him, 'Simon son of John, do you love me?' He said to him, 'Yes, Lord; you know that I love you.' Jesus said to him, 'Tend my sheep.' He said to him the third time, 'Simon son of John, do you love me?' Peter felt hurt because he said to him the third time, 'Do you love me?' And he said to him, 'Lord, you know everything; you know that I love you.' Jesus said to him, 'Feed my sheep* (John 21:15-17).

Like Peter, we certainly love the Lord and we are ready to protest this love. Unfortunately, like Peter's response to the first two questions, often this love remains an intellectual or academic assent, a head response. It was only after Jesus addressed the same question for the third time that Peter's response welled up energetic and passionate from the heart. He felt hurt, and, knowing the Peter of the Gospels, possibly he was also a little angry. It is easy to say we love God, but is this love the energy of our life, the conviction of our beliefs and the stimulus of our relationship, all welling up from inside of us as part of who we are and of our primal spiritual DNA? Unless this love invests the totality of our being at the deepest level of mind and heart, our protestation of love will remain a rational or cultural level, a "good-boy/nice-girl" assertion; certainly not the expression of a relationship with our God getting hold of us and compelling us into total acceptance of his energy in us and towards each other in community.

Love is a hallmark of John's Gospel and the key to discipleship, both as the gift of being loved unconditionally by our God, and as a life-commitment to unconditional love for each other through incarnating the values and attitudes of the Good Shepherd towards his sheep (John 10). That is what loving God means: awareness of being caught up in an energy that invests the wholeness of who we are and explodes in the reality of what we live. Only then Jesus seems satisfied.

The reassurance of God's unconditional care and loving presence in our life must become energy for action, because the Word of God does not allow for privacy. The Word always carries a universal social dimension, enjoining on the disciples a missionary intent. Faith in the God of love transcends any form of privatisation and individualism, detached or unaware of any other member of the community. We are precious in God's eyes because we belong with others, and others will discover their preciousness to God through our life lived with them. Gifted by God's loving and life-giving presence, in turn each disciple must become a wounded healer, bearing such gifts to the whole world. Aware of being shepherded into safety and fulfilment by our God, now we have no option but to become shepherds and bearers of peace and salvation. Failing this awareness and commitment to community on our part, Jesus' life and death on our behalf becomes devoid of energy for the whole world. Then our claim to faith could well turn into that plundering action of betrayal, destruction and death of the flock against which the prophets warned us centuries ago (Ezekiel 34:1-10), and Jesus himself pointed out with great realism (John 8:8, 10).

Within the scenario of table fellowship and intimate friendship mixed with darkness, uncertainty, confusion and denial, Jesus elicits from Peter that triple declaration of love. Yes, Peter, the broken and rough man who had denied his Lord, has not lost the love for his Lord, or as Pope Francis would say, 'sinner but not bad'.[50] Each assertion of love by Peter is met with a very clear injunction on the part of Jesus to reach out of himself, to go and feed God's flock and look after God's sheep.

> *'Peter, do you love me?... Feed my lambs... Look after my sheep!* (John 21:15-17).

In this way, Jesus points out the indissoluble link between our relationship with God and the mission to foster and nurture this relationship with the whole world. Now that he has experienced the care, love and healing presence of Jesus, Peter has no other option but to become a carer, a lover, and a healing presence for others. Mission can only be the outflow of recognising God in our life, and allowing God to enter into intimacy with us.

Throughout the Fourth Gospel, this is the first and only instance where we encounter an explicit missioning, and such that enjoins on Peter the divine expectation not only to become a shepherd, but, in doing so, to move away from the gatherer for himself that was Peter the fisherman to a guardian and a nurturer of others. Peter could catch fish (except that night, apparently!) but minding sheep would have been utterly unknown to the fisherman of Capernaum. Peter knew nothing about shepherding, yet his protestation of faith in the Lord commits him to become Peter the shepherd, minding sheep and lambs. It does not matter

---

50 Pope Francis, *The Name of God is Mercy*, 2016, 37-47.

if Peter knows nothing about animal husbandry, because when God calls he calls us *out of* where we are and *into* something else, often something we do not know. The fisherman must become a shepherd.

The Christian community is not a social, cultural, political, racial, or any other form of ghetto. Nor is it a conglomerate of gregarious individuals jealously guarding their private patch with God, bearing a personally distinctive badge, and congregating under some artificial religious banner. Central to Christian faith is the absolute and active conviction of oneness within a living integration of people who acknowledge, love, and accept each other, energised by the Shepherd-God, who is prepared to lay down his life for them, and leading them securely into personal and communal fulfilment of life and love.

As Christians, we cannot and must not claim exclusivity and even less perfectionism at any level of our community. Indeed, Jesus himself has strong words of condemnation for the leadership that seeks personal fulfilment and destroys and pillages the Christian community (John 10:11-13). As a human reality, no church is perfect and we must own the truth that often individuals and indeed shepherds will wander and go astray, leaving the community to bear the scars and weaknesses of brokenness and infidelity. The temptation to control is a powerful and destructive energy in all of us, choosing to break through the enclosure of community and love, rather than following the shepherd through the gate of fidelity.

Dependency and availability

If we are prepared to accept that our God stands by us, seeking us and safeguarding us whatever our daily experiences, then we can journey on and be shepherds to each other with courage and hope, safe in the unshakable conviction that we are loved even in our individual or collective unfaithfulness, that we are enlightened in our darkness, and that we are strengthened in our weakness and brokenness. However, this security comes at the cost of abandonment and trust, as the last words of Jesus to Peter forcibly point out. Those words represent the very bedrock of that oneness of life and relationship that underscore not only John 21, but the whole of Johannine faith and discipleship.

> *When you were young you put on your belt and walked where you liked; but when you grow old you will stretch out your hands, and somebody else will put a belt around you and take you where you would rather not go* (John 21:18).

Accepting the living and healing presence of God in our life and becoming wounded healers for each other means to become paralytics for the kingdom, relinquishing all control on one's life and becoming totally dependent on God. We have to become instruments of God's love and peace, but mission is not something that we do, nor is discipleship something we take on for ourselves, according to our own agenda or personal endeavours. Mission is the inescapable consequence of letting God univocally into our life, as we become instruments of his love and life to others. In those final words of forewarning, Jesus is not talking about chronology but about relationship of mutual love. The deeper we delve into God's love and allow ourselves to be taken over by this divine energy, the more we become aware of our inadequacy and insufficiency in responding to God. Taking his cue from the human process of growing physically older, Jesus speaks of growing into that state of mind that has no longer any reference to self, having abdicated all that self to total openness and total availability to God. The more we grow into a loving relationship with our God present in absence, even if unknown and unrecognised, the more we feel that we are no longer arbiter of our lives, whatever shape that life may be.

Only when we reach this state of total insufficiency, abandonment, and complete reliance on God, are we ready for discipleship. At that final injunction demanding total dependency and lack of personal control of one's life, Jesus turns to Peter and says, "*Follow me!*" (John 21:19). Although John opens his Gospel narrative with a dramatic and frenetic calling of the disciples in a variety of circumstances and of real down-to-earth human interactions (John 1:35-51), the Fourth evangelist never uses the technical term, "Follow me" except now, at the very end of the story. When we have lost all control of our own self and abandoned our life into the totality of God, then we are ready for discipleship, because then God will be free to shape us and use us as instruments for his greater glory and the transformation of the world. Then "God alone suffices", as Teresa of Avila would proclaim, and God alone becomes the energy standing there on the shore, in the night, inviting us even when we do not know or fail to recognise him. We just have to let go and embrace total dependency and absolute destitution, trusting in God and on God's terms alone. Then we will be true disciples not because of what we would have done or achieved, but because of our readiness to let God do with us what God wants, and as God wants.

Destiny

The Kingdom – Presence in Absence
Mark 16:15-20; Matthew 28:1-10

So when they had come together, they asked him, 'Lord, is this the time when you will restore the kingdom to Israel?' He replied, 'It is not for you to know the times or periods that the Father has set by his own authority. But you will receive power when the Holy Spirit has come upon you; and you will be my witnesses in Jerusalem, in all Judea and Samaria, and to the ends of the earth.' When he had said this, as they were watching, he was lifted up, and a cloud took him out of their sight. While he was going and they were gazing up towards heaven, suddenly two men in white robes stood by them. They said, 'Men of Galilee, why do you stand looking up towards heaven? This Jesus, who has been taken up from you into heaven, will come in the same way as you saw him go into heaven (Acts 1:6-11).

Confusion and promises fulfilled

At the end of the liturgical cycle of Easter centred on Jesus' appearances to his disciples after his resurrection, the liturgy puts before us the last such encounter in what Christian tradition has come to know as the Ascension of Jesus to the Father.

On the last evening of his earthly life, Jesus gathered his disciples in the upper room, the place that was to become the hub of the followers of Jesus. In an atmosphere of intense emotion and in the intimacy of a ritual meal, Jesus engaged in a long conversation, in a mantra-like persistence on the theme of love, mixing expressions of deep sentiments with down-to-earth realism. Warning his followers about what lay ahead, he made no secret about the fact that very soon, he would no longer be with them, and they would be looking for him in vain.

At that long Last Supper conversation, Jesus spoke at length to his disciples about his leaving them, telling them persistently that he would be going home *"to prepare a place"* for them, while at the same time repeatedly reassuring them that he would not leave them orphan or alone. Not that such reassurance contributed in any way to ease their pain when events precipitated rapidly both for Jesus and for his disciples, as within a few hours they saw him hanging dead on a cross and his body entombed in a grave.

Yet, within a few hours, unbelievably, he was in their presence again, keeping his promise that he would be back with them (John 14:3) after rising from the dead. However, the alternate current of presence and absence continued, and soon after he left them for the second time, and this time definitively, when he would return to his Father and our Father, to his God and to our God, as he had told them many times before that he would (John 20:17).

This hide and seek sequence of Jesus dying and rising, appearing and disappearing, sharing a meal and vanishing from their eyes only threw the disciples into deeper confusion, a roller coaster of contradictory emotions, a bewilderment of cosmic proportion. As he had warned them, the disciples are truly lost, not knowing what to make of him, of his dying and of his being with them again. Yet, through it all, they became gripped by the power of an experience that had no human rationale beyond the fact that only God could have brought this about. They had seen Jesus dead and buried and yet there he was, inside a locked room, asking them for a piece of fish to eat. As they stood, their minds numb with confusion and fear, he greeted them with the gift of peace. They were running away, trying to forget and pretend it had never happened, and he falls in step with them on the road, sharing their pain and enlivening their hope. He is back from the dead, totally himself, and yet they will never be able to hold onto him as they did before (John 20:17).

During that central revelatory conversation at the Last Supper (John 14:12.28), Jesus had already primed his disciples for the pain of separation, repeatedly foreshadowing the fact that he would leave them and go away. Likewise, after his Resurrection, in the encounter with Mary, distraught for the loss of her Master and searching for him as a dead body in an empty tomb, the risen Jesus reassures her of his living presence beyond death, but points beyond the here and now telling her,

> *Do not hold on to me, because I have not yet ascended to the Father. But go to my brothers and say to them, "I am ascending to my Father and your Father, to my God and your God* (John 20:18).

Such a strange mix of reassurance and warning will remain obscure to the disciples for a time; but to us, with the hindsight of two thousand years of Christian Tradition, it has the flavour of a preamble to some momentous event representing the climax of the Gospel narrative, and the final fulfilment of Jesus' life and mission. Clearly, Jesus is saying goodbye to his disciples, but a goodbye full of promise and expectation.

In the Gospel narratives, Jesus leaves the disciples not once but twice, the second time definitely and forever as he returns to the Father in that unique and mysterious event that the Christian Tradition calls the Ascension, the event that reproposes the same pre-resurrection scenario. Each time the disciples face the confusion of extremes and all the transforming consequences, and each time they are called to make sense of unexplained and unexpected loss, abandonment and confusion (Acts1:6-11). In both cases, the disciples have to deal with a situation of immeasurable loss and of hopeless emptiness. At the same time, in both cases, the disciples are caught up in an event that becomes a turning point in their individual stories, as well as in the community story. In both cases, in the end, the deep sense of loss somehow explodes into a sense of wonder and joy that defies human words, and transposes those who lived through it into a totally new level of reality and self-understanding. Thus, Jesus' Ascension to the Father is more than just physical hovering in the sky, but a revelation that the Lord has now ascended to a totally other level of reality, a level that defies time and space, nearness or distance, physical absence or personal presence. Jesus' Ascension is both the fulfilment of a promise and a confirmation of a destiny. At the last supper, Jesus had expressed his earthly goodbyes from his disciples precisely in word of contradiction, of presence in absence, of down to earth realism pointing to final destiny.

> *Do not let your hearts be troubled. Believe in God, believe also in me. In my Father's house there are many dwelling-places. If it were not so, would I have told you that I go to prepare a place for you? And if I go and prepare a place for you, I will come again and will take you to myself, so that where I am, there you may be also* (John 14:1-3).

The post Resurrection disciples and the believers of all times will always be trapped in a confusion of extremes, an interplay of presence in absence, of intimacy without possessiveness, of fullness of life when all the evidence points to death. Jesus is there, but he is no longer theirs. The disciples can not only no longer hold on to the Lord as their possession, but precisely when they reach out to him as they knew him, the Risen Lord constantly distances himself from them, as the end of the Emmaus event beautifully declares (Luke 24:13-35). That is the dominant constant of the biblical narrative, highlighting the twin event of Resurrection and Ascension as the one experience of the Lord without any personally physical experience of his sensory presence. This is also the call for all of us when we claim faith in Jesus, dead and risen, and forever the living revelation of God with us.

Ending and beginnings

Ascension celebrates the fulfilment of those anticipated predictions, although the disciples will be forever caught in the dilemma of opposites to the end, and, as Matthew says in his narrative of the Ascension, those first eyewitnesses failed spectacularly to understand the meaning of Jesus' words. "*On that mountain some doubted*", (Matthew 28:17). As such, the context of today's celebration carries a significant element of closure. Together with the celebration of Pentecost, this gathering on the mountain of Galilee brings to conclusion not only the liturgical cycle of Easter, but the earthly story and mission of Jesus. At the same time, the final words of Jesus clearly declare the very opposite of any departure or conclusion. Instead, they speak of new beginnings and of presence now and in the future. The closing line of Matthew's Gospel, "*I am with you always, to the end of the age*" (Matthew 28:20), was Jesus' welcome greeting into a totally new reality for those who stood by him on the mountain, wondering and confused at what was happening to them and around them. Once again, we have that interface of beginning and endings, of future and past, and of presence and absence which intertwine and dominate the Easter narratives and our post-Easter liturgical season.

Just as the Resurrection had been the supreme proclamation revealing the eternal, unfailing and life-giving presence of the Lord beyond and in spite of the finality of death in the human story, the final earthly goodbye of Jesus to those who followed him is the absolute reassurance of this eternal presence beyond and in spite of his physical absence in their future story. Ascension celebrates the continuity of God's eternal presence-in-absence in our lives and in our world, in life and in death.

While Matthew and Mark hint at this duality of perspective, Luke clearly highlights both dimensions of ending and beginning by giving us two diverse narratives of the event, each connecting a story of past and future at the same time. At the end of his Gospel, Luke says,

> *while he (Jesus) was blessing them, he withdrew from them and was carried up into heaven* (Luke 24:51).

However, things do not end there. The third evangelist picks up the same event as the opening lines of the Book of Acts with an obvious forward intentionality and mission. Those very same disciples are repeatedly told that they are now to be his witnesses and his instruments in the Galilees of this world and for all time.

> *You will receive power when the Holy Spirit has come upon you; and you will be my witnesses in Jerusalem, in all Judea and Samaria, and to the ends of the earth.* '*When he had said this, as they were watching, he was lifted up, and a cloud took him out of their sight* (Acts 1:8-9).

Going home

On the mountain, he is true to his word, fulfilling the promise made to his immediate followers and to all believers for all time. In Jesus' rising to a new level of reality, in the midst of confusion of extremes, we are given a glimpse of our own future destiny and a commitment to live by in our present reality.

In Jesus' mind, leaving his disciples was never meant to be a separation from the present but a projection into a future of total union with the Father for himself and for all those who claimed fellowship and discipleship. Jesus' persistence about going to the Father to prepare a place for his disciples speaks clearly of going home and homecoming, and never of closure and abandonment. The pain of leaving is a function of the joy of embracing home.

The final and definitive physical appearance of Jesus to his disciples taps directly into that perennial and natural yearning of the human heart which seeks *to be at home*, tending unceasingly to reach beyond purely sensory evidence and the limitations of time and place, beyond the measurable and foreseeable. When you love someone, this person is present to you near or far, in life and in death. Ascension celebrates yearning for fulfilment, for homecoming, and for oneness, and it celebrates our roots and our destiny at the same time. At the Last Supper, Jesus spoke at length to his disciples about his leaving them, telling them persistently that he would be going home, "*to prepare a place for them*", while at the same time repeatedly reassuring them that he would not leave them orphans or alone, and promising that he would come back and take us home with him (John 14:1-3).

> *'I go to prepare a place for you. And if I go and prepare a place for you, I will come again and will take you to myself, so that where I am, there you may be also* (John 14:2-3).

That is Jesus' going-away promise and a reassurance of our inalienable destiny. He has ascended to the Father, and where he is we are all meant to be, in an eternal oneness of togetherness with each other and with the God who gave us life, and whose heart yearns just as much for our return to him as ours longs to go back home where we belong.

Allow me to share a cherished personal memory. On the last day of one of my visits to my elderly mother, the day before my departure that would take me across half the world to the other side of the globe, she gave me a precious going-away gift, one that I will treasure for the rest of my life. In the course of a casual conversation, she commented with a glint in her eyes and a wavering in her voice, "I would love you to stay a little longer, but I know that in order for both of us to enjoy your next visit home, you must go away now". That insight of a ninety-year-old seemed to echo strongly the words of Jesus when he told his disciples that it was necessary for him to go away, so that they might have fullness of life, peace, and joy in the power of the Spirit. Jesus went home so that we too might be at home.

Home is where the heart belongs, and one of the most powerful yearnings of the human heart is to find a home, to be at home, or to go home. In our normal parlance, homecoming does not refer exclusively to geographical or temporal categories. Home carries strong connotations of time and place, of emotions and of memories. All of us have experienced moments when "we feel at home", while thousands of kilometres away from our place of residence. Home is where one belongs in freedom and peace, where affections are expressed and lived out in mutual joy, where one is welcomed and where encounters and relationships blossom and are re-energised.

Ascension celebrates Jesus' homecoming as the blueprint of our own destiny – the final and eternal union with the Father. Today, we are reminded that our destiny is total union with God and with each other, precisely the kind of union which our heart yearns for and which God has destined for each of us, from eternity and for eternity. Jesus' Ascension is more than just a physical hovering in the sky before disappearing from human sight, but a revelation that the Lord has embraced a deeper and eternal horizon of reality that defies time and space, nearness or distance, physical absence or personal presence. In that raising to a new level of reality by Jesus, we are all given a glimpse of our own destiny in the future, and of a commitment to live by in the present reality for the rest of our earthy living years.

At the end of that long conversation with those he calls *children* and *friends*, after repeatedly reassuring us not to be afraid and to trust him, he places us into the hands of the Father in one of the most emotional and stirring prayers of all time on our behalf.

> *They were yours... I am asking on their behalf... on behalf of those whom you gave me, because they are yours... I am no longer in the world, but they are in the world... I am not asking you to take them out of the world, but I ask you to protect them from the evil one... Sanctify them in the truth;... so that they also may be sanctified in truth. Holy Father, protect them in your name... so that they may be one, as we are one . . . so that they may have my joy made complete in themselves* (John 17:1-14).

Wherever we may be and whatever our hearts may yearn to embrace and to hold, we rest on one absolute certainty: with his last human breath, Jesus placed us in the hands of the Father while we journey towards home, to be one with him and with each other. In these terms, the celebration of Jesus' return to the Father, rather than a departure becomes the fulfilment of his ultimate wish, and a mission for us to live his presence in oneness with each other, in the sure knowledge that in Jesus' physical absence we are in the hands of the Father and energised by the Spirit. As Jesus is with the Father, so we will be with him and with each other, in the Father's embrace forever. That is our destiny, but also a commitment for us who are left with the memory and the promise of his presence. The message is one of hope now, commitment to joy now, and unconditional love now.

The presence-absence of Jesus in the life of the disciples has all the flavour of a call to a spectacular transformation and new beginnings into a world of hope, of energy and a renewed sense of presence, because transformation and new beginnings are the very raison d'être of the Easter-Ascension-Pentecost liturgical season. Because of Ascension, the disciple is called to live through the struggles and dilemmas of making sense of the words, actions and promises of Jesus on the one hand; and on the other, of dealing with personal experiences, full of those questions, confusion and uncertainties that the first followers of Jesus experienced preceding and following the Resurrection experience.

After the Ascension, the early disciples had only the memory of Jesus, of what he did and of what he said, but a memory of an extraordinary, all-transforming experience, and a deep sense of having been chosen, befriended, called by name by Jesus, as well as of having been repeatedly left orphaned. Are we such people of transformation, of new beginnings, of renewed energy and of fresh awareness? Alternatively, do we just celebrate a series of empty rituals, perhaps gazing at events of the past like the disciples looking up into an empty sky, with no significance and even less bearing on our daily lives?

Not passive observers but committed actors

The return of Jesus to the Father marks the end of his human story. However, the celebration of God's action in the world through Jesus can never be simply an exercise of memory or ritual. Matthew ends his Gospel narrative with Jesus' mandatory injunction to *"go and make disciples of all nations"* (Matthew 28:19), and hence we are not passive spectators but primary actors in the story of humanity that Jesus lived and left behind to us – a humanity now and forever impregnated with the energy of God who, through Jesus' life and mission, will be totally and forever immersed in our human condition.

From this perspective of presence-in-absence, Ascension takes on a totally new meaning and becomes a pivotal event in the ongoing Christian story, intertwining into one past, present and future. The message of the whole Easter liturgical season is not about loss and loneliness, but about our way of life here and now, and about our perspective on the future. More than closure today we celebrate a beginning, projecting us into a future reality of love, peace and joy. Ascension is not a looking up into an empty sky, but a commitment to becoming ever more grounded on this earth, and instruments of that future of eternal love, peace, and joy in our daily reality.

At the Ascension of Jesus, the disciples stood gazing into the heavens, worrying about the destiny of Jesus, wondering, once again, about the absurdity of another good-bye, of more unanswered questions, and of further loss and loneliness. In our personal experience, at times the sense of loss can be so chronic and all-pervading that even idle wondering and speculation seem to relieve the boredom of asking questions such as "where is your God?" But the message of the Easter season is not about speculations. It cuts deeply into the sameness and practicality of our lives and, like a fiery sword of light, it challenges, and it must reshape our praxis and our perspective.

As I stand there with the disciples looking into the sky, I hear those words addressed to me personally, as *promise of companionship* as well as *words of mission*:

> *Go therefore and make disciples of all nations, baptising them in the name of the Father and of the Son and of the Holy Spirit, and teaching them to obey everything that I have commanded you. And remember, I am with you always, to the end of the age* (Matthew 28:18-20).

Today and forever, like the first disciples, we need to hear those words challenging us and heed the command spoken by the messengers of God,

> *Men of Galilee, why do you stand looking up towards heaven? This Jesus, who has been taken up from you into heaven, will come in the same way as you saw him go into heaven'* (Acts 1:11).

There is a strong sense of earthiness in the message to

> *'Go into all the world and proclaim the good news to the whole creation* (Mark 16:15),

a message projecting the disciple into a future presence and action that will bring presence in absence and peace in turmoil precisely in the earthiness of everyday life.

While leaving us to till the earth we stand on, the absence-presence of Jesus who ascends to the heavens to prepare a place for us is not some other-worldly, pie-in-the-sky dream, but a presence in spite of physical absence. This is the presence that only the heart knows and yearns for, a presence that makes us feel at home and radiates at-homeness all around us. In the end, the physical absence of Jesus in our world will only be redeemed by our presence to each other, as people embracing home and committing ourselves to the Jerusalem of our daily lives. Through liturgy and spirituality, Ascension becomes a commitment to a present and a future energised by memory of the past. Any attempt at holding on to the sensory and visible meets with the same injunction of the angels to the women at the empty tomb, at the very first announcement of Jesus' living presence beyond and in spite of death.

> *Go quickly and tell his disciples, 'He has been raised from the dead, and indeed he is going ahead of you in Galilee; there you will see him* (Matthew28:7).

Jesus himself greets the grieving women at the tomb by reassuring them with the words

> *'Go and tell my brothers to go to Galilee; there they will see me (Matthew 28:10).*

Galilee is the place of realistic practicalities, of down-to-earth simplicity, of ordinariness and of commonality, of heart-people with little regard for the strict Judaic observance or the legalistic convolutions of Jerusalem. Galilee is "the Galilee of the Gentiles'" (Matthew 4:15), the potpourri of cultures, ethnicity and traditions where reality is what you see, and what you see is never quite perfect or what you expect to find. In the Gospel narrative, Galilee is the setting of Jesus' self-revelation and mission, and our Galilee is the place where Jesus is to be encountered, and where our presence as disciples must witness to his presence in absence. The ordinary, the everyday, the unexpected and limited Galilee of our lives and of the life around us are both the place of encounter and of mission for the believing disciple.

There is a strong sense of realism in the words of Jesus, and the disciples are to stop gazing into an empty sky outside of themselves but embrace the reality of each day where they stand. They must look for and build the kingdom of God's living and active presence where they are, and there find the Lord, as much as bringing the Lord to others. The presence of Jesus in the Spirit is not some otherworldly pie-in-the-sky fantasy or fiction, but a presence in spite of physical absence enabling us to assume a new self-awareness of who we are and a new vision as to what we do, both as individuals and as a believing community. Sometimes this presence and mission may appear to us as inadequate, or even as terrifying as handling snakes and drinking poison (Mark 16:18). However, the physical absence of Jesus in our world will only be redeemed by our presence to each other, as people who know the presence of God in their own lives, and are committed to the kingdom right here and now.

No looking up to heaven

The Fourth Gospel has no official missioning in its story. And yet all the Easter narratives are pregnant with the injunction to go and proclaim what the disciples have witnessed (John 20:17; 20:23;

21:17). The missionary dimension is not an optional extra for the Easter-energised person. On the contrary, discipleship cannot be genuine unless the Good News is proclaimed by those who, beyond any sensory evidence, claim and incarnate belief in its message. The disciples are missionary by their very nature, but the mission is not their own. They are entrusted with the mission, and we cannot lay any entitlement to it except the claim to instrumentality and stewardship. The message proclaimed is not of our own making, nor do we possess the Risen Lord that we proclaim.

To Mary who wants to hold Jesus as her own possession, and so never run the danger of ever losing him again, Jesus says,

> *Do not hold on to me, because I have not yet ascended to the Father. But go to my brothers and say to them, 'I am ascending to my Father and your Father, to my God and your God* (John 20-17-18).

On that injunction, Mary of Magdala went and announced to the disciples, "*I have seen the Lord*", and became the first messenger of Good News, enjoining on the disciples the Lord's command to go and do the same to the whole world. Jesus' word to "*go and tell my brothers and sisters*" are not just an invitation, but a challenge to our authenticity as believing disciples in whatever life-journey we embrace. The drive to mission must stem from deep inside the heart of the one who claims to have seen the Lord, as an energy that comes from the Lord and leads to the Lord. The disciples never possess the Risen Lord as an exclusive, private and personal relationship, but are inalienable instruments proclaiming to the whole world by their lives what they have seen and experienced in their own lives.

Anything short of this theological understanding of mission makes for personal advancement or professional expertise, but not necessarily for discipleship and evangelisation. The disciple is to go and proclaim to the whole world that *"the Lord is risen"* (Matthew 27:40; Mark 14:58; John 2:19), even if all our senses seem to deny that presence. Our faith becomes authentic and credible only when we live by the spirit of joy and hope embedded in the Easter event, and others experience that joy and peace in us and through us.

Ascension challenges us to understand Church as a community where we belong and as the visible evidence of an eternal and life-giving presence of a God of love, compassion and hope. The Church is never and can never be a consumer of ritual legalism or a number in a sectarian club. First century Palestine spoke of the *"Galilee of the nations"* (Isaiah 8:23; Matthew 4:14-16), not as a geographical identification but as a way of being and living. Like Church for us, Galilee had a universal and people-centred connotation, linking together people of the most diverse backgrounds, social status, economic, and religious persuasions. Galilee meant life lived in the full gamut of daily experiences of work and family, struggles and success, relationships and beliefs. That is the place to which Jesus sent his disciples to carry on his mission of healing and salvation. In the potpourri of our busy suburban streets and tenement houses, in our family struggles, in our exhilarating encounters, in the boredom and difficulties of making ends meet, in giving life and in sharing love – that is the Galilees where we are sent to proclaim the living, healing, and affirming presence of God.

And we *must* do it; we have no choice, or we renege on our

very identity of believers. Unless this happens, we will be those people standing with our feet on the ground and looking into an empty sky, without understanding and without hope. Unless we become responsible instruments of peace and concrete down-to-earth committed love, the Ascension of the Lord will only degenerate into the ultimate act of separation of God from our world, his work, life and death a meaningless sophism lost in some old dusty history books. If we do not become actors of presence and instruments of life and love, not only will the world be poorer, but we will have betrayed our personal protestation of faith, and indeed we will never be able to recognise or find the very God in which we claim to believe.

In a world of efficient organisations and structures based on hierarchical systems of operation to ensure success as the ultimate and exclusive value, we may be tempted to point to the Church as the institution chosen by Christ to ensure efficiency and success in proclaiming Good News and continuing his work through time and space. However, if we do not feel personally responsible for the mission as a life-long realisation of our Baptismal claim, no institution will ever touch and transform the life of people or make God's saving presence a reality in this world. Individually and collectively, we are responsible in our time and our space, and we are weak, and sinful, and broken. This Church, called to incarnate the mission left by Jesus, carries all the frailty and weakness of humanity, and cannot make any claim to absolute perfection, nor give any guarantee of success. As someone facetiously put it, "If you want a perfect Church, please join it. Just remember that from that moment onwards, your chosen Church will no longer be perfect".

Our efforts may often appear insignificant, our vision may

be blurred, and our resolve weakened. Our witness will know rejection and attract contradiction. But Jesus is there, yes, to the end of time, and on that one certainty we commit ourselves to a world grappling with uncertainty, brokenness and searching for a meaning in the emptiness of sky and tomb. The metaphor of the vine (John 15:1-5) and of the potter (Jeremiah 18:1-6) powerfully illustrate that frailty and brokenness are inherent to our humanity, and they will always be part both of the human story and of the preciousness of each individual in the eyes of God. Jesus reminded us very clearly.

> *You did not choose me but I chose you. And I appointed you go and bear fruit, fruit that will last* (John 15:16),

and in that one choice on his part lies our greatest challenge, both in terms of commitment and of trust on our part. We will be truly disciples sent out to meet the Lord in the many Galilees of our lives, only when we are prepared to stop looking into the empty sky of speculation and theory, and enter completely into the reality of the Galilees of our lives. When we become presence to each other through serving without imposition or control, and through receiving service with openness and trust, then the vine will bear abundant fruit and the whole world will know presence and love of God through peace, joy and hope. Then, as the old storyteller would have ended, "we would have lived happily ever after" in the reality of our daily life, and in the realisation of God's dream of oneness with each other.

When our commitment to human promotion, to justice and

peace has become the lived reality for everyone in the world, then we will have finally understood Ascension, we will have listened for the first time to the parting words of Jesus, and we will have become leaven of life and love for our world and time. Only then will God become present and visible once again amidst the confusion and darkness that may surround us. Then, we will have become true disciples committed to the God with us here, and we will be journeying on our destiny of fullness of life and love together as a community and with our God.

Kingdom-Person

Mary – The First Disciple of the Kingdom
Luke 1:1-56

Of the four evangelists, only Matthew and Luke give us what we call the infancy narratives. However, while Matthew stresses decidedly the Jewish heritage of Jesus by focusing on the role of Joseph, as if to prove the old adage that 'behind a great man, there stands an even greater woman', Luke gives Mary the greatest prominence in the Gospel infancy story. In the Lukan narrative, Myriam of Nazareth plays multiple roles. She is the main character leading up to the events of Bethlehem before the birth of Jesus. Secondly, she is the one person who brings about the physical presence of God in human history. Finally, the story of Mary projects the reader beyond the physical birth of a Saviour in a stable fit only for animal shelter, and into a unique and personal relationship between God and humanity. Mary is both the human instrument in God's plan two thousand years ago, as well as the first and ultimate exemplar of what it means to accept and incarnate God in the reality of our personal and collective stories. Mary gives flesh and blood to the central reality of faith, consisting of a gracious all-evocative God intersecting with the fragility of the human story.

In the Christian Tradition, there is a symbiotic relationship between Mary and God, an intense relationship summed up by God's messenger at the Annunciation in the words *"Greetings, favoured one! The Lord is with you"* (Luke 1:28). Later, in the house of Elizabeth, Mary herself will express the same sentiments about

God looking *"with favour on the lowliness of his servant"* (Luke 1:48) and lavishing *"his mercy on those who fear him from generation to generation"* (Luke 1:51). Thus, from the very beginning of the Lukan narrative, mercy stands as the fundamental element encompassing Mary's life as *the favoured one*, and in her understanding of God as *the One who lavishes mercy* on her, and on the whole of history.

Mary: the challenge of presence

Whether we gaze at the pious figurines of Mary in the piety stall, or try to find meaning and personal significance in her most diverse representations through the ages, I propose that *presence* is the operative word. Ever present to God, she makes God present to the world, and becomes a challenge to us to see and accept God's presence in our own personal lives. When dealing with the mother of Jesus, it is easy to slide into some pietistic attitude or mushy sentimentality meant to warm our hearts and make us feel good that we have prayed repetitiously, even if absentmindedly, many pious words, or engaged in some personally meaningful Marian devotion. Mary is not an idol or a goddess, nor a superwoman endowed with extra-terrestrial entitlements denied to the rest of us poor mortals. Mary is not and can never be a mere devotional appendix to the Christian tradition, and we can never and must never exhaust our relationship with Mary into tallying up as many rosaries or wordy prayers in a day as we have hours to live. Nor can we transpose Mary of Nazareth out of her cultural context and embalm or clone her into our daily humdrum. That is not making Mary present, neither in her life story nor in our life. That is idle pietistic nonsense, reducing the Mother of God to a goddess, a personal insurance to turn to when we need favours. This would be disembodying Mary from her identity of a fully human being responding to a fully divine presence.

Pope Francis has no doubts about this. Addressing the youth of the world on 27 January 2019, in Panama, he said:

> Mary, the young woman of Nazareth, did not appear on the social networks of her time, she was not an influencer. However, without wanting or even seeking what happened to her, she became the woman who has had the greatest influence on human history. This is Mary, the "influencer" of God. In a few words, she was able to say "Yes" and trust in the love and promises of God, the only energy capable to make all things new.[51]

Ever-present to God in mind and heart, she makes God present to us. Mary was a living and active presence that walked our journey two thousand years ago. That is what underlies Luke's narrative: a presence for us today who claim discipleship; a presence as real as the air we breathe; as present as our own mothers are present to us, dead or alive, near or far, forever challenging us to be aware and responsive to this presence.

At the end of the infancy narratives, Luke sums up all the mysterious events of Bethlehem by projecting the reader into the long Nazareth years of Jesus, in one brief, all-embracing comment: *Mary treasured all these words in her heart* (Luke 2:19). Much more

---
51 Pope Francis. https://www.lastampa.it/2019/01/27/vaticaninsider/il-papa-ai-giovani-di-panama-maria-linfluencer-di-dio-5J5aHy8QMV80JBo2clObiI/pagina.html
- (Translation is mine – Accessed 18/01/2019)

than a memory of the mind, or some verbal expression of heart-warming sentimentality, motherly presence is a matter of the heart, a living and active presence, affecting and energising our whole journey of life. Mary is not just someone to admire or pray to. She is the primal and ultimate exemplar of discipleship expressed and lived through faith and mission, in a constant awareness of the mind and stirring of the heart.

'To reflect, ponder and store things up in the heart!' This, I propose, is the essence of what Mary the Mother of Jesus stands for in our Christian Tradition across the last two thousand years. This is also the fundamental call of discipleship. Having given her personal response to God's call, Mary becomes the pattern of a life totally caught up in God to the very core of one's being. Aware of this, God whose "*mercy is on those who fear him from generation to generation*" (Luke 1:51), she is the person who reflects, ponders and stores the message of her merciful God in her heart, and then goes on to live and proclaim this divine merciful presence through a life energised by faith, committed to service, and embraced in thankfulness.

That is why Mary holds such a pride of place in every religious tradition down through the ages, beyond any personal or private devotion. Authentic Marian devotion becomes the key to that intimate relationship with God which justifies and informs discipleship above all else. In this awareness of the active presence of a God of love and mercy incarnated by Mary, we have the blueprint of the life of faith, and we draw the energy by which to respond to our God in our daily experience and forever. It is not a matter of pleading with Mary for personal needs, or of pleasing the Mother of God with personal devotions, but of allowing ourselves to be stimulated and energised in our own life by this template of human response to God's presence, through a life of faith, service and of thankfulness.

This is the template for the concrete life of the believer today, the pattern for incarnating the most diverse charisms expressed through the most diverse cultures and individuals across the full span of history. Charism is what keeps us rooted deeply to the reality in which we live, commits us to the mission, and at the same time projects us to an eternal destiny with God. Thus, Mary is the incarnated charism for all time bringing God into play in her life and in the life of others, in this way fulfilling her own destiny of becoming one with her God. Beyond any personal or private devotion and pietistic sentimentalism, she is the first disciple and the exemplar of discipleship.

There is no denying the Church's wisdom over the centuries in perpetuating Mary's unique position in the history of salvation as the Mother of God. However, I propose that the greatness of Mary lies outside and beyond theological categories, to be found instead in her humanity as Myriam of Nazareth, the young girl who had her life plans upset by God, and in return responded with courage born of faith and trust in the God who *"looks with favour on the lowliness of his servant"* (Luke 1:48).

Mary was a normal woman of her time and place, who, through her response to God in her own culture and in her individuality, will always challenge us to reflect, ponder and store in our hearts the awareness that God will always look with mercy and favour on those who place their trust in divine Mercy and Love personified. As a normal woman, she gave her response to God, and she will always be the first disciple and the exemplar of discipleship, and of the human relationship with God for all time.

Long before Jesus comes into play, the evangelist Luke brings Mary into centre stage where she is the main actor in a triptych of lived and living discipleship and faith leading up to the climax of God's presence at Bethlehem and on Golgotha. The story of Jesus is introduced by Mary's personal call (*Annunciation*), her response in faith and service (*Visitation*) and her explosion of joy and thankfulness at realising what God has done for her and through her (*Magnificat*).

Mercy in struggle and faith

> *In the sixth month the angel Gabriel was sent by God to a town in Galilee called Nazareth, to a virgin betrothed to a man name Joseph, of the House of David; and the virgin's name was Mary. He went in and said to her, 'Rejoice, so highly favoured! The Lord is with you'. She was deeply disturbed by these words and asked herself what this greeting could mean. But the angel said to her, 'Mary, do not be afraid; you have won God's favour. Listen! You are to conceive and bear a son, and you must name him Jesus. He will be great and will be called Son of the Most High. The Lord God will give him the throne of his ancestor David; he will rule over the House of Jacob for ever and his reign will have no end'. Mary said to the angel, 'But how can this come about, since I am a virgin?' 'The Holy Spirit will come upon*

you' the angel answered 'and the power of the Most High will cover you with its shadow. And so the child will be holy and will be called Son of God. Know this too: your kinswoman Elizabeth has, in her old age, herself conceived a son, and she whom people called barren is now in her sixth month, for nothing is impossible to God'. 'I am the handmaid of the Lord', said Mary 'let what you have said be done to me'. And the angel left her (Luke 1:26-38).

The story of the Annunciation is one of the most dramatic events of the Gospel narrative. It plunges us into the very heart of the mystery of God, and represents the critical turning point in the Christian story and of the whole of humanity. As much as a moment of revelation of God's plan for humankind, Mary's response to the divine invitation becomes the moment of incarnation in time, the very instant when divinity becomes personified and reaches its ultimate and eternal expression by God entering world history, and becoming literally and physically one of us in full humanity.

Any encounter with God inevitably produces a crisis-situation, causing us to question our jealously guarded values, enjoining on us to look at things in a new way, to do things differently, and to change our behaviour. Any onrush of the divine into the human story, disturbs jealously guarded certainties, it provokes doubts and questions, and even fear and struggle. That is precisely the scenario into which Luke introduces Mary to the world.

Contrary to some shallow pietism, the first announcement of God's messenger with Mary was not in terms of any idyllic excitement, and pious sentimentality. On the contrary, it was an experience of deep human struggle expressed through a dialogue full of questions, promises, anxiety and hope. And understandably so, when we consider that the main character is a teenage girl suddenly confronted with a revelation that is as stunning as it is disturbing. Beyond any theological speculation, in her peasant ignorance she would have shared the cultural and religious traditions of her people that spoke of a Messiah that would set her people free and re-establish the glories of the Davidic kingdom. Nevertheless, to be a direct instrument of such divine intervention was probably not in Mary's agenda. Here is the fulfilment of centuries of promises, of expectations, and of apparently hopeless dreams of her people, and that qualification that *"he will be called Son of the Most High"* is a reality check. Probably for the first time, she realises that the child she is to bear, to nurture, and to care for is no ordinary child. Undoubtedly, Mary's contribution to the history of God's intervention in human affairs remains unique. Nevertheless, she is asked to make herself available for something extraordinary about to happen *to* her and *through* her, but beyond her understanding. Nonetheless, she was called to embrace her unique call, and not told.

Faced with such an unexpected and in some way unwanted demand, she baulks, and doubts, and her first reaction is to look for excuses to avoid the confrontation. Although we can safely surmise that Myriam of Nazareth would be quite unaware of the full implications of such a request, even so she did not like it. Luke structures the dialogue with God's messenger completely on her reservations and hesitation. She questions not only her ability to undertake such a task, but she questions the very authenticity of the call that claims to be from God.

Her life plans for the future would have been very simple. Her betrothal to the village carpenter assured her of a comfortable livelihood. Her days spent in the simplicity of home, interrupted only by the mandatory daily to and fro to the village water well with her friends, would make of Myriam of Nazareth the loving wife and the devoted mother. Suddenly she is confronted with a proposal that will take all this away from her. Her dreams for the future vanish, her plans are shattered, and she is left with an uncertain promise that she neither understands nor, at first, wants. She is simply made aware that God has other and very different plans for her.

A distorted, pietistic devotion to Mary may lead us to believe that Mary would have been incapable of even considering refusing God's call, totally available, always ready. However, that would mean denying Mary all possibility of free response, and consequently it would mean to destroy Mary as a real person and, ultimately, undermine the whole concept of incarnation. To say that Mary doubted does not destabilise in any way the uniqueness of her role within the history of salvation and of her position in the Christian tradition. Rather, Mary's doubt sublimates her into becoming the living model of human response to God. Like every living person, Mary too had to make her journey of faith, which ultimately is a blind trust in God, without securities or guarantees beyond the weakness and liminality we experience within ourselves.

As for each of us, Mary was *called* by God to cooperate in the establishment of the kingdom. But a call demands a response, and such a response will only be truly human when it is given in freedom. In the end, life begins to make sense only when we accept our human condition as man or woman called by God with all our struggles and limitations. Then we will experience true personal freedom. Then God will burst into our living frame changing not only our own selves, but the whole world *in* us and *through* us.

Yes, Mary was free to refuse her cooperation, and in her full humanity she doubted, she hesitated, she was afraid. But also, in her full humanity, she accepted the challenge of faith and she answered "*Yes!*" Her availability was only a consequence of that blind act of faith in a God who was the centre of her life and considered her "*highly favoured*". In the end Mary's "*Yes*" is the result and an expression of her awareness of being the object of God's love and merciful outreach into her life, embracing her completely with her questions, her doubts and her uncertainties. Mary is the human instrument of the personification of what Pope Francis calls Divine Mercy, both as a gift (God's mercy towards us) and as a commitment (Mary's mercy-full journey of life).

Aware of being the highly favoured object of God's mercy, Mary was and remained a woman of her time and of her culture. In that time and that culture, so diametrically opposed to ours, she gave her free response to God in faith, just as we are called to give *our* free response to God in our time and in our culture. However, faith is not a once-and-forever *Yes!* The first moment of abandonment in faith to God becomes authentic and real in the never-ending *yeses* that we have to incarnate through the turmoil, joys, and boredom of each day. The qualification of *highly favoured* by God then became the energy to confront her life of faith and of commitment to witness God's loving presence to others.

It takes faith to be rejected by everybody when you are desperately trying to find support and shelter as you are about to give birth to your child, knowing that *"the child to be born will be holy, and will be called the Son of God"* (Luke 1:35).

It takes faith to see a child, your child, born in a lurid stable, amid beasts of burden, and admit that God's message at Nazareth has come true, and here is the King of Israel, the One sent by God, the Creator of the universe.

It takes faith to have him lost in a crowded city, and your anxiety is met with a reminder by a twelve year old that *'I must be in my Father's house'*(Luke 2:41-49) doing my father's business; or watching him grow up, learning a trade and say, "He is not like the rest of these children".

It takes faith to being rebuffed at a wedding banquet when you are trying to help someone out of a sticky situation, knowing full well that *"nothing is impossible to God"*! (John 2:1-12).

It takes faith to see your son nailed to a cross, condemned to die the most excruciating and ignominious death of a rebellious criminal, abandoned by his friends, insulted and derided by most, crying in agony to the God who has abandoned him, and say to yourself "here dies God!" (John 19:25).

It takes faith to let that first '*Yes*' grow and become real in your flesh for a whole lifetime on the strength and conviction that you are the highly favoured one of God. This is the greatness of Mary, and this is the challenge thrown at us every day. Like for Mary, God looks with favour on us in our full humanity. Are we prepared to accept that guarantee of divine love, as we are, and live by it? In that life-long "Yes" Mary stands as the first disciple, and we gamble the authenticity of our claim to discipleship precisely in our life-long readiness to live as people who know they are the beloved of God. Mary lived by the reassurance that beyond her doubts and fears and misunderstandings God was with her, *the favoured one* of God, and that *nothing is impossible with God*. The same reassurance is ours if we accept that we are embraced by God's love in our full humanity and personal struggles, inadequacies and uncertainties, mostly not knowing why or how.

We are called to accept limitations and face seemingly impossible situations with hope, trust and availability, in spite of questions and doubts gnawing at us on all sides, and have the courage to take the plunge blind, even when we know fear and bewilderment, and to walk on in the dark, simply on the strength *nothing is impossible to God*.

We will be true disciples and not just devotees when we are prepared to incarnate God with us through those attitudes of availability, trust, and faith of the Favoured One of God.

Historically, God entered the human story by Jesus taking human flesh in the womb of Mary. Likewise, God will become a reality in our history and our world whenever, docile to the movement of the Spirit, we make ourselves available to God's message of love and mercy, as Mary did.

This is the greatness of Mary and this is the challenge thrown at us every day we claim discipleship of Jesus. Mary was not a superwoman, or someone endowed with divinely infused gifts not available to the rest of the human race. She was a woman of her time, steeped in her culture and of down-to-earth realism, who simply said "Yes" to God with trust and abandonment, because she believed beyond any logical rationality that God's name was Love and Mercy personified.[52] The result of this conviction was God's

---

[52] Pope Francis, *The Name of God is Mercy*, Bluebird Books for Life, 2016

eternal presence in the down-to-earth reality of each day, for each individual, for the whole of humanity, and for all time. That is what makes her the first disciple, a divinely conceived blueprint for all of us who, as disciples and believers, are called to give our free response in faith to God in our time and in *our* culture.

Energised by Mercy into commitment

> *Mary set out at that time and went as quickly as she could to a town in the hill country of Judah. She went into Zechariah's house and greeted Elizabeth. Now as soon as Elizabeth head Mary's greeting, the child leapt in her womb and Elizabeth was filled with the Holy Spirit. She gave a loud cry and said, 'Of all women you are the most blessed, and blessed is the fruit of your womb. Why should I be honoured with a visit from the mother of my Lord? For the moment your greeting reached my ears, the child in my womb leapt for joy. Yes, blessed is she who believed that the promise made her by the Lord would be fulfilled'* (Luke 1:39-45).

When we encounter experiences of great delight or of deep suffering, or we face a radical turn of events rushing unexpectedly into our lives and conditioning our story to the very depths of our being, the chances are that we have to tell someone. As if propelled by an unbearably painful compulsion, the more personal the event, the greater is the urge to tell or to reveal it "in the strictest confidence". The experience of God belongs to this category of secrets that demand revealing. When we experience God in our lives and allow ourselves to be touched and transformed by the experience, we cannot hide it any longer, and its freight of joy and pain inevitably flows out into what we do or say, but especially through who we are.

The secret that Mary carries is to be revealed. She just knows with the deep knowledge of the heart that God is totally caught up in humanity, in her flesh and blood, in real time and place, in every skerrick of human history, whatever the human condition may be. Once she accepted such a God with her, then someone else must know and experience the same secret. Mary cannot keep it inside any longer, and Elizabeth, the woman condemned and scorned as having been punished by God with barrenness, has to discover that the God of hope and joy has chosen her too. Against any cultural or religious taboos that condemned her barrenness as a punishment for some unspecified wrongdoing in her long-lost past, she too is God's favoured one, and the result of this revelation is joy and hope. The very presence of Mary, the woman who has accepted the touch and embrace of God's love, generates joy, peace, and hope in Elizabeth,

And so, Mary, very womanlike, her bewildering secret in her heart, sets out to tell someone, even if that means undertaking a long and perilous journey, simply because someone needs to know and must know God's presence of love and mercy in the reality of one's life. Having been told that her cousin Elizabeth, the woman rejected and enslaved by social, religious and cultural taboos, and yet the woman who, although long past childbearing age is to bear a child, Mary does not display any of the hesitation that accompanied Gabriel's original revelation. Confronted with the unbelievable and mind-shattering announcement of the angel that she is to be the beloved of God, chosen to be Mother of the Messiah, Mary baulks at the idea, she hesitates, and her final *Yes* to God comes only after considerable struggle of faith. By contrast, there is no hesitation here, no dialogue or anxious questioning. In Luke's words, there is an unrestrained urgency about Mary undertaking this journey. Regardless of the peril or distance, Mary just *"set out and went with haste to a Judean town in the hill country"* (Luke 1:39) to her cousin Elizabeth. Without hesitancy, she undertakes a dangerous journey simply driven by the realisation that someone is in greater need than she is right now, and this someone needs to experience in the flesh the love and care of God. Having given her "Yes" to God and allowed God into her life and into the flesh and blood of human history, she is driven by a totally new energy and intent. Someone must know that God is now part of this human story and the human story is enmeshed with the divine.

Mary's almost instinctive decision is quite bewildering and even more difficult to accomplish considering the socio-cultural-geographical context. The two hundred kilometres separating Nazareth from Ein Karem, the village not far from Jerusalem reputed to be the place where the encounter between Mary and Elizabeth occurred, do not make for a pleasant drive, even in the comfort of today's air-conditioned coaches. Twenty centuries ago, it would not have been any more pleasant, and certainly much longer and much more risky for a young expectant mother.

The journey of service she decided to undertake was long and tiring. Besides, Nazareth was not exactly what you would call a thriving metropolis, hardly buzzing with excitement and life. But Nazareth was home with friends, and security. Why then, leave it all behind for the unknown dangers of Samaria and beyond? Yet, unlike her response to the original announcement by Gabriel, Mary's only concern is for Elizabeth, who needs reassurance and affirmation that our God is truly a God of love and mercy, totally caught up in the human story, in her story. She has no second thoughts about undertaking this risky journey into the unknown, simply because, having said *Yes* in the first instance, she believes that now she has no choice but to repeat the *Yes* of her mission to others.

The love of God compels here without alibis or personal considerations. This is the response to God's gift of loving mercy at its best: availability in service and love for others, so that through our human presence others too will know and experience the favours of God's love. That original *Yes* to God uttered in the darkness of Nazareth gave human flesh to the divine and made God "Emmanuel", God-with-us, real and active in our world, for all eternity. Only a continued *Yes* to God on our part will make incarnation real and life-giving today, for all time, for us and for the whole world.

Let us not be pietistic but realistic. Our commitment as disciples does not immunise us from personal and collective experiences of unfaithfulness, desolation, and loneliness, nor are we ever strangers to doubts and insecurity. These are as much part of our psychic and spiritual DNA as the consolation of a successful venture and the courage of facing the unknown. The crucial question, however, is precisely about availability. How do the negative and less appetising aspects of daily life affect our availability to the mission and to the sense of joyful hope that marks the encounter between Mary and Elizabeth?

Incarnation is a very real event that not only took place within the body of a virgin two thousand years ago, but it is an event that *takes place* in each man, woman, or child who dares to make the step to meet the other at the concrete level. Only through such a step into personal availability, will God become truly present, and his love become life-giving in human history and in each and every concrete daily situation. Only through such stepping into personal availability to each other, will God be a living and concrete reality in human history, and God's mercy and love redeemed from a level of platitudes to become a living energy in every concrete daily situation. Mary calls us to stop gazing into the dim past with mushy sentimentality and instead become actors now of God's living and loving presence by daring to step into the shoes of another person and making God's loving presence a concrete reality present for that person now.

Service to others is not something that the Christian can dispense with or excuse themselves from. Service is the irrevocable and inevitable consequence of one's protestation of belief in a God of mercy and love. Otherwise, our protestation of faith is pointless. Christ declared that he came to serve and not to be served (Matthew 20:28), and Mary proved the point well before the events of Bethlehem, not because of any special preview of what her son was going to say or do, but because she realised very quickly that she could not escape the practical implications of her act of faith in God. She experienced Emmanuel in the flesh, and others had to discover the same presence through her availability to service.

Availability to God in the openness of faith can only be manifested in real terms through availability to others in the service of fellow human beings, as James the apostle reminds us.

> *No one has ever seen God; but as long as we love one another God will live in us and his love will be complete in us* (1 James 4:12).

As believers, we do not commit ourselves to service out of some economic benefit or vague altruistic intent, but in order to testify to the presence and love of God among those who need it most: the unwanted, the tired, the lonely and the helpless. To these and to thousands who have lost focus and sense of life, we must offer the possibility of experiencing love and hope as God's gift to them, and reawaken in them an awareness of the life-giving presence of God in their marginality, whatever their situations. And we, the believing disciples who know that the God of love and mercy is with us, must do it. A non-committal, live-and-let-live is one of those ambiguous platitudes by which we compromise everything we stand for. Such a self-centred attitude, besides nullifying the living presence of God in our own life, also nullifies the place of Mary of Nazareth in our Christian Tradition as the exemplar of faith, the epitome of discipleship, and the instrument of God's love in which we claim to believe.

The mutual encounter of two women both confronting a similarly unexplained situation was the spark that ignited joy and peace in the midst of rejection, uncertainty and doubt. Mary brought the God in her womb to bear on another yet unborn child, and the result was joy (Luke 1:44). Devotion to Mary is an outward-looking and other-reaching commitment to bring peace, joy and hope where it is most needed, at the concrete level of here and now. Of course, the very word "commitment" could very well be an ambiguous platitude, banded around indiscriminately. In our devotion to commitment and service, we can easily jump on the bandwagon and become just another efficient social structure with a hollow "Christian" label attached to it. But joy is not the artificial product of external, artificial, and often false publicity, and of unbridled consumerism of advertising. Our commitment must be Good News for those who meet us, and the result must be joyful hope, as the encounter of Mary and Elizabeth incarnated. The very first line of Pope Francis' first encyclical letter places both the source and the result of true joy in the heart of every person who becomes aware of the presence of God in their life.

> The joy of the Gospel fills the hearts and lives
> of all who encounter Jesus.[53]

Goodwill, joy and hope are not platitudes that we exchange for one day of the year like Christmas wrappings. Joy is the hallmark of the encounter of Mary and Elizabeth, and joy must be both the message we proclaim and the witness we give. If I truly accept that mercy and love are the actualisation of God with us, then I have good reasons to rejoice because God knows my struggles and my dreams. If I truly accept that God is in my life as intensely and intimately as the God-child was in Mary's womb, then I can hope because, with God in my story, the future is secure, and I have nothing to fear. If I truly believe in Emmanuel, then others must discover this presence through me, and I have to become a gift of love, peace and joy to others. Youngsters will truly leap for joy, and the elderly will smile with gratitude and peace when they see us joyful in our daily drudgery. People will look forward and struggle on to another tomorrow when they see us hopeful in our weakness. The whole world will rejoice and be transformed if our lives celebrate the Good News of joy and hope that comes from our

---

53 *Evangelii Gaudium.*

deep and lived conviction that God is love without qualifications, and loves us unconditionally.

Thankfulness for God's mercy

> *My soul proclaims the greatness of the Lord and my spirit exults in God my saviour; because he has looked upon his lowly handmaid, Yes, from this day forward all generations will call me blessed, for the Almighty has done great things for me. Holy is his name, and his mercy reaches from age to age for those who fear him. He has shown the power of his arm, he has routed the proud of heart. He has pulled down princes from their thrones and exalted the lowly. The hungry he has filled with good things, the rich sent empty away. He has come to the help of Israel his servant, mindful of his mercy – according to the promise he made to our ancestors – of his mercy to Abraham and to his descendants for ever* (Luke 1:46-55).

There comes a moment in the life of every person who has accepted the call to faith and service when one stands inevitably alone with God and asks the question, *Why?* The smile of a child, the power of the storm, the angry loneliness of defeat, the peaceful fading away of an old person facing death and reminiscing about life – they all speak of a presence that cannot be encapsulated by physical categories, and yet affect us at the deepest level of our psyche.

Mary experienced one such moment when nothing more made sense, and she can only burst into a personal and yet cosmic expression of thankfulness: the *Magnificat* (Luke 1:46-55). Awareness of being grasped and gifted unconditionally by our God of mercy and love must stimulate us to pause and to remember with joy and gratitude what this God has done. In turn, this memory of giftedness becomes stimulus and energy for the future, whatever that may be. Each of us is the converging point of a thousand dreams, from God, through to our parents and the events that shaped us for who we are. And yet we live as though the past has drifted away into nothing. We look and plan, and we do not realise that tomorrow is but yesterday's dream brought to fulfilment. Too often we do not like to look back to our past. So many mistakes, failures, foolishness! The temptation to forget and pretend is probably the immediate palliative that comes to mind. No, it is better to forget, and pretend that the past is gone forever! But then we will be unable to look forward to our future. Honesty demands that we admit that only God could have unravelled the messed-up threads of our life, given the predicaments of time and situation. We have lived through that past, and we have survived, and grown, and have given life. Therefore, we will live, and survive, and grow, and give life in our present and in God's future.

This is Mary's song and prayer: a *thankfulness* for what has been, so that we are enabled to entertain a *hope* for what will be. Only the trusting poor can rejoice in their memories and hope in their dreams, and Mary in her destitution and total abandonment to God gives thanks for both memories and dreams. Confronted with God, Mary looks back in order to see forward. In her thankfulness for what God has done *for* her and *through* her, she can only go back to the wonders God has wrought in the past, and in that past she can see and acknowledge the power and love of God at work for her personally and for her people collectively.

> *He has looked upon his lowly handmaid, yes, from this day forward all generations will call me blessed, for the Almighty has done great things for me* (Luke 1:48).

In her ecstasy of contemplation, full of exultation and unexplained excitement, all she can say is: *He has! He has! He has!* and therefore, because of that past, *He will! He will! He will!*

The future will hold its traps and uncertainties. But, because of what has been in the past, we can have hope for the tomorrow for the hungry, the poor, and the lowly that dwell deeply in each of us and all around us. The traps and uncertainties are no longer threatening and death-dealing. The future is pregnant with possibilities screaming fulfilment. But it is the past that tells us that these possibilities can be brought to realisation only by the lowly who have the courage to lean on a God, whose name is Mercy, and whose energy for life is Love.

If we are able to incarnate this looking back in anamnesis, in order to see forward in our own life dreams and possibilities, then, like Mary and because of Mary's life story, we are truly a God-gifted people for a God-enriched world. The future is God's, but God leans on you and me to build a kingdom of faith, hope and love. Mary truly prays the prayer of the poor: *May your will be done,* and in Mary's words one can hear resonate the famous saying of Dag Hammarskjöld, *For all that has been, Thanks! For all that will be, Yes!*

Mary stands as the first and ultimate disciple, who in her abandonment and trust brings God into the reality of human flesh and blood. May we too have the courage to incarnate in our own flesh and blood Mary's attitudes of complete *faith* in our God, whose name is Mercy, total *service* of love, compassion to each other, and deep *thankfulness* for the love with which God embraces us! In this conviction, we will be energised into bringing healing, peace and joy into our own life and into the whole world, in spite the brokenness and sinfulness that weighs us down, and hems us in on all sides.

May the memory of Mary's life impel us into accepting the silent but stirring presence of God in our lives, committing us to be instruments of loving presence for a world that needs to discover and accept through us the God-enriched gifts of compassion, hope and joy! Let us allow ourselves to be propelled by that unbearably painful compulsion projecting us into revealing the secret of a God totally caught up in human affairs. Let us live as people who know with the knowledge of the heart that *God is with us*, and lead others to discover that they are *beloved* of a God obsessed with lavishing mercy and love, indistinctly and unconditionally, on every human being.

www.ingramcontent.com/pod-product-compliance
Lightning Source LLC
Chambersburg PA
CBHW051935290426
44110CB00015B/1984